THE PRACTICE OF
MARRIAGE COUNSELING

EMILY HARTSHORNE MUDD, M.S.W., Ph.D.
Executive Director, Marriage Council of Philadelphia

The Practice of

MARRIAGE COUNSELING

ASSOCIATION PRESS · NEW YORK · 1951

27801

March 1952

Printed in the United States of America
American Book–Knickerbocker Press, Inc., New York
55

To the inspiration and memory of my brother
EDWARD YARNALL HARTSHORNE, Ph.D., 1912–1946
whose work and faith were in the betterment of human relations

To our own young people
EMILY and WILLIAM, HARVEY, MARGARET, JOHN
and to the young men and women
with whom many of my working hours have been spent
and in whose strength I believe so deeply

Three Forewords

*E*ACH INDIVIDUAL INVESTS LIFE with feelings which make life tolerable and zestful, or unhappy and intolerable. They are determined by early experiences in the family. The satisfactions, happiness, and wisdom of a husband and wife determine to a great extent whether their children will enter into society and contribute constructively, or whether they will represent dissonant and destructive forces, with great personal unhappiness and often emotional and physical ill-health.

Psychiatrists and social scientists view with concern the social scene, with its rapid changes, conflicting pressures, and new frustrations—whether war, inflation, unemployment, economic uncertainty, or inadequate housing. Increasing divorce rate and the decreasing influence of the family are alarming indices of social and personal tensions.

The study in this book presents an account of fourteen years' experience of the Philadelphia Marriage Council in tackling one of the most important problems in our society. It is a unique and major contribution. The sociological and historical backgrounds are given. Records of service are shown ministering to obvious personal and community needs. Examples of actual interviews are presented. Perhaps the most valuable part of the book is the discussion of the philosophy and methodology of marriage counseling—an analysis of the elements and process of counseling. As such it will be eminently useful to people who are not just marriage counselors but whose profession or friendliness brings people to them for help—whether

vii

they are in religion, education, law, medicine, or just friendly people. It will be of especial interest to psychiatrists, to whom marital problems increasingly come, and whose education and experience in this field need enhancement.

With the increase in marital tensions and their psychoneurotic and psychosomatic ramifications, it is heartening to read these reports of successful short-term psychological counseling, focused around specific problems. This research shows that adjustive change can take place through specific experience with trained counselors in people who would never consult a psychiatrist.

The recognition of the value of this work is attested by a grant from the Federal Security Agency, Public Health Service, National Institutes of Health. It is gratifying that through the publication of this study its principles may be used by a widening group of counselors. Any facility that society can develop to strengthen the individual, lessen prejudice, dispel ignorance, superstition, and intolerance, lessen fear, soften hate, increase understanding and co-operation, deserves our gratitude and support. This book will contribute to better human relations in the family, in society, and, may we hope, ultimately internationally.

KENNETH E. APPEL, M.D.
Professor of Psychiatry
University of Pennsylvania

Philadelphia
April, 1951

MARRIAGE COUNSELING HAS DEVELOPED in the last two decades as a new and distinct area for the application of co-ordinated professional skill of the social caseworker, the physician, the lawyer, the educator, and the minister. The need for these services has been recognized and has been met in a variety of ways. This particular presentation of fourteen years of experience emerges out of one important type of structure which, by its name, indicates that it is uniquely set up for the one purpose—to provide a counseling service for young married people or for those contemplating marriage.

The Marriage Council of Philadelphia, under the continuous leadership of Mrs. Emily Mudd, has become one of the important contributions to this field of professional endeavor. Through its direct service to young people and the important research which has been based on and grown out of this service and the educational activities which have been carried on, this organization has achieved a leading place in the field of marriage counseling. This book represents a careful analysis of this experience and adds to the body of knowledge so needed in broadening our understanding of the marriage relationship.

It has been my privilege to be associated with this organization from the beginning. It was started as a small and modest effort to find how social work skills, co-ordinated with other skills, could be developed in this special field. Under Mrs. Mudd's leadership the organization has grown and new skills have been developed in the helping process. The fact that the staff have developed a clarity in the function of the agency has enabled them to help those who seek its service and to refer clients to other professional resources out of and beyond their own areas of competence.

> FREDERICK H. ALLEN, M.D., *Director*
> *Philadelphia Child Guidance Clinic*

Philadelphia
April, 1951

*T*HIS VOLUME IS appropriately entitled *The Practice of Marriage Counseling.* First of all it interprets the rise of marriage counseling in the context of changes taking place in American society. Second, it offers the most recent and complete survey of the organization and development of different types of marriage counseling services in the United States. Third, it analyzes the theory and the procedures of counseling upon the basis of intensive study of the case histories of a selected marriage counseling center.

This is the first book which describes in a systematic way the actual operations of a marriage counseling center. It provides the kind of knowledge which people interested in the workings of this new type of service wish to know: the way it is organized, how persons in need of counseling find out about it, their characteristics and their problems, the philosophy and practice of counseling, and the qualifications and training necessary for a person to become a marriage counselor.

The use in this book of the experience and data of the Marriage Council of Philadelphia is unusually valuable. It is the only center in this country, and in the world, that possesses in high degree all four activities essential to the complete development of marriage counseling, namely, counseling clients, integration of its work with other community agencies and institutions, training of students in marriage counseling, and an ongoing and significant research program.

The author, Emily Hartshorne Mudd, has been director of the Marriage Council of Philadelphia since its establishment in 1932. She utilizes in a telling way the records of 2,559 consecutive cases interviewed from 1936 to and including 1949, by dividing them into the prewar, the war, and the postwar periods.

A valuable feature of this book is the first presentation in the literature of a series of detailed case studies exemplifying the actual process of marriage counseling. These cover a wide range of problems of concern to engaged as well as to married couples. These cases will be of interest not only to marriage counselors but to teachers and students of courses in marriage counseling, in the family, in preparation for marriage, and in family social work. Most valuable is the record of progress from one visit to the next, showing the relation of counseling procedures to changes in attitudes and behavior.

Although this book is addressed primarily to those engaged in counseling, and to teachers of courses in this and related fields, it should also attract readers from the wider public interested in knowing more about the nature and actual workings of marriage counseling. Its publication marks a real advance in marriage counseling practice.

Ernest W. Burgess, Ph.D.
Professor of Sociology
University of Chicago

Chicago
April, 1951

x

Preface

THIS STUDY HAS TWO main purposes—to examine the development of marriage and family counseling in the United States, and to record details of its practice. It is neither light nor easy reading. It attempts, with care and persistence, to winnow out available information useful to professional persons, doctors, social workers, ministers, teachers, lawyers, and others whose daily work involves them in formal or less formal marriage counseling. This material should answer questions also for the intelligent lay reader—those husbands, wives, and parents who want to know what marriage counseling is and what kinds of situations in marriage present difficulties.

The general interest of the sociologist in society and of the psychiatrist, the psychologist, and the caseworker in the individual can never be identical. However, the interdependence of these professional groups is increasing. The writer, responding to impetus from training in social casework and in sociology, attempts to relate the detailed case material and the counseling procedures—the essence of this book—within a broad social perspective. The caseworker may well be restive in the first chapters, the social scientist in later sections. Effort has therefore been made to organize the presentation so that readers may readily turn to their particular interests.

The variations and similarities among services in this field, certain characteristics of persons who use them for counseling, how they come to these services, the kinds of situations for which help is sought, and the type of help given are all discussed. Summary reports covering the organization, staff, source of support, methods of counseling, and type of program offered in the functioning services from all parts of this country in which marriage counseling can be obtained are presented.

A total population in one functioning service, consisting of 2,559 consecutive cases seen in a fourteen-year period between January 1, 1936, and December 31, 1949, is analyzed in detail. The data are so divided that, through the use of a few statistical devices, men and women clients and the periods before, during, and after World War II can be studied independently. This material was considered against the background of (1) current events of national and international importance, as these might affect marriage counseling and family life; (2) developments within the particular agency studied; (3) general population and local figures for the geographic area from which the members of the group are drawn; and (4) the professional development of marriage and family counseling in the United States.

It should be emphasized that the cases studied represent a population sufficiently large to justify the expectation that results derived from it have fairly stable characteristics. A sampling problem of one kind would arise if a part of these cases were considered and from them attempts were made to generalize conclusions over all cases. A sampling problem of a different nature arises when we consider the extent to which these cases are representative of some larger population. At present there is little if any knowledge about characteristics of the population from which people are drawn who constitute samples in marriage counseling agencies. We cannot evaluate the possible influence of selective factors, nor the extent to which the present sample is representative or nonrepresentative of persons who in one sense or another require the services of marriage counseling. Furthermore, it is not the intention of this study to generalize its conclusions beyond the population who sought marriage counseling.

The sections on case histories of clients and the process of counseling reflect as accurately as possible the theory and practice of marriage counseling at the Philadelphia Marriage Council. (Identifying particulars of persons and places have been removed meticulously from all cases.) The interrelationships between client and counselor during the entire contact with the agency are presented. The theory and practice of marriage counseling are related to those of social casework. Evidence presented indicates that sound marriage counseling is also a constructive supplement to psychiatric practice.

This material is presented with humility inasmuch as no systematic investigation can disclose completely the unspoken communication between two persons and its effect on each, but with conviction that when counselors work with constructive methods and attitudes, in the majority of cases their clients will be helped.

It is hoped that this study, although but a beginning, will serve as a catalyst for systematic, scientifically sound supplementary studies in marriage and family counseling.

ACKNOWLEDGMENTS

This study was made possible in part by grants from the Lessing Rosenwald Foundation in 1947–50, for which I am most grateful. These covered technical assistance in statistics, rendering of graphs, and typing of the manuscript. It could not have been made without permission from the Board of Directors of Marriage Council to use the case material and office records, and to take leaves of absence from routine agency work.

My professional introduction to this field was due primarily to Karl de Schweinitz who, with the help of a small group, enthusiastically negotiated the experiment of opening a Marriage Council in Philadelphia and subsequently implemented my training at the Pennsylvania School of Social Work. To Dr. Virginia P. Robinson, who supervised my first cases at Marriage Council during 1934–35 and subsequently served on the agency case committee, I owe the beginning belief in myself as a counselor which was basic to subsequent work. To Drs. Frederick H. Allen and Kenneth E. Appel, for sixteen years intermittently President of the Board of Directors and Chairman of the Medical Supervisory Committee of the agency, and to the other members of these committees, I am indebted for leadership, encouragement, sound judgment, and dedication to basic client service through the application of scientific principles and the belief in human values and human beings.

I wish also to express appreciation to Dr. James H. S. Bossard and other members of the Department of Sociology of the University of Pennsylvania for their interest in the formulation and completion of the study. To Dr. Malcolm Preston, Associate Professor of Psychology, University of Pennsylvania, I am indebted for suggestions and guidance in the statistical analysis of the data.

To my husband, Dr. Stuart Mudd, I am deeply grateful for valuable and continuing criticism and suggestions as the work progressed and for critical review of the manuscript. Without his belief in the worth-whileness of the project, his willingness to forego many evenings of companionship, and his pressure to put this experience in writing, this work might still be unfinished.

To my fellow counselors on the staff of Marriage Council between 1936 and 1944, Dr. Elizabeth Kirk Rose, Mrs. Charlotte Freeman, Mrs. John Everton, and Mrs. Herbert Gaskill, whose case records constituted almost half of the cases used during those years, I extend my warm thanks. To Mrs. Katharine von Minckwitz, counselor during 1945–46, I express appreciation for assisting in tabulating the cases studied and for contributing to the thinking on the dynamics of counseling. Members of the more recent staff of Marriage Council—Mrs. Hazel Froscher, Mrs. Margery Klein, Mrs. Virginia McLean, Dr. William V. Fittipoldi, Dr. Morton Schwab, and the counselors-in-training in 1949, Dr. Chester R. Dietz, Dr. Thoburn R. Snyder, and Dr. Janet Fowler Nelson—gave valuable help through discussions of case material and counseling method which aided in the formulation of Chapters 8, 9, and 10.

Thanks for secretarial assistance are tendered to Mrs. Evelyn Lewis, Mrs. Harriet Moss, Miss Lydia Harmer, and Mrs. Estelle Rosanoff, and finally my very warm gratitude and friendship is tendered to Mrs. Elizabeth Swartley, Marriage Council's indefatigable office manager who always found time, enthusiasm, and good will to ferret out the endless necessary references, help in practical details, maintain calm, and impart strength to carry on through steadfast loyalty and devotion to the work of the agency.

The manuscript was read critically by Dr. Earl D. Bond, Dr. James H. S. Bossard, Dr. Lovett Dewees, Dr. Janet Nelson, Dr. Robert L. Laidlaw, Dr. Ernest Osborne, Dr. Abraham Stone, Dr. Walter Stokes, and in part by Mr. Ralph Bridgman and Mr. Frank Hertel. The friendly professional interest of these referees was a source of great encouragement and their suggestions were incorporated in the manuscript to its definite improvement.

EMILY HARTSHORNE MUDD

Philadelphia
May, 1951

Contents

Contents

List of Tables and Charts

1

Marriage Counseling as an Expression of the Times

AT THE PRESENT TIME it is practically incumbent upon the worker who deals with the adjustment of individuals to develop a philosophy which relates his practice to the broad perspective of world environment. Such perspective enables him to see not only the needs of one person but to visualize those needs in relation to the immediate community and in the larger context of national and international pressures and demands. He accepts quite naturally the realization that, if civilized mankind is to survive, the study of human relationships must become an even more important science than the science of annihilation. He knows that individuals must be able to live satisfyingly with themselves and with those about them and that this ability is the goal of the modern concept of mental health in the United States.

It is recognized that one method through which individuals can hope to live with more satisfaction is to change institutions, social systems, and governments in order that present conflicts may be ameliorated or eliminated. There is no disagreement in the following material with this contention. However, in the last analysis it is the basic will to do, the initiative and ability of the individual man and woman and of the leader, be he scientist, reformer, priest, minister, rabbi, philosopher, politician, or statesman, which will influence and control the possibilities and probabilities of constructive change.

It is in the family constellation that the first experiences in living with others are found for each individual—the husband

1

and wife with each other, parents with their children, and children among themselves. These experiences set the pattern for future interpersonal relationships (Benedict, 1934).[1] It was with the conviction that "destiny is not something wholly visited on us but is in great part our own creation and responsibility" (Appel, 1950) that the author became interested in marriage counseling and its inherent possibilities for fostering the inborn capacity of people to do something themselves about their own living; to make their interpersonal relationships more satisfying; to promote and release the feelings and attributes of love; and to minimize the cultivation of hostility and hate.

THE STUDY OF THE ABNORMAL LEADS TO THE SEARCH FOR PREVENTIVE MEASURES

Individual and group behavior of human beings has been the object of study and exploration by many disciplines for a long time. It has been more common to consider behavior that is arresting, spectacular, ominous, and abnormal rather than the more usual conditions of normality.

The study and treatment of pathological manifestations in all fields have led increasingly to the exploration of causative factors in maladjustment and finally to attempts at measures for prevention of abnormality, and the conflict which is so often the causal factor. The so-called preventive approach has been illustrated in recent decades in various branches of the medical, psychological, and social sciences, particularly in pediatrics, in the mental hygiene movement, child guidance clinics, school guidance, personnel programs in business, industry, and government, and in marriage counseling.

University departments such as Institutes of Human Relations, Bureaus of Applied Social Research, Departments of Social Relations, and so on, have been established at Chicago, Columbia, Harvard, Vassar, Yale, and other institutions of higher learning. Such departments, as well as private foundations, government bureaus, and other sources, are attempting to evaluate the behavior of people in different phases of living by

---

[1] See the alphabetized list of sources in the Bibliography.

means of action and service programs. Research to weigh techniques and results of efforts to aid adjustment, and finally to study adequate adjustment itself, is the essential cornerstone for progress in this field.

A science of human relationships should furnish knowledge of practical as well as theoretical value for promoting adjustment. These facts should exert pressure to change outmoded institutional forms in law, in education, in marriage, in government. New approaches and conditions should serve to curtail the increase in conflict, neurosis, divorce, and mental disease which is now evident in this country. They should foster attitudes of mind which do not divide all ideas into two groups, one regarded as dependable, sound, and true, the other as unproven, unreliable, misleading, and false. They should foster the realization that there is a third category of ideas—hypotheses not yet known to be valid that might be true if by research they could be proven (Gregg, 1948). "Exact science about human nature itself will deliver man from his present gloom, and will purge him from his contemporary shame in the sphere of interhuman relations" (Pavlov, 1928).

ACCELERATED CHANGE HAS PROMOTED NEW COMPLEXITIES

There are increased complexities at present in the social setting in which human beings must carry on. The post-World War II era has been labeled The Age of Anxiety—anxiety about ourselves and the universe. Psychology and psychiatry have given us an understanding of maladjustment, have begun to make us aware of sentimental illusion, have given us the possibility of growing up. "Philosophy," says Edman (1949), "can teach us to have a generous hope, to extract human values and wisdom from facts discovered by science." [2]

With the acceleration of change within almost all aspects of our culture, differences in the functioning of families have multiplied. They perform a wide range of activities which vary according to cultural backgrounds, financial status, and locality. Continuity of income may be uncertain due to the na-

---

[2] Quoted from address, entitled "Philosophy and Our Current Anxieties," given by Professor Irwin Edman at the annual meeting of the Phi Beta Kappa Associates, 1949.

ture of modern industry and labor relations. With the increase of mechanical equipment, the skills required of husbands and wives are often dissimilar to those learned in the parental homes. Technology has invaded the home as well as the factory and values have been influenced accordingly (Bossard, ed., 1950).

According to Kingsley Davis (1950), "The combination of increasing longevity, a slightly earlier age at marriage, and a tendency to control fertility and bunch reproduction in ages below thirty has freed married women for economic pursuits and led to a new conception of marriage as a personal rather than a community or kinship matter. Marriage, divorce, and reproduction have accordingly become much more responsive to current fashions—and the new family structure seems to be integrated with the general character of modern society."

Because of these and many more complex factors, certain difficulties and disasters are apparent within the relationships of which the family is composed and on which at present it depends basically for survival. An interweaving of multiple causes from which conflicts, inadequacies, and frustrations accrue complicates diagnosis and correction. Responsibility for results is evaded by individuals, communities, and on the national level. Modern circumstances of family life and current ideologies are among those factors which may make a flight from reality all too easy.

Activities and duties formerly handled within the family itself, whether for better or worse, are now shared by the community. Marriage and family counseling is one community facility which has developed for the purpose of promoting personal and social adjustment within the family by aiding those individuals who feel inadequate to utilize their own strength, and of furthering knowledge concerning the dynamics of relationship between husband and wife.

DEVELOPMENT OF MARRIAGE COUNSELING

Marriage and family counseling in some form has been carried on informally and semiformally throughout the ages. Families, friends, members of the learned professions, and unschooled individuals, persons of good and bad repute; nature's

4

great symbols, the sun, moon, and stars; gods, goddesses, magic, and even the Devil have been called upon to help find the desired mate, smooth the peregrinations of love, realize the values and solve the conflicts, disappointments, and desperations of conjugal life. Men and women of all walks of life have tried through the ages to minister to each other in this respect and are still trying. Others have exploited one another and are still doing so (Steiner, 1945).

The twentieth century continues to produce no little variety in methods of mate selection and of assistance in marriage adjustment. One of the more formal attempts has progressed through a series of steps based one after the other on experience. This is marriage counseling as it has been practiced by the physician (Dewees, 1938), (Dickinson, 1931), (Laidlaw, 1950), (Levine, M., 1943), (Stokes, 1951), (Stone and Stone, 1939); minister (Dicks, 1947), (Goldstein, 1945), (Hiltner, 1949), (Wood, 1949); teacher (Bowman, 1947), (Groves, 1941); psychologist (Adams, 1946), (Nelson, 1947); lawyer (Alexander, 1948), (Bradway, 1938); social worker (Berkowitz, 1948), (Hollis, 1949), (Ware, 1940), and other professional persons as part of their professional duties and especially as this is carried on in centers specifically oriented for this purpose (Bridgman, 1932), (Carden, 1942), (Fisher, 1936), (Gaylord, 1942), (Groves, E., 1940), (Mudd, 1938, 1951), (Stone, 1949). This work, as surveyed in these articles, has begun in the last decade to enlist scientific interest, scrutiny, and experimentation.

Following World War I, the first center for information and advice on sex was established in 1919 at the Berlin Institute for Sexual Science, directed by Magnus Hirschfeld. Three years later, in 1922, the social services of the municipality of Vienna founded a public and official "Center for Sexual Advice" in Vienna. Later a number of Leagues for Sexual Hygiene were established in Germany, in Austria, in Denmark, in Sweden, and in other countries, and a number of marriage consultation services began to be organized under their auspices (Stone, 1949). Gradually the idea came to be accepted that individuals faced with sexual and family difficulties should receive help and advice from special centers established for that purpose. In 1932 there were more than one thousand marriage consultation centers in Germany and Austria (Kopp, 1938). Although operating under a variety of names, they had the common purpose of directing public opinion toward the betterment of national health in relation to the family. The rise of Nazism with its submergence of the individual put a stop to such centers except as they were used for "purification" of the race. Marriage counseling as an aid to individual adjustment was continued only in the democratic countries.

In the United States the development of marriage preparation and aids in marital adjustment has proceeded along several distinct lines: the establishment of functional courses in marriage and the family in schools and colleges, the evolution of sound literature in this field, the development of research, and the organization of marriage counseling services. Concurrently state and national councils and conferences have promoted interest and activity in all phases of this development.

COURSES ON MARRIAGE AND THE FAMILY

Even before Ernest Groves, one of the earliest and most persistent pioneers in this field (Groves, 1937), established his course in "Marriage and Family Relations" at the University of North Carolina in 1936, courses in "The Family" had been offered at the University of Chicago in 1893 under Dr. Charles R. Henderson in the department of sociology, at Stanford University in 1901, and in 1908 a survey (Bernard, 1908) indicated about a score of such courses were being offered in departments of sociology, theological seminaries, and teachers' colleges. In 1939 marriage courses were studied by J. S. Burgess (1939) and Groves (1941). More recently it was estimated that courses on marriage and the family are now being given in approximately 632 universities and colleges (Timmons, 1948), (Bowman, 1949), and a large number of high schools throughout the country. These vary in content and method from the older and more conservatively named course on "The Family" to lectures or courses specifically oriented and focused on marriage and family relations. Although surveys have been made in the hope of determining the extent of these courses, in some instances the respondents have included ap-

6

parently such a wide range of activities that it is questionable whether the units counted are really comparable. It is hoped that funds for a systematic study will be forthcoming.

In their inception some of these marriage courses emphasized sex education, then health and the physiological aspects of adjustment. Some reflected repercussions of the feminist movement and were developed by open-minded members of departments of home economics whose interest progressed from a focus on child life to home management, to family life. In the main all of these courses represent attempts to prepare young people for the functions of marriage and parenthood. Some are elective with voluntary student attendance; some carry academic credit. A "rough outside estimate," given by Bowman (1949) indicates approximately fifty thousand students registered yearly in these courses. Texts have evolved through the experience and insights of the last decade; these include Baber (1939), Becker and Hill (1949), Bowman (1948), Duvall and Hill (1948), E. Duvall (1950), Fishbein and Burgess (1947), Folsom (1943), Foster (1950), Himes (1940), J. and M. Landis (1948), Leclercq (1949), Nimkoff (1947), Waller (1938).

The present trend in college courses is to emphasize, in addition to the history and sociological functions of the family, the importance of personality development and the dynamic quality of interpersonal and interfamilial relationships as these are reflected in both constructive and conflicting behavior. As greater understanding of the actual role of family adjustment in the early conditioning of the child is admitted by all scientific observers (Allen, 1942), (Appel, 1946), (Bossard, 1948), (Osborne, 1951), (Powdermaker and Grimes, 1940), (Wolf, ed., 1941), courses in marriage and family relations are becoming more functional (Lamson, 1949) and including detailed study of the child in addition to the parent as an integral part of the family group. The concept recently advanced by Bossard (1949) that, realistically, "education for family living must be education for group living" holds fascinating portent for future education and group counseling.

To function successfully the courses should have teachers with sound information in the many related fields. These teachers should also have attitudes and personality attributes which enable both student and teacher to discuss and absorb ideas and information freely and comfortably. Teachers are being called on increasingly to do both formal and informal individual counseling in conjunction with their courses (Bowman, 1947), (Timmons, 1948). At present there is a dearth of such teachers and a correspondingly great need for additional training in the professional schools from which individuals may be called on for group work, teaching of this type, and for counseling when conditions permit adequate space, time, and training. Something of the need and the natural limitations of the teacher-counselor will be discussed in Chapter 3, "Less Formalized Marriage Counseling."

Increasing effort is being made by many high schools and community organizations, such as the Y.W.C.A., Y.M.C.A., Y.M.H.A., churches, synagogues, and club groups to make material similar to that given in the colleges available with suitable adaptations to the young men or women who do not get to college (Gaskill and Mudd, 1950), (Landis, P., 1946), (Ryan, 1949).

Training seminars have been conducted for ministers, doctors, teachers, and other professional groups in marriage counseling in a few communities either as part of the activities of functioning marriage counseling centers (Mudd, 1951) or specific professional organizations or educational institutions (Brown, Groves, and Rusbad, 1947). Such seminars study marriage counseling as it is related to day-by-day practice in these professions. Intensive training in marriage counseling on the graduate level is being developed increasingly in the postwar years by some of our universities and colleges. (See footnotes, pages 34, 35.)

BIBLIOGRAPHICAL AND REFERENCE MATERIAL

Books and articles, learned, popular, and "forbidden," have been written through the ages in all languages on marriage and sex behavior. This material was at first largely romantic, descriptive, and often erotic. With the advent of the early Freudian era some of it became analytic, using predominantly inductive methods. In the last decade there have been many

8

contributions based on academic discussion and theory and a lesser number on clinical findings.[3]

RESEARCH

As a field of endeavor attains sufficient interest for professional scrutiny and participation, the way it functions and the results of its work almost inevitably are investigated through research procedures. Some of the earlier pioneer studies in this field in the United States appeared during the last two decades: Davis (1929), Dickinson (1941), Dickinson and Bean (1931), Hamilton (1929), L. Hutton (1937), C. Landis (1940). Results based on experimental findings are adding new facts and forming the bases of new hypotheses for behavior and education (Cottrell, 1948). A few projects of importance in different areas of the general field are mentioned:

1. Studies in Child Development, and the like, at the Yale Medical School (Gesell and others, 1928–49); Iowa State Child Welfare Research Station; Child Development Institute, Teachers College, Columbia University; California Institute of Child Development; Research in Child Behavior at the Rochester Child Health Institute (Aldrich, Spock, 1945–50); the University of Chicago, Committee on Human Development and the William T. Carter Foundation for Child Helping (Bossard and co-workers, 1940–50).

2. Studies in Prediction of Success or Failure in Marriage (Burgess and Cottrell, 1939), (Kelly, 1941), (Locke, 1947–48), (Terman, 1938).

3. Studies in Delinquency in Boston under Eleanor T. and Sheldon Glueck.

4. Studies in Marriage Counseling at the Marriage Council of Philadelphia (Mudd, Preston, Peltz, Froscher, 1939–51).

5. Studies in Animal Sex Behavior at the American Museum of

---

[3] In the United States no bibliography in this field would be complete without listing works from such recognized contributors as the following (listed in bibliography): Alexander and French, Allen, Appel, Baber, Becker, Bergler, Bossard, Buck, Burgess, Butterfield, Cottrell, Cuber, de Schweinitz, Duvall, Elliott and Bone, Ellis, English and Pearson, Fisher, Folsom, Foster, Frank, Groves, E. and G., Hart, Hill, Himes, Kinsey, Pomeroy and Martin, Koos, Landis, C., J., and P., Mead, Menninger, K. and W., Mowrer, Nelson, Nimkoff, Plant, Popenoe, Rogers, Saul, Stokes, Stone, Strain, Strecker, Waller, Wood, Young, Zabriskie.

Natural History in New York under Dr. Frank A. Beach (Beach, 1947–50).

6. Studies in Analytic Psychology under Dr. Franz Alexander at the Institute of Psychoanalysis in Chicago (Alexander, French, and others, 1946 to date).

7. Studies in Human Fertility at the Wistar Institute of Anatomy and Biology under Dr. Edmund Farris (Farris, 1946–51).

8. Studies of Human Sex Behavior at the University of Indiana under the auspices of the Rockefeller Foundation and the National Research Council with Dr. Alfred Kinsey in charge (Kinsey, Pomeroy, and Martin, 1947 to date).

9. Studies of Movement in Social Casework at the Institute of Welfare Research, Community Service Society, New York, under Dr. J. McVicker Hunt, (1948–51).

10. Studies in Population and Family Organization at the Bureau of Applied Social Research at Columbia University (K. Davis and others, 1950).

A comprehensive survey analyzing the contribution of research to marriage and family counseling and recommending needed research in this field was prepared by Burgess and his co-workers in 1948 for the National Conference on Family Life.

The years 1946 and 1951 have seen increased interest on the part of government agencies in furthering knowledge and understanding of mental disease and its prevention through large-scale research programs. The passing of the recent National Mental Health Act is concrete evidence of this fact. Appreciation of the deleterious effect of mental breakdown on family life and the saving to individuals and communities by preventing this calamity is seen in certain of the research projects financed under one of the Research Divisions of the United States Public Health Service (Reynolds and Price, 1949).

NATIONAL AND STATE COUNCILS AND CONFERENCES ON FAMILY RELATIONS

Groups in the United States interested in the advancement of cultural and other aspects of family life have organized councils or conferences for the general dissemination and exchange through meetings and journals of ideas, information, and techniques in the different fields of specialization related to marriage and family life. Best known and most active among these groups at the national level are the Family Service Association of America with its 238 member agencies, the National Council on Family Relations with headquarters in Chicago, State Councils in twenty-five states and Regional Councils in five sections of the country, the National Catholic Welfare Conference, the Central Conference of American Rabbis, the National Council of the Churches of Christ in America, the National Conference on Family Life held in Washington in 1948, the Mid-Century White House Conference on Children and Youth held in Washington in 1950, and the American Association of Marriage Counselors organized in 1943, in New York, by a group active in clinical work in this field.[4] This Association is the first to recognize the potentials of marriage counseling as a social and scientific discipline. Definition of professional standards, development of counseling techniques, exchange of clinical experience, and certification of professional services are among its major concerns.

Other organizations well known at the national level have had interest in marriage counseling and have made recognized contributions to its progress. These will be discussed in detail in Chapter 3. Among annual conferences having national renown are the Groves Conference on Conservation of Marriage and the Family, which has met for nine years at Chapel Hill, North Carolina (*Marriage and Family Living,* Spring, 1949, issue) and the Pennsylvania State College Annual Institute on Marriage and Home Adjustment, which held annual meetings in 1944–46. Summer institutes in this field conducted under the auspices of educational institutions are in demand increasingly.

MARRIAGE AND FAMILY COUNSELING SERVICES

According to the section report on Marriage and Family Counseling (National Conference on Family Life, 1948), in the United States at that date there were about 300 active marriage or family counseling centers functioning in approx-

---

[4] See Appendix A for complete addresses.

imately forty of our forty-eight states; 240 of these were member agencies of the Family Service Association. The centers were organized and run in a variety of ways in different communities. A bird's-eye view of these services constitutes the content of Chapter 4, and is supplemented by reports from thirty-five of the functioning agencies reproduced in the words of their executives in Appendix B. These reports furnish information also on the background, training, and experience of currently practicing marriage counselors and on facilities for further training of present and future marriage counselors.

SUMMARY

It is generally conceded at the mid-point of the twentieth century that human relationships must become the subject of scientific scrutiny. Unless better methods of getting along together are evolved, the acceleration of destruction can hardly be expected to be followed by a civilized world. The family is the kernel in which relations begin. Marriage as the beginning of a family unit is a vital testing ground. Marriage counseling is one product of the times to assist in the promotion of more adequate marriages. Marriage and family counseling has been carried on throughout the ages, informally, semiformally, and recently more formally. In the twentieth century it developed first in German-speaking Europe, and later in England and the United States. The rise of Nazism arrested growth on the European continent. Development in the United States has been along the following main lines listed chronologically: (1) as a by-product of the daily practice of professionally trained individuals, (2) as an adjunct of other community agencies, (3) as a service focused on marriage counseling.

Marriage counseling in the broad sense has as its purpose the promotion of more adequate preparation for and adjustment in marriage. This purpose has been fostered by several approaches: (1) courses on marriage and the family in schools and colleges, in community groups, and in family counseling centers; (2) improved source and reference material; (3) intensified interest, promotion, and active participation in research. The formation of national, state, and community councils and conferences has promoted interest and activity in all of these approaches; (4) organization of marriage and family counseling centers; (5) an increase in the number of qualified professional persons in private practice in the field of marriage and family counseling; (6) more inclusive and higher standards for background and supervised in-service training in marriage counseling, and more available facilities.

2

Current Events
Affecting Marriage Counseling

MARRIAGE COUNSELING should be considered in relation to the times in which it functions if any significant understanding of its place in contemporary society is to be obtained. The people who use such a service and the problems they bring to it may be expected, in part, to reflect daily events in the world about them. It is therefore essential for the counselor and those working with or studying the family to be familiar with daily events as well as specific and general trends of the times (Boie, 1937). For this reason the following section highlights events of international, national, and specific importance to families in the United States during the years 1936–49 in which the 2,559 consecutive cases studied came to Marriage Council of Philadelphia. Thus the problems of the clients and the variation in intake may be considered against a picture of the continuities and discontinuities of the period.

ECONOMIC DEPRESSION TO WAR ECONOMY

Between 1936 and 1949 the American people went from the midst of economic depression into abnormal economic prosperity and the beginning of inflation. In December of 1936 there were still nine million unemployed in the United States. Strikes and labor disputes abounded, leading to the new law for fair labor standards for minimum wages and maximum hours. The inflated prosperity of 1941–44 was due to the production demands of war and Lend-Lease requirements. In 1949, as the last of the 2,559 cases studied was seen, increas-

14

ingly high taxes, economic difficulties, and job insecurity were once more in the offing. The swing from depression through war economy (Thomas, 1925), typical of the United States as a whole, was reflected in the unemployment and public relief figures of Pennsylvania. These conditions are important considering that 86 per cent of the persons who came for marriage counseling in the clinic studied resided in this state at the time counseling was sought. (See Table 2.)

In Pennsylvania, public dependency rolls showed 1,719,000 persons receiving federal and state assistance in 1933, with only slightly fewer in 1937. However, between February, 1939, and July, 1945, public dependency followed a steady downward course, primarily as a result of the rapid increase in employment opportunities brought about by World War II. This decline was concentrated for the most part among employable persons and their families; but substantial decreases also occurred among cases of families containing no employable members, as relatives of recipients obtained jobs and assured the support of family members formerly dependent on public aid (Komarovsky, 1940), (Stouffer and Lazarsfeld, 1937). As economic conditions improved, an increase was reflected, as might be expected, in the marriage, birth, and divorce rates of the country at large and in lesser degree in the Philadelphia area. (See Table 1.) With the defeat of Germany and, later, Japan in 1945, the six and one-half year downward trend was brought to a halt and the dependency rolls again turned upward due to labor-industry disputes and the difficulties of reconversion. By 1949 a total higher than any since 1942, but still considerably less than the prewar years, had been reached, to begin to decline once more as war in Korea gripped this and other nations in 1950–51 (*Public Assistance Reviews,* 1936–49).

THE EFFECTS ON FAMILIES OF ACCELERATED CHANGE

The economic shifts of the last two decades along with advances in science, mechanical inventions, increased methods of communication, transcontinental air travel, mobility and greatly increased transportation of millions of young persons due to war, postwar rehabilitation, and war again (Mautz and

15

Durand, 1943) have all combined to give the American family of the last decade experiences, perspectives, and values greatly different from those of the American family of 1936 (Cavan and Ranck, 1938), (Mead, 1947), (Sorokin, 1950).

The demands of World War II caused families to be uprooted and members separated to meet the needs of the armed forces and industry. After the first bill for compulsory registration of men between eighteen and forty-five in June, 1940, and its enactment into law followed by the first draft registration in November, 1940, the number of marriages increased. Many of these involved persons from different parts of the country and, later, different nationalities. Men and women were frozen for the duration of war in jobs declared essential. Rationing of food and gas was introduced. By 1943 all able-bodied men under a stipulated age not in essential industry were in the armed forces. Living costs had risen 25 per cent since 1941. Thus personal freedom was invaded on a large scale and trends reflecting family life of "normal" times suddenly disappeared, to be superseded by dramatic variations apparent in many phases of living (Ogburn, ed., 1943), (Abams, ed., 1943).

Marriage and birth rates rose further during the first years of actual war, tapered down during 1943–44 when many men were in overseas military service, rose again to an all-time high after demobilization in 1946 and 1947, and then again began to taper off. By this date thirty states required premarital examination for venereal disease. The divorce rate did not fall during the active war years but rather continued to rise steadily to an all-time high in 1946, after which it dropped appreciably through 1948. (See Table 1.) The number of persons over sixty-five was increased appreciably. Disability or illness of parents, physical or emotional neglect, discord between parents and between parents and children, necessitated seven out of every thousand children in the United States receiving specialized casework services in June, 1950. According to the Mid-Century White House Conference on Children and Youth, this was a small fraction of those known to be in need of protective and foster care.

In addition, the economic vagaries and shifting customs begun before the war, and greatly accelerated by war and its

16

aftermath, have altered the cultural status of groups within our society, the relationship of individuals to each other, and the values held important (Bossard, 1941), (Hughes, 1942), (Hill, 1949). There were not only appreciably more women, fewer single and more married, over fourteen in the United States in 1949 than in 1940, but there were over three and one-half million more married women working, over two million more than the single women in the labor force.[1]

TABLE 1*

MARRIAGES, DIVORCES, BIRTHS PER 1,000 POPULATION
IN THE UNITED STATES AND PHILADELPHIA
1936–1949

Year	Marriages		Divorces			Births		
	U.S.A.	P.	U.S.A.		P.	U.S.A.		P.
	Number	Rate	Rate	Number	Rate	Rate	Number	Rate	Rate
1936	1,369,000	10.7	6.9	236,000	1.8	0.8	2,144,790	16.7	15.3
1937	1,451,296	11.2	7.3	249,000	1.9	1.0	2,203,337	17.1	15.5
1938	1,319,143	10.2	6.8	240,000	1.9	0.9	2,286,962	17.6	16.0
1939	1,375,063	10.5	8.0	251,000	1.9	0.8	2,265,558	17.3	15.6
1940	1,565,014	11.9	7.5	264,000	2.0	1.0	2,360,399	17.9	16.2
1941	1,679,000	12.6	8.4	293,000	2.2	1.0	2,513,427	18.9	17.8
1942	1,758,000	13.1	8.9	358,000	2.3	1.3	2,808,996	20.9	21.8
1943	1,577,000	11.8	7.7	359,000	2.5	1.4	2,934,860	21.5	22.2
1944	1,445,000	10.9	6.7	400,000	2.9	1.5	2,794,800	20.2	19.7
1945	1,618,331	12.3	7.4	502,000	3.6	1.7	2,735,456	19.6	19.6
1946†	2,291,045	16.4	10.8	610,000	4.3	2.6	3,458,000	23.3	20.2
1947	1,992,878	13.9	9.6	483,000	3.4	2.3	3,876,000	25.8	20.6
1948	1,802,895	12.3	8.8	405,000	2.8	1.9	3,702,000	24.2	20.6
1949	1,585,440	10.5	7.6	386,000‡	2.6	1.7	3,581,000	23.9	19.7

* *Bureau of the Census Population Series*, 1, 2, 3, 4, Washington, D.C., *Statistical Abstracts of the United States*, 68th Ed., 1947, United States Department of Commerce, Bureau of Census, Washington, D.C.

† Figures for Marriage and Divorce for years 1946–48 obtained from: *Vital Statistics Special Reports, Provisional Marriage and Divorce Statistics*, United States, 1948. Federal Security Agency, Vol. 31, No. 16, November, 1949. Figures for Births for years 1946–48 for the United States obtained from: *Vital Statistics Special Reports, United States Summary of Vital Statistics*, 1948. Federal Security Agency, Vol. 34, No. 50, June 1, 1950. Figures for Philadelphia from Chamber of Commerce, corrected for nonresidents.

‡ Divorce figures for 1949 obtained from Federal Security Agency—Public Health Service, National Office of Vital Statistics, Washington 25, D.C., *Marriages and Divorces, Crude Rates: Continental U.S., Territories and Possessions, 1949.*

[1] *Census Release*, Series P-50, No. 22, April 19, 1950.

A leveling off in the standard of living took effect as lower income groups raised their standards and higher income groups lessened theirs (National Resources Committee, 1938), (Folsom, 1943), (Bossard, 1944). Other aspects of our culture such as entertainment, diversion, and manners, particularly as they are reflected in music, education, business, professions, vocations, and recreation, all give evidence of significant difference (Bossard, 1950), (Ellis, 1948), (Johnson, 1949), (Sullivan, 1946), (Watkins, ed., 1947).

Change is inevitable. However, during the last two decades the rate of change has greatly increased over any other similar period of time (Zimmerman, 1949). This accelerated rate with its accompanying lack of time for assimilation contributes greatly to the anxiety, restlessness, and apparent unhappiness felt by many persons. An adjustment to one type of stress and strain has no sooner been made than a new orientation is demanded. Values maintained under the authoritarian restraints of earlier generations are being rebelled against as irrational although there is as yet little secure familiarity with a new and more realistic set of cultural values.

The transition from world to national to community events no longer requires the fabulous seven-league boots of the past. Communities consist of families and today's families include men, women, and children, many of whom have lived through the kaleidoscopic years of 1936–49. Young people have been caught up in the fluidity of this period, whether they wanted to be or not, and older people have held their breath and "taken" it because there was no way out. Millions of all ages, unable to keep pace, have fallen by the wayside and are to be found in our overflowing state and private mental hospitals and sanitariums (Appel, 1950), (Menninger, W., 1948), (Odegard, 1946), (*Patients in Mental Institutions, 1944*, 1947), (Stern, 1942), (Truesdell, 1947).

THE HUMAN NEEDS OF MEN AND WOMEN ARE FOCUSED IN MARRIAGE AND FAMILY LIFE

And while these years were passing, men and women were living together in love and hate, in sickness and health, in poverty and wealth, in war and peace, as they have since the beginning of time. Others, separated by the exigencies of war, were waiting to live together in the hope of fulfilling their dreams, or in the dread of repeating a past replete with conflict and disappointment. In the years following demobilization men and women once more faced each other for better and for worse in a world scarred by the ravages of total war, shadowed by the A- and H-bombs, and fearful of the unfocused, all-pervading uncertainties of two incompatible ideologies.

Studies of human development show that human behavior can be modified throughout life by human contacts and that social institutions also have plasticity. Yet both are resistant to change. The family, like other institutions, imposes its imprints early on its members, who, in turn, perpetuate the traditional pattern to which they have been molded. "It is the men and women in whom these patterns of attitude and behavior have been incorporated who present the immediate resistance to social, economic, and political change. Thus prejudice, hostility, or excessive nationalism may become deeply embedded in the developing personality without awareness on the part of the individual concerned, and often at great human cost." [2] In contrast to these negative attributes, attitudes of acceptance of difference, of kindness and tolerance, could be nurtured in the family to help men and women live with each other and with their fellows.

The very living together in family life has been difficult for many persons although desperately desired by most. Evidence of this is found in the fact that, although the divorce rate rose steadily until 1946 in the United States, remarriage increasingly has absorbed the divorced. As it became increasingly evident that these difficulties presented hazards to national and international health, ideas as to how these hazards might be lessened and approaches for furthering adjustment and preventing difficulties in marriage and family living came into existence. Marriage counseling services are one evidence of

---

[2] Ideas in this paragraph and the direct quotes are taken from the *Statement* by the International Preparatory Commission, International Congress on Mental Health, London, August, 1948. Used with permission.

an attempt to meet the needs of the times for more comfortable and constructive family life and to utilize professional resources toward the goal of more stable and healthy communities. These services and others in this field cannot solve the disturbances, some of which, as we have indicated already, are inherent in cultural complexities. However, as world upheaval and family disruption once again dog the footsteps of many citizens, they should be able to help. The question might well be raised as to whether the prognosis for more comfortable family adjustment will become less optimistic as war again infringes on the nations. If this is the case, will a greater need for more marriage counseling arise? In all probability it will. And when it does, it will be the responsibility of the professional persons interested or working in the field to see that this work matures healthily with the challenge.

SUMMARY

This section has presented a brief survey of events of national and international importance which affected family life in the United States during the thirteen years in which the 2,559 cases seen in a marriage counseling office were studied.

Emphasis was placed on the following facts: (1) The years from 1933 through the first part of 1939 were years of economic depression in the United States, with a large amount of unemployment and labor unrest. This resulted in privation and conflict for many families and in public dependency, despair, anxiety, and resentment. (2) In 1940 the imminence of World War II initiated new industries and greatly implemented production of all kinds, thus beginning to eliminate unemployment and economic privation. Introduction and passage of the draft bill this same year and, later, requirements for workers in essential industry vitally affected the status of all families containing men between eighteen and forty-five. Internal migration was greatly accelerated. Taxes and living costs rose. (3) On December 7, 1941, war was declared by the United States on the Axis. The following years show the stresses and strains on family life of a country engaged in war. (4) Following the surrender of Germany and Japan, from 1945 to 1949 American families were faced with the problems of demobilization, continued internal migration, the conversion of industry to postwar needs, climbing living costs and the beginning of inflation, all climaxed in 1950–51 by the United Nations war in Korea. (5) The transition from old to as yet unfamiliar new value systems was mentioned together with the recognition of the plasticity of human behavior and institutions and the vital potentials of the family in fostering attitudes conducive to living together in harmony. (6) Marriage counseling is mentioned as one means of assisting family members to meet individual and group problems under the complex conditions of accelerated change as evidenced in this period. (7) As stresses and strains of war again create added disturbance to marriage and family life, it is predicted that there will be increased demand for more marriage counseling. The professions involved in this field will have the responsibility for guiding this growth toward healthy maturity.

3

Less Formalized Marriage Counseling

IT IS GENERALLY conceded that of all the marriage counseling that takes place, the most of it is very informal. The
majority of those who wish clarification and assistance in mar-
riage-connected problems go first to the nearest and most obvious source of help—their relatives, friends, their family
physician, minister, priest, or rabbi, their teachers, or some
third party, just on the basis of an understanding of their backgrounds. The turning to someone known and trusted, or trusted
though unknown, is natural and will continue, even when
formal marriage counseling services with specially trained personnel are more easily available.

Relatives and friends are often sought because they know
through first-hand experience the individual personalities involved, the factors surrounding the situation, and are emotionally linked to the persons seeking counsel. But it is to the
physician, the minister, priest, or rabbi, and the teacher that
in all probability come the greatest demands for marriage
counseling help: the physician because he automatically comes
in contact with the couple contemplating marriage as they
fulfill the state requirements for premarital health certificates
or later when maladjustment produces symptoms of physical
distress; the minister because the ritual of the wedding ceremony, the customs of the church, and the growing practice of
requiring a preliminary interview before marriage bring contact at periods fraught with emotion; the teacher because the
young man and woman are in daily contact with him or her,

and in certain classes discuss subject matter directly related to dating, mate selection, and marriage.

It therefore seems important to understand something of the areas dealt with, the procedures, techniques, advantages, limitations, and pitfalls which may occur in this type of discussion between someone with a problem wishing assistance and the person turned to who, although trained and experienced in his own profession, may not be technically trained in the counseling field. Following this it should be possible to suggest criteria from the experience of technically trained marriage counselors which may be helpful to those persons who are precipitated into counseling through their other duties and who, for one reason or another, do not see their way clear for long and arduous professional training in this field.

Perhaps it should be emphasized at this point that in discussing counseling which is less formalized we do not refer to the spurious "psychologist" with no college degree, the "personal adviser" advertised in the classified directory, or the host of unorthodox, unethical, fly-by-night, irresponsible, money-making adventurers who play upon the heartaches of troubled humanity and exploit their needs. These should not be considered in any sense as marriage or family counselors, nor should their performance be discussed within the same framework. Reputable marriage counselors almost invariably are on the paid staff of a recognized community organization, or they have memberships in one of the recognized national professional associations, or they have graduate degrees in medicine, social work, psychology, sociology, or a related field.

No systematic studies have been or probably could be made of either the extent of the rather informal counseling of physicians, ministers, and teachers or of procedures they may employ. The writer, herself inexperienced in this type of work, will draw upon presentations of points of view on marriage counseling prepared by a committee of physicians, a committee of clergy of various religious affiliations, and by a committee of teachers for the section on Counseling and Guidance of the National Conference on Family Life.[1]

[1] Permission has been given by the National Conference on Family Life held in Washington, May 6-8, 1948, to use the unpublished report

Physicians

The *Index Medicus* for the years 1943–48, according to this report, does not contain the heading, "Marriage Counseling." Papers dealing with the various medical and psychiatric aspects of marriage are scattered under many different headings. It is well recognized that continued maladjustment in the personal relationships of marriage and family life often lead to disturbances which give rise to many varieties of medical symptoms. Patients with such symptoms are found in the offices of most physicians and hospital clinics. They absorb a vast amount of medical time, often with little satisfaction to themselves or to the physician. It is in this area that physicians are becoming aware increasingly of the effectiveness of marriage and family counseling as they use its techniques within their own practice or refer to facilities in the community organized for such service (Stokes, W., 1951). In addition, forty states (Mackay, 1946) now require a medical examination for physical fitness for one or both partners before granting a marriage license. Because of this, physicians come in contact with thousands of young persons at a time when real preventive work is possible.

Physicians, the report states, should be aware of the following in connection with marriage counseling:

That the emotions have an important influence on health.

That the majority of normal people have problems in marital and family relationships which may cause tensions, anxiety, and conflicts, and which may interfere with good health.

That problems often arise early in marriage and that much serious damage may occur during the first year.

That the majority of people have had inadequate preparation for marriage and family life or no education, or what is much worse, much misinformation.

---

prepared for the section on Counseling and Guidance by a committee of 24 persons, all with recognized positions in medicine, psychology, law, social work, teaching, etc., of which the author was Chairman. This material was also used as a report by the Preparatory Commission, International Congress on Mental Health, London, 1948, and summarized in Basic Materials used by working groups, World Federation for Mental Health, Geneva, Switzerland, 1949.

That inadequate medical service is given when the only answer to timid questioning is a pat on the back with advice to "let nature take its course."

That the premarital examination, compulsory by law in an increasing number of states, presents a most important opportunity for the preventive and educational aspects of marriage counseling. Taking a Wassermann alone is inadequate, and does not even fulfill the requirements of the law. Only by direct examination can it be determined whether the man and woman about to be married are free of gonorrhea and have physical anatomical fitness for marriage.

That it is equally important to ascertain psychological fitness and readiness for marriage. The wise physician will take this opportunity to allow the couple sufficient time, both separately and together, to ask their questions, encourage them to express their fears, anxieties, ascertain their knowledge about sex and particularly their attitudes toward each other. The physician should be a qualified educator of the couple in the anatomy, physiology, and psychology of sex life in marriage. It is realized, however, that because of the lack of adequate training, many physicians at present are unable to qualify in this role.

That many couples will be helped more than they realize by a fuller knowledge of techniques of the sex act. Care should be exercised to allow each couple freedom to choose and develop their own methods of attaining mutual satisfaction. Advice on family planning is a common request at the premarital interview. The prescribing of a safe method of child spacing acceptable to the individual in the light of his or her religious affiliations helps in sexual adjustment, since fear of unwanted pregnancy frequently leads to fear of sex life. Models and illustrations are helpful also. The physician should also encourage pregnancy as soon as conditions are favorable for children, for the ultimate fulfillment of marriage and family life is parenthood.

That he must be aware when the problem is one of sexual adjustment per se, or when it is only one of the symptoms of a deep-seated neurosis or beginning mental illness. He must be able to make the differential diagnosis between what lies in the field of the family physician and what should be referred to a psychiatrist or specialist in marriage counseling.

That he should accept the view that prevention of divorce is as important as prevention of disease, and that prophylactic measures are better than curative ones. Religious factors are important.

25

That he should be familiar with the community resources which can co-operate with him in the establishment of a stable family life. He should initiate and co-operate in the establishment of such resources if they are not yet available.

Clergymen

The minister's emphasis, as reported, whatever the particular problems of the married state, sexual, social, financial, or religious, is that marriage is to be seen as a relationship of two personalities with all that they have and all that they are. Though it has many particular adjustments they all fit into a pattern of living which is ultimately of the personality and of the spiritual nature. Marriage is a venture with God, with destiny and with future generations, as well as a personal venture of a man and woman with each other. The minister is particularly concerned with the total meaning of the various types of adjustment. He emphasizes the importance of emotional maturity and of the spiritual foundations upon which firm human relationships must be based. He also thinks of the little family in relationship with the larger family, the church, for in the life of the church the little family gains an enhancement of its values in a social and spiritual setting related to God and to the highest values and meanings of life.

The minister is concerned with three kinds of love, of which God is the Giver: romantic love which draws a man and woman together, conjugal love in which they build a pattern of creative co-operation in fulfilling domestically the meaning and purpose of love, and a third kind of love which is somewhat like the love of God, who loves us not because we are always lovable but because love is the most creative force in bringing out the best in people. That is, people learn to love on principle and not merely on emotional impulse. The family as a part of the tissue of humanity has its part in making life what it ought to be for its members and, in some measure, for the world in which they live.

Among the functions of ministerial counseling the following are listed: listening, information giving, reminding, interpreting, providing a steadying influence, offering techniques and resources and aid in reorganization of life, and assurance of

26

forgiveness.[2] Twelve suggestions as to procedure in counseling are offered which are characteristic of the way in which many ministers approach counseling. They are: (1) create a counseling atmosphere, (2) let the approach be to the counselor, (3) respect the sacredness of confidence, (4) take an objective point of view, (5) be a good listener, (6) hear both sides whenever possible, (7) get the person or persons to tell enough but not too much, (8) look for the deeper problem beneath the apparent ones, (9) help the counselee to solve his own problem, (10) remember that the solution of the problem must be based on available resources, (11) use the resources of the community, (12) get individuals and families adjusted to life and to God.

From another source comes the statement that the clergyman is in an ideal position to serve young engaged couples in premarital counseling even though he is not always adequately prepared to do so.[3] Premarital counseling is not new to religion. For years the clergy have helped plan the wedding and have given incidental advice which might help a couple in their marriage. Only recently a few ministers have systematically studied how they might better prepare couples for marriage and then purposely set up a program of counseling. (The Protestant Episcopal Church since 1931 has required their clergy to undertake premarital counseling with the couples they marry.) Only a relatively small percentage of clergymen are undertaking this task, and a still smaller number feel their program to be in any way adequate. A clergyman according to one point of view should never feel that premarital counseling is the sole means of preparing young people, but should conceive of it as a necessary part of a total program of family life education (Staples, 1949). This may well include courses

---

[2] Author's Note: "Assurance of forgiveness," from the viewpoint of the caseworker, psychiatrist, or marriage counselor, belongs specifically to the minister. The implication of moral judgment here is one of the significant differences between the clergy and the attitude of the marriage counselor.

[3] From a statement prepared for the Training Center in Family Life, Health and Social Relations at the University of California in the summer session of 1948. Used with permission.

of instruction at the various age levels, parent education, literature, sermons, talks, visual aids, and so on. The following objectives of premarital counseling are listed:

.To help a couple face their relationship with each other realistically and frankly in the light of the distinctive features which each may bring to the marriage in order that they may better understand each other, their backgrounds, and the goals of their marriage. To do this not through lecturing or giving advice, but by guiding them in thinking through their own situation so as to gain new insights and reach workable solutions. Identity of thought and action is not necessary, but a common direction and purpose are essential.

To anticipate some of the common problems of young married couples so that later they may not be taken by surprise, but may prepare themselves to master each new situation as it develops.

To help a couple face and overcome a sense of inhibition or reticence in facing certain issues in regard to sex, family spacing, or other points where it may be difficult for them to express their feelings.

To help those who have had domestic failures to understand the factors which wrecked the previous marriage in order that they may be avoided in the new relationship. (This applies to those churches which permit remarriage and to those cases in which the minister feels he may do so.)

According to Sylvanus Duvall (1947) the minister can be educated to perform limited, but invaluable, service as a counselor in marriage and family relations. "At present his training in this area is insufficient both in quantity and in quality. Clinical experience in counseling with relatively normal persons," he feels, "might prove a far more valuable preparation for the minister than experience in a hospital, working with cases of more extreme derangement." [4]

Books by Dicks (1947), Fosdick (1943), Goldstein (1945), Hiltner (1949), Liebman (1946) and articles by Federal Council (1945), Robert (1950), Schindler (1942), Wood (1948, 1950), and the monthly journal, *Pastoral Psychology,*

---

[4] In this connection it is of interest to note the residencies in psychiatry available for ministers at St. Elizabeth's Hospital, Washington, and elsewhere. For details write Chaplain Bruder, St. Elizabeth's.

add further worth-while thinking on the counseling done through religious representations.

Educators

Children and young people look to teachers for counsel, continues the report for the Washington Conference, in time of difficulty and anxiety just as they seek advice from any older, more experienced person in whom they have confidence. They are more likely to request counsel in their family problems from their teacher in this area of subject matter, if they have such a course. This is a natural result of family situations being more clearly defined and focused for students in such courses. They see some hope of understanding the situation and having it resolved. The attitude of a teacher is likely to be more receptive to talking over a situation that has already been brought to light in his course. There is usually some ground for the student's confidence that the teacher of such a subject-matter field will know how to direct the student toward the solution of his problem.

In the preliminary report of a recent sample study of some eighty teacher-counselors in college courses in the family life area in some seventy colleges and universities over the United States, no counseling was indicated as mandatory on the student. Instead, students sought out their teachers to talk over their problems with them. This was done in the most informal and casual manner, the teachers frequently disclaiming any title to counselor and regarding their services as incidental to their teaching duties. With few exceptions teachers gave their time in student counseling voluntarily and without compensation in addition to their salary for teaching. Counseling to be of any value frequently becomes very time consuming and some of these teacher-counselors estimated that they gave from 1 to 25 per cent of their spare time for counseling services. Some fifteen of these teacher-counselors indicated that their counseling services were ignored by the administration in respect to recognition in the form of salary or promotion and that the status of counseling was inferior on their campuses to that of teaching. A few teachers did not interpret their work as including counseling and did none of it. In other instances, the college or university maintained a regular counseling bureau for students and the teachers did little counseling on their own responsibility, referring students who so desired to such a central office.

Expression was unanimous among these teachers as to the need of students for counseling services in love, marriage, courtship, and family problems, some of them employing such words as "pathetic" and "desperate" to indicate the intensity of the need. Private offices, or rooms, were available for counseling in most cases but a few teacher-counselors felt greatly handicapped by having to share offices or look for a vacant classroom to carry on interviews.

The counseling interviews of the seventy-three teacher-counselors varied from twenty minutes to three hours, on the average; the longer periods and the greater number of interviews per student tended to be associated with the teachers having the more technical preparation for counseling and the wider reputation as counselors. Counselors varied from one to one hundred or more counseling interviews in an academic year, the modal average being two or three.

Some teachers believe that teaching and counseling have reciprocal advantages for each other in that teaching serves as a sifting device to select out for counseling those persons who have unresolved problems and anxieties (Pritchett, 1949). The teacher is readily available and can be consulted without the student being conspicuous. The atmosphere of the classroom and the faculty office is normal and somewhat optimistic and the student takes little risk of being thought of as freakish or abnormal because he talks over his worries with his teacher.

Many teachers and officials, however, find themselves called upon to render advice or opinions on matters for which they are quite unprepared. A professor, for example, who appears to be human, tolerant, understanding, and approachable, may be quite an authority on medieval history but has had no formal training or background for analyzing or understanding the nature of emotional problems of human beings. He knows nothing about casework, interview or counseling techniques, or the deeper underlying psychiatric or psychoanalytical interpretations. In spite of all this he may, of course, on a common-sense basis help many students work their way through the maze of emotional difficulties.

Obviously a faculty member who attempts to deal with the intimate personal questions of students is handling dynamite. There are no stock answers and even now, according to the same report, although some teacher-counselors are fitted by training and experience to do good work in marriage and pre-marriage counseling, much of the informal counseling that goes on in the colleges and universities is done by persons who think in terms of direct or evasive answers, assume attitudes of praise and blame, give heart-to-heart pep talks and advice.

In some problems the student would be exposed to disciplinary measures if his college knew the whole story. The teacher is handicapped in such situations and sometimes has difficulty disassociating himself from his college sufficiently to provide full assurance that the student's confidences will be maintained at all hazards. Some problems not subject to disciplinary action are of such a nature as to cause the student to think there is danger that he will be lowered in his teacher's estimation or his credit standing in the course may suffer if he discloses all the facts. (This point has been referred to as an argument in favor of noncredit courses in this field.) Under these circumstances it is evident that good counseling is impossible. The teacher, however, has the opportunity of rendering a genuine and in some cases a much needed service by helping create in the minds of young people an attitude of normal acceptance of professional counseling services, and by referring the necessary cases, when facilities are available, to professional experts in marriage counseling or other appropriate specialties.

Another analysis, made in 1950 by Beatrice Marion,[5] of 120 questionnaires returned by teacher-counselors in thirty-eight different states, reports in summary: "The counseling picture presented by our survey would seem to be something like this: Many instructors of supposedly functional courses are doing no counseling. Those who report counseling reach less than one-fourth of the students in their classes. Interviews are thirty to

---

[5] Unpublished report by Mrs. Beatrice Marion at the Annual Meeting of the National Council on Family Relations, Denver, September, 1950. Used with permission.

sixty minutes in length, averaging two to a client. Half keep no records, most charge no fees. The counseling is nearly always optional, frequently suggested by the instructor who usually does it in addition to a full teaching load and with a constant sense of frustration because of inadequate time and facilities" (Timmons and Caraway, 1947).

An arrangement utilizing professionally recognized community resources in this field for combining teaching and counseling of undergraduate college students has been under way for some seven years in the Philadelphia area. Swarthmore College in 1942 and Bryn Mawr College two years later requested Marriage Council of Philadelphia to conduct a series of discussions, financed through the college treasury, on personality development, dating, courtship, and marriage adjustments.[6] A committee of students recommended that the series be held in the evening in an informal setting and that attendance be voluntary, carrying no credit. Marriage Council accepted these recommendations, assigned staff personnel as discussion leaders, and arranged that adequate reading material be purchased by the college and made available on a reference shelf throughout the series. The deans recommended the series be open at Swarthmore to senior men and women and engaged juniors, at Bryn Mawr to students in the three upper classes after passing the Hygiene examination. Announcement of the course was made through the student paper and the dean's office. Seventy-five to one hundred and twenty students have registered for the course yearly at Swarthmore, at first more women than men but since the war about equal numbers. At Bryn Mawr the group has varied from forty-five to eighty-five.

Shortly after the initiation of the course each college requested Marriage Council to furnish counseling service to any student in the course who so desired. This was arranged by having an experienced counselor from Marriage Council, sometimes the same person as the discussion leader, sometimes a different staff member, available on the campus for the necessary number of days, the cost being covered by the college and

---

[6] For staff background requirements and experience at Marriage Council of Philadelphia, see agency report in Appendix B.

no charge made to the student. The counselor was briefed in the college recreational, medical, and psychiatric facilities. Marriage Council sent to the dean's office each year a general report, without names, of the types of situations for which students sought counseling but arranged that the counselor would have no disciplinary responsibility whatsoever to the college. Records of the interviews, similar to other agency recordings, were made and kept in the agency office.

Approximately 8 to 18 per cent of the students in the courses signed up for individual counseling. A few more sought out the agency later for premarital service as their own marriage approached or for specific or more involved adjustments before or after their marriage. Counseling interviews on the college campus were scheduled for one-half to one hour and were predominantly one contact. If more than two interviews were indicated, arrangements had to be made for the student to come to Marriage Council at his own expense or to continue work with the college psychiatrist. The majority of student problems were connected with weaning in parental relationships, behavior in connection with dating, choice of a mate and engagement adjustments, and, with engaged students, general preparation for marriage.

The students have requested the continuation of this series of discussion meetings yearly and both the colleges and Marriage Council feel it serves a constructive place in student life. Evaluation of these counseling contacts is in process along with evaluation of other agency counseling and will be published at a later date. (See section on Follow-up of Counseling, p. 196.)

College, secondary, and elementary school administrators are sometimes severely criticized for not entering completely and enthusiastically into a program of courses and counseling in marriage and family life subjects "to meet the crisis of the family in our times" (Rockwood and Ford, 1945). The schools and colleges have probably the widest contact with all the children and youth of our country of all our social institutions, except the family. They reach these young people at a period of life when ideals and attitudes are being formed and when lifelong choices are being made (Gruenberg, 1946). Such courses well directed, continues the report, with more time for competent counseling of students in their problems and anxieties supplement that part of the work of the dean which has to do with family relations and constitute strategic spots at which to attack the disorganization of family life in the future.

But administrators are also responsible for seeing that such important programs are inaugurated soundly. The material of family life education, if not wisely planned and presented, may not only fail to be helpful but may influence adversely progress and improvement of family life. Teachers and counselors in family living subjects must know their limitations, be mature in judgment and well-balanced emotionally, as well as being informed in the fields in which they teach and counsel. Administrators cannot be justly blamed for delay until those conditions are reasonably assured of fulfillment and careful, systematic study of the effect of the courses is begun.

That training for teacher-counseling in this field is as yet difficult to obtain is borne out by a recent survey of "Content of Theory Courses in Marriage Counseling" (Morgan, 1950). This reports that nine universities offer training courses,[7] all on the graduate level with the exception of two. Six universities offer advanced seminars in this subject and five, practicums or internships in marriage counseling. Course content follows closely the requirements set down by the American Association of Marriage Counselors. These universities recognize that marriage counseling involves many disciplines such as law, medicine, religion, social work, and others and is interprofessional in character. In the advanced work, use is being made of recordings of counseling interviews, case studies, and actual counseling situations.

It is not appropriate to leave the subject of teacher-counseling without considering the situation in the high schools as

---

[7] For further information, make contact with the following universities: Denver, Drew, Florida State, Merrill-Palmer, Ohio State, Pennsylvania State, Southern California, Utah, Utah State Agricultural. In addition, courses in marriage counseling are offered at the Free Synagogue, New York, New School of Social Research, New York, and the American Institute of Family Relations. Since the survey, Teachers College, Columbia, offers special work in marriage counseling.

well as in the colleges. From an experiment of recognized success come the following comments:

Because of the wide range of maturity represented in the groups, individual guidance and assistance, rather than mass instruction, is attempted. The young people who are planning marriage in the immediate future receive special help with their problems and are directed toward reliable sources of information. The sex aspects of marriage are not overemphasized; on the contrary, the many, many more important phases of the marital relationship are stressed.

Affirmatively, it is obvious that pupils need to learn how to live more successfully and happily in their present family relationships in order to develop into the kind of mature, stable, well-adjusted personalities that will have a better than even chance of establishing strong homes through marriage. Therefore, the individual family set-up is studied, problems are aired, suggestions and possible solutions are considered, new avenues of thinking and behaving are opened up.

And finally, the limitations of any human relationships program must be kept in mind. We must be reasonable creatures. A course in human relationships is not a magic formula for the world's ills. It is not a cure-all for divorce. It will not automatically create happy homes. It will not change human nature overnight. It will not insure understanding and wisdom and health and happiness in all homes, present and future. But, it will *help!* Churches do not close their doors because sin continues to be so popular. Health clinics do not cease to function because patients are plentiful. . . . In this area results may not be measurable. . . . Here may be the place to inject a word too seldom used in education—faith—faith in the ability of children to learn, to grow, to absorb, and to change.[8]

Community Organizations

Efforts of value in the promotion of constructive relationships within family groups, especially between parent and child, are currently under way nationally, on a large scale, through yet other important community organizations—the Young Men's and Young Women's Christian and Hebrew Associations. Here we find organized group activities for young people of various ages, together with their parents, utilizing

---

[8] Elizabeth S. Force, teacher, Social Behavior and Family Relations Courses, Toms River High School, Toms River, New Jersey.

alternately the facilities of the Y, the school, and the home. Staff members are encouraged to undertake preliminary vocational guidance interviews with interested young men, and are frequently called on by the young people who get to know them to discuss personal situations, related to dating, courtship, and choice of a mate, in which anxiety, doubts, fears, or confusion may be present.

Only a small proportion of the staff secretaries who lead groups or deal with the problems of individuals in such organizations have professional training in the field of family life. However, where kindliness, consideration, and tolerance are present and the young person is enabled to talk out and think through his ideas and plans, without dogmatic directing, these contacts often furnish great comfort and relief, whether or not they should be considered marriage counseling. The importance of enabling these staff personnel to become acquainted, through systematic reading and staff seminars, with what can be done helpfully and with the least potential danger to the young person on this less formalized level might well be considered carefully by these and other organizations involved.[9] The organization also has a responsibility in connection with the volunteers whose services they accept. It is this group in particular who often need help in realizing what they should know, and how and when to refer to professional sources.

The Individual

In addition to these institutionally connected sources of talking things over, there is found in almost any neighborhood or group of friends an individual to whom others quite naturally turn in their troubles. Very often this is a woman such as

---

[9] Within the last few years the family agencies which heretofore have given individualized service to a family and its members, have become interested in the possibilities for working on adjustment through group discussions. The Family Service Association of America has put this on their program and some member agencies are accepting assignments for staff members. It is hoped that in this way a new professional group—caseworkers—will be available to educational institutions and community organizations such as churches and Y's for group discussions, and possibly combined with individual counseling.

Pearl Buck describes her mother to be or other authors depict, the family doctor, the friendly judge, or the humane priest, minister, or rabbi with broad sympathies, strength of character, and deep faith in human beings. Such a person often does not think of himself as a counselor, but his usefulness is not necessarily less on that account, for he is a "natural" in applying what are conceded currently to be basic principles in successful formal marriage and family counseling: the art of being a stimulating listener, and faith in the ability of the other person to find, with help, a solution to his own problems. From such a person others receive refreshment, encouragement, and faith to try again.

Marriage Counseling in England [10]

In England, training for marriage counselors is also a matter of considerable importance, as marriage guidance has been subsidized in part by the government. A *Syllabus for the Training of Marriage Counselors* was issued in 1949 by the National Marriage Guidance Council. This presents an outline for six one-hour lectures with auxiliary reading, and states in brief the requirements which must be met by persons desirous of becoming marriage counselors, as follows:

"Approval is given by the National Marriage Guidance Council on a fivefold basis: (1) nominations by properly constituted local M.G.C., (2) approval by a National Selection Board, (3) attendance at the lecture course, (4) satisfactory completion of the written work, (5) evidence of sound casework during a period of probation to be determined according to the circumstances, but normally of not less than one year."

The syllabus defines the concept of the marriage counselor "as a general practitioner, working as a member of a team which includes specialist consultants in five fields, medical, psychological, ethical and spiritual, social, and legal. By this arrangement the counselor is constantly learning by co-operation with his colleagues, and is supported by specialist knowledge and skill upon which he can call as soon as he is confronted

---

[10] The full story of this work in England is told in a book, *Marriage Counseling*, by David R. Mace, obtainable for $1.50 from the National Marriage Guidance Council, 78 Duke Street, London W 1, England.

with a situation which is beyond his competence. Thus every safeguard is provided against false confidence and the cultivation of superficial, rule-of-thumb techniques. The good counselor is always learning and always improving his skill.

"But two things are necessary before this process can begin. We must be sure that the counselor is a suitable person for the delicate and responsible task of dealing with marriage relationships. And we must give him a basic equipment of knowledge so that he may have an intelligent grasp of the implications of his task. The first requirement has been met by the techniques of selection which have been worked out and applied by the National Marriage Guidance Council. The second has led to the provision of a course of instruction."

Apparently, the situations in which people find themselves in interpersonal and marriage relationships are much the same the world over. But what constitutes a problem to one person under a certain set of conditions is not necessarily a problem to another person. Within this truism, this author believes, lies the most vital principle for all those persons professionally trained or untrained who attempt to be of help to others seeking assistance in perplexity or trouble.

Although there is general acceptance among professionally trained counselors that on-the-job supervision in actual marriage counseling cases is the way to learn and carry on really professional counseling, nevertheless it is realized that whole areas of this country do not have either professional marriage counseling service or training possibilities. For such circumstances the counseling principles which follow have been compiled in the hope that they may be of practical assistance. They are familiar to professionally trained counselors and are illustrated in great detail in later chapters in this book on "Case Histories of Clients" and "The Process of Counseling." They have become real and substantial to the staff of Philadelphia Marriage Council in our eighteen years of counseling experience in this field. As stated they can be applied quite simply through patience and effort in situations, either before or after marriage, by less formal counselors or by those individuals to whom people in trouble turn, even if they do not consider themselves counselors. They are offered only as suggestions, certainly not as a prescription. They are in no sense final and should be modified and improved by the continuing experience of persons doing this type of work. Much more specific suggestions have been published in "Some Things the Teacher-Counselor May Do and Should Not Do," by Henry Bowman (1947), himself a leading teacher-counselor. It seems important also to mention here that it is obvious a person can assimilate only so much of the ideas of others. Being the individual he is, he must in the last analysis use himself, with all that he has acquired, as best he can.

SOME PRACTICAL SUGGESTIONS

1. *It is important always to protect completely the identity and confidences of the man or woman seeking help.*

2. *It is usually unwise to let a person talk too long at a time—he may become too upset;* an hour is a good general average. Emergency situations in which time limits have to be met necessarily may be exceptions.

3. *Behavior, thinking, or feeling should not be condemned because it is different from that of the counselor's.* Instead, raise questions in a kindly and understanding manner which will enable the person seeking help to appreciate and think through the social, religious, and other implications in his or her past or present conduct for himself and for others concerned. Give the person the chance to tell the story in his own way.

4. *If the person has difficulty in telling his story or repeats the same material over and over, help him out by asking how he feels about any of the following:* what his problem is and why it is a problem to him; what about his partner and how does he or she feel about the situation; what about his partner's background and growing up; how does he get along with his father, his mother, his in-laws, and whether they are involved in this present problem; how he feels about children of his own; how he feels about his job; how he feels about difference of opinion; and what he himself feels are the alternatives and possibilities.

5. *Ask questions only if the person gets stuck or repeats over and over, and only as many as the person has time and incli-*

nation to answer. By being a friendly, kindly, tolerant, interested listener, give assurance of caring about what is going on and believing in the possibility of working something out in the future. It can often be said that other persons of this age, and so forth, have had the same type problems and been able to work them out. In so doing indicate willingness to continue being of assistance *if this is desired.* This process of listening and occasionally questioning enables the person to gain perspective and relieve anxiety. It also gives the person the opportunity to try over again and in different ways to express his situation. By doing this consistently the verbalization often becomes more logical and more realistic and the person becomes able to start working on his problem.

6. *Do not be fearful of pauses.* Sometimes a person will be gathering courage to ask about something *very important to him* and will do so after a waiting period when nothing is said. A question raised too soon on a different subject than what is in the other person's mind may shut off this important question. Often it is best just to repeat with a slight questioning inflection the last remark the person has made, rather than introduce a new idea.

7. *No matter how hard a person pushes do not advise him, tell him what to do "if I were you" or how to do it.* A decision to be valid should be a real part of the person who makes it and should grow out of his feelings and attitudes about his situation.

8. *If information is desired suggest pertinent authoritative reading material in either pamphlet or book form.* Stress the fact that in many fields of science authorities have different points of view because continuing experimental work adds new facts which in turn reshape current opinion. It is often an advantage to read more than one author.

9. *Legal questions should be referred to a lawyer or legal aid service.* The local bar association can make suggestions of personnel.

10. *Medical questions should be referred to a doctor or hospital.* The local medical society can make suggestions of personnel.

11. *Remember that in most instances the person seeking*

help is the one who does the work. He is offered the opportunity of finding a different use of himself by testing out new ideas, feelings, and behavior during a period in which he can use the counselor as an objective sounding board. He responds to interest and caring by sharing a new and often fearful part of himself in a relatively safe and impersonal environment. If he is allowed to do this without the counselor inserting his own feelings, ideas, controls, without being too active, in the majority of instances he will be able to change his attitudes and develop new and unused parts of himself.

12. *If the situation is very complicated, involves persistent conflict for one or more persons, if the person continues to be in violent opposition to someone else and has many symptoms of physical disturbance or outward nervousness such as tics, twitches, and so on, make a careful and sincere effort to refer the person to a trained and experienced psychiatric service.* If no such personnel is available in the community, consult with an experienced, older local professional individual, if this can be done with the client's permission or, if not, without disclosing his identity.[11]

13. *If there is no one to refer to or consult with, be more than ever careful not to argue, blame, or recommend action of any kind.* Try to serve as an outlet, a sounding board, and a kindly listener.

---

[11] Important points are raised by Dr. Walter Stokes in the "Legal Status of the Marriage Counselor," *Marriage and Family Living,* February, 1951.

4

Functioning Marriage Counseling Services in the United States

THE PURPOSE of this chapter is to present an accurate account of the inception, functioning, and growth of recognized marriage counseling services in this country as of 1950. Practical details necessary for initiating such work in other communities will thus be made available. In this connection such factors as the reasons for which people seek counseling and the kind of settings in which a service functions are essential to an understanding of personnel requirements and budgets. Such facts may be stimulating also, either positively or negatively, to individuals who wish marriage counseling before or after their marriage, for themselves, their families, or friends. Following this over-all picture of marriage counseling services, the five successive chapters will furnish, for the critical examination of the reader, detailed and comprehensive clinical experience from one functioning service on marriage counseling in practice. This information has been released from the service with which the author has been associated closely for a period of years and has had systematic experience.

METHOD OF EXPLORATION

In order to examine a variety of functioning services, the co-operation of national organizations whose programs included interest, participation, or promotion of marriage counseling was solicited through their directors.[1] These organizations

[1] All national organizations approached are listed alphabetically, with addresses, in Appendix A.

were asked for a brief statement of the relation of their work to marriage counseling and for information as to existing functioning services initiated under their auspices. Certain of these groups stated definitely that no marriage counseling had been initiated under their auspices; others reported functioning services. As a result, a group of marriage and family counseling services representing a variety of different sources were invited by the author to prepare statements about their work for possible inclusion in this book.

It must be borne in mind clearly, however, that statements referred to in this chapter and reported in detail in Appendix B do not constitute a complete coverage of the organizations functioning in this field.[2] For instance, when a national organization, such as the Family Service Association of America, reported a large number of member agencies offering service in this field, a few examples only of their work could be included. These were selected because of the known activity of the agency executive in this field of marriage counseling, and to represent different sections of the country. It should also be realized that the inclusion of a report does not indicate approval or endorsement of the service by the author or any other person or group. Effort was made to include services whose directors were on the 1950 membership list of the American Association of Marriage Counselors. However, services reported are not limited to this membership. Efforts were also made to effect representation from as many geographic areas as possible. Services organized as a business enterprise, no matter how professionally adequate, are not included because of the almost insurmountable difficulty of attempting to

---

[2] None of the National Associations approached claimed to have reliable and comprehensive lists of all functioning marriage counseling services for distribution. The American Association of Marriage Counselors reports through their secretary, Dr. Janet Nelson, the appointment in 1950–51 of a committee to work actively on plans for systematic evaluation of existing marriage counseling services with recommendations in regard to accreditation. This committee, of which the author is chairman, will welcome information from any functioning marriage councils. Lack of complete comprehensive information may have caused, inadvertently, the omission of some services from this report.

locate, select, or classify such enterprises or to obtain objective and unbiased statements.[3]

The reports utilized do, we believe, make available something of the similarity and variation in auspices, development, and procedure of these services during the two recent decades, as well as current trends. If some present an overly rosy impression it may be because the actual picture is optimistic, or the director reporting thinks it optimistic, or wants us to think so. The contemplated evaluation by a professional group should, at least in part, solve this dilemma.

The directors of all services approached received the same form letter requesting concise information on the following items: date of initial organization; sponsoring auspices; means of support; physical set-up; staff personnel including background, training, and experience; client population and the range of problems they presented; method and philosophy of counseling; source of referral; fees required; length of client interview and contact, and type of records kept; educational work; in-service training and research. Responses were edited if necessary and returned to the executives for final correction and release in the late autumn of 1950. Names and addresses of the thirty-five functioning services which furnished material are listed in footnotes in the text following statements from the national groups under whose auspices they were first initiated. A complete listing of these services alphabetically under the states in which they are located is found in Appendix A. The detailed reports of work from each director, following the order in which they appear in the footnotes, constitutes Appendix B.

SPONSORING AUSPICES ARE EXPLORED

Discussion follows of national organizations or groups whose programs include active interest through participation in or promotion of marriage counseling.

---

[3] An example of a service of this type run by a professionally trained person is found in Family Relations Institute, 1035 Juniper St., N.E., Atlanta 5, Ga., Mrs. James E. Barbee, LL.B., Ph.D., Director.

Child Study

"Most groups concerned with child study and parent education are primarily study or discussion groups and are organized in widely differing ways and under a variety of auspices. Few are in a position to offer individualized professional assistance to supplement their group program," according to Mrs. Mildred B. Beck, Director of the Child Study Association of America, which is devoted to parent education in its broader aspects. "Its varied program is carried on through a Family Counseling Service [4] parent discussion groups and is supplemented by a general educational program based on lectures, conferences, and publications. The counseling deals with *family* counseling rather than marriage counseling as such. The service is concerned with the parents' adjustment to each other as well as with their own personal difficulties, but primarily as these problems affect the development of the children."

This focus of study groups on parent-child relationship apparently is accepted in general by persons interested in child study throughout the country; only one such organization claims specific work in marriage counseling. This is the Association for Family Living in Chicago.[5] Its name as well as its history indicates that its purpose and scope have changed since its beginning.

Family Relations

The National Council on Family Relations is a national clearing house of interprofessional interests in marriage and family life. The Executive Secretary is Dr. Evelyn Duvall. Through its journal, *Marriage and Family Living*, national, state, regional, and local council programs and projects of twelve national committees conduct a basic program to

---

[4] Family Counseling Service, Child Study Association of America, 132 East 74th Street, New York 21, N. Y., Mrs. Mildred B. Beck, Director. See Appendix B for a descriptive report of this service, pages 257-58.

[5] Marriage Counseling Service, Association for Family Living, 28 East Jackson Boulevard, Chicago 4, Ill., Freda S. Kehm, M.S., Ph.D., Director. See Appendix B for a descriptive report of this service, pages 258-60.

strengthen family life through research, education, and counseling. It maintains a large membership open to persons with professional interests in marriage and the family. This group does not conduct functioning marriage counseling services under its auspices but aids the field of marriage counseling in general by helping to develop sound procedures, by fostering competency through its National Committee on Marriage and Family Counseling, and by encouraging sound counseling and guidance for members of the related professions, community leaders, married couples, parents, young people, and all who want to meet family problems wisely.

Family Service

For over one hundred years Family Service agencies have extended individualized help to troubled persons and families —at first, mainly to those in economic difficulty. "Over the years," report Cora Kasius, Editor of *Social Casework* and Frank Hertel, General Director of Family Service Association of America,[6] "both function and method have undergone several revisions. Since the development of public assistance and social insurance measures, in the past two decades, family service agencies have directed their programs toward offering casework help with problems of personal and family adjustment. The majority of local agencies are nonsectarian and are supported by voluntary contributions derived in the main from community chests. Local agencies operate from a single office in small communities or in a series of district offices in large cities.[7]

---

[6] List of member agencies or information regarding use of local agencies can be obtained by writing to the national office. For address see Appendix A. At the close of 1950 there were 238 member agencies, including 6 public, with 13 pre-member affiliates.

[7] Family Service, 312 West Ninth Street, Cincinnati 2, Ohio, Mrs. Anna Budd Ware, M.A., Executive Director; Family Service of Los Angeles Area, 355 South Broadway, Los Angeles 13, Calif., Mrs. Blythe W. Francis, R.S.W., Executive Secretary; Jewish Family Service, 113 West 57th Street, New York 19, N. Y., M. Robert Gomberg, Ph.D., Executive Director.

See Appendix B for descriptive reports of these three services, pages 260-66.

Family Service Association's standard for the casework and supervisory positions in member agencies is graduation from an accredited school of social work. In 1949, 85 per cent of the two thousand professional casework staff met this standard. Of the 15 per cent who had incomplete training, a number had plans for completing full training within a specified time.

The problems for which persons seek help cover a wide range of personal and family difficulties. The presenting problem resulting from disturbed family relationships may be expressed in various forms—marital strain, parent-child difficulties, illness, poor work adjustment, and so on. The focus of the problem may shift as treatment progresses, often moving from superficial concerns to more fundamental ones. Family Service Association studied 31,000 cases given casework consideration, in 1949. Fifty per cent of the problems were those of difficulties in family relationship. Of this group, 65 per cent involved marital difficulty.

Psychological and psychiatric concepts have been incorporated in casework philosophy and method. The client's situation is viewed in terms of the social reality and of the emotional factors affecting the difficulty. Treatment is designed to help partners gain some understanding of their individual part in creating the difficulties. The diagnostic use of the caseworker-client relationship as a means for bringing about modification in feelings, attitudes, and behavior has come to be accepted as the chief medium of treatment.

The approach in each situation is based on an understanding of the client, his relationship to his problem, and the treatment that seems best aimed to help him toward a solution. Among the families seeking help with marital difficulties, all degrees of severity are found. Many families now seek help with disturbed relationships in the early phase of their difficulties. Casework help with this group is directed toward relieving the partners of some of their emotional tensions and toward helping them gain some understanding of their part in creating the difficulties. Through such techniques as reassurance, support, suggestion, clarification, and interpretation, the person is helped to achieve a more mature level of emotional development. The free discussion of childhood and adolescent sexual fears and taboos, and a reorientation to adult sexual standards, particularly with women, often is an important factor in reducing tension and in fostering greater maturity. In some instances, the marital maladjustment is but one expression of a profound personality disturbance in one or both partners. Psychiatric referral or consultation is usually arranged in such cases. Psychiatric consultation is available to the staff in well over half of the agencies to further the understanding of the personal and family dynamics and to aid in planning appropriate treatment goals.

In the past two decades the trend generally has been to incorporate in the regular program a fee plan on a sliding-scale basis, free to those who are unable to pay. The fee scales vary according to agency from twenty-five cents per interview to ten dollars.

In general, weekly interviews of one hour are arranged with clients, although the frequency varies somewhat according to the individual situation. Contacts range from short-time help to continued treatment of emotional difficulties which may extend over a period of a year or two.

In the past few years, a number of family service agencies have extended service to include group educational activities, to make available, on a broader basis, principles of personal adjustment and family relationships. Various subjects have received attention, including parent-child, marital, and boy-girl relationships.

RESEARCH. One study, based on 100 cases of marital difficulties treated by family service agencies, has been published, *Women in Marital Conflict* (1949). It analyzes various factors affecting marital adjustment, both social and psychological, and also the effectiveness of various treatment techniques. A reprint pamphlet of eight articles from *Social Casework* (1949), written by caseworkers in family service agencies, and an authoritative book, *Principles and Techniques in Social Case Work* (1950), also have been published.

IN-SERVICE TRAINING. Supervised training for staff members is routine in all member agencies large enough to employ several people. Family Service agencies are used by many accredited schools of social work for the field work placement of students.

Interprofessional Auspices

There is another very natural approach to setting up marriage counseling service in a community where interest is felt by many different professional groups. This might well be termed interprofessional sponsorship, and is illustrated by several of the services recognized for their continuing work over a period of years as well as some of more recent origin.[8] Usu-

---

[8] Marriage and Family Council, Inc., Chapel Hill, N. C., Mrs. Gladys H. Groves, Director; Marriage Council of Philadelphia, 1422 Chestnut Street, Philadelphia 2, Pa., Emily H. Mudd, Ph.D., Executive Director; Marriage Counseling Service, American Institute of Family Relations,

ally the original sponsorship in this type of organization comes from locally well-known representatives of religion, education, social work, medicine, psychology, law, and allied professions. Organizations initiated in this way have the practically automatic advantage of being precipitated into an interchange of professional points of view and method from the beginning, and continuously. To survive they must work out procedures acceptable to many different groups in a community.

Law [9]

The legal section of the Report on Counseling and Guidance of the National Conference on Family Life states:

It is the duty and prerogative of the legal profession to advise concerning the law and to assist in its administration. It should be the duty and prerogative of the marriage counselor to advise concerning the emotional and social problems which arise out of the marital relation. There need be no conflict between the two professions and, indeed, their work, each in its own sphere, should be of value.

Marriage counselors should know the legal resources of the community and work co-operatively with community sponsored legal agencies and local bar associations. Marriage or family counseling services should have access to reliable legal advice wherever possible, either through consultation with and/or membership of locally prominent lawyers on committees and boards of directors.

Because the profession of marriage counseling is new, many lawyers are unacquainted with the services which the marriage counselor is prepared to offer. This ignorance sometimes breeds prejudice. From a public relations standpoint, it is necessary that recognized practitioners of marriage counseling make plain to the Bar that no attempt is being made to usurp any of the historic functions of lawyers. Once this task has been accomplished, the marriage

---

5287 Sunset Boulevard, Los Angeles 27, Calif., Paul Popenoe, Sc.D., Secretary and General Director, Roswell H. Johnson, Ph.D., Director of Department of Personal Service; Pre-Marriage and Marriage Counseling Service, 421 West Grace Street, Richmond 20, Va., Mrs. Beatrice V. Marion, Director.

See Appendix B for descriptive reports of these four services, pages 266-74.

[9] Cf. Chapter 3, footnote 2.

counselor will secure the earnest and sympathetic interest of many lawyers.

As a practical example of the cementing of this interest, a marriage counseling service has been initiated recently under the auspices of a family court.[10] It is hoped that, by making assistance in adjustment available, before court action, to those persons who apply for separation or divorce, many couples will be able to work out their difficulties and continue their marriage.

Marriage Counselors

"The American Association of Marriage Counselors," according to its President, Dr. Robert W. Laidlaw, "is a professional organization which concentrates its work specifically on marriage counseling. It has this stated purpose: To establish and to maintain professional standards in marriage counseling. This purpose shall be furthered by meetings, clinical sessions, publications, and research in this field. Its membership is open only to those who meet its detailed requirements for clinicians in the field, or for affiliates whose work in this or related fields is well known, and for associates whose background, training, and beginning practice is sufficiently advanced to enable them to gain professionally by meeting with the more experienced counselors." The Association was initiated in 1943. At present no marriage counseling services are functioning under its auspices.

Mental Health

Among national groups with far-sighted and active programs of great importance to family life has been the National Committee of Mental Hygiene, recently amalgamated with other groups in this field to become the National Association for Mental Health, Incorporated. This group through the years has emphasized mental health. Through its promotional auspices, the mental hygiene and child guidance clinics now found

---

[10] Marriage Counseling in a Family Court, Juvenile and Domestic Relations Court of Lucas County, Toledo, Ohio, Ralph P. Bridgman, M.A., Director.

See Appendix B for a descriptive report of this service, pages 274-79.

in many areas of the country were initiated and have flourished. According to Dr. George Stevenson, its medical director, this group is "interested in marriage counseling because such work attempts to aid individuals to achieve marital adjustment and therefore indirectly (if this goal is attained) aids in the promotion of good mental health. Although members of this group have been active in marriage counseling, the organization itself has not sponsored any services focusing on marriage counseling. It has continued its main focus on aid to individuals with their own personality adjustment and reorganization."

Planned Parenthood

The Birth Control League of America, organized in 1921 by the courageous pioneer, Margaret Sanger, had as its major objective—to enable women to control the number of babies to whom they gave birth. In increasing numbers, women who sought birth control services brought to the attention of the clinicians the existence of other types of problems in their marital relations. Many had problems of sex adjustment, others wanted babies and couldn't have them, still others wished their daughters could enter into marriage more adequately prepared than their mothers. To meet these needs, the birth control clinics expanded their program to include infertility treatment services and to some degree, depending on local facilities, premarital and postmarital counseling. With a broadened program of service, the name of the organization was changed to the Planned Parenthood Federation of America, Incorporated.[11]

According to Dr. D. F. Milam, Medical Director, the Federation, after considering carefully unmet needs for education and counseling in the areas of marriage, parenthood, and family life, formulated its policy, which states in part:

Planned parenthood organizations should co-operate in community programs providing education for marriage and parenthood, but should initiate them within the framework of their own organizations only when qualified staff is available.

---

[11] Information regarding local facilities can be obtained by writing to the National Office. See Appendix A.

Later, in an attempt to clarify its position with regard to premarital and marriage counseling, "Standards for Education and Preparation for Marriage and Parenthood" were developed. In addition to the content of the program and the qualifications of personnel responsible for education and preparation-for-marriage programs developed by the Planned Parenthood affiliates, these standards include several types of service which seem essential to a complete program: (1) general education on marriage and parenthood; (2) consultation with individuals and couples either before or after marriage; (3) marriage counseling.

Marriage counseling is limited in either premarital or post-marital cases as follows:

Marital problems relating to the sexual aspect of marriage are suitable for Planned Parenthood marriage counseling if the difficulties are on a superficial level and accessible to short-term treatment. Marriage counseling requires an understanding of the attitudes responsible for the difficulties, and the treatment of the patient when the origin of these difficulties is readily determined. Where difficulties arise from deep-seated personality problems, referral to appropriate psychiatric services should be made. If the patient has problems in other areas of family relations, referral should be made to appropriate sources of help.

"The contribution of Planned Parenthood in this field is primarily that of providing the individuals or couples with pertinent information regarding the sex harmony of couples and regarding child spacing, through its counseling service as described above." Detailed examples of clinics functioning in this way are found in statements from affiliated services.[12] In addition to the services which furnished reports, Planned Parenthood Federation states that premarital consultation is available in five affiliated clinics.

Other reports of services initiated originally under local Ma-

---

[12] Marriage Counseling Service, Mothers' Health Center, 44 Court Street, Brooklyn, N. Y., Lena Levine, M.D.; Margaret Sanger Research Bureau, 17 West 16th Street, New York, N. Y., Abraham Stone, M.D.

See Appendix B for descriptive reports of these two services, pages 279-82.

ternal Health or Planned Parenthood members illustrate work in clinics not affiliated with the national association.[13]

Psychiatric Auspices

Very recently a leading psychiatric treatment center has crystallized interest in the potentialities of marriage counseling by initiating such service as one of its departments.[14] This experiment includes counseling for individuals both before and after marriage and in-service training for marriage counselors. It is the first effort of its kind by a psychiatric center and reflects consideration on the part of analytically oriented psychiatrists in the techniques and procedures of casework and counseling as these may be applied to problems focused on marriage.

Religion

Undoubtedly the clergy of Catholic, Jewish, and Protestant groups, with the sanction of their religious organizations,[15] are carrying on daily marriage counseling with many thousands of men and women. They also are educating young people for marriage in discussion groups and in conferences with the couples for whom they perform the marriage ceremony. Religious groups also publish pamphlets and books and promote extensive distribution of materials in this field of marriage and family relations. Statements in connection with marriage counseling, which reflect the attitudes of the three groups mentioned, follow in alphabetical order.

"The approach of the Catholic Church to marriage counsel-

---

[13] Consultation Service of the Maternal Health Association, 2101 Adelbert Road, Cleveland 6, Ohio, Mrs. Byron E. Jackson, M.S., Director; Family Service of Reading and Berks County, 620 Franklin Street, Reading, Pa., Mrs. Charlotte K. Hutchison, M.S., Executive Secretary.

See Appendix B for descriptive reports of these two services, pages 282-85.

[14] Marriage and Premarriage Counseling, The Menninger Foundation, Topeka, Kan., Robert G. Foster, Ph.D., Director.

See Appendix B for a descriptive report of this service, pages 285-86.

[15] National organizations representing these groups are listed in Appendix A. Reading lists and pamphlets are available upon request as well as suggestions regarding local marriage counseling facilities.

ing springs from its traditional attitude towards marriage itself," says Dr. A. H. Clemens, Associate Professor of Sociology of the Catholic University of America, Washington, D.C., to whom we are indebted for the statement which follows:

The Church has ever taught that marriage is always a natural contract subject to immutable natural laws; that it is ever a social institution with social goals as well as personal; that it is generally a legal contract; and that in the words of St. Paul: "This is a great Sacrament," when effected by baptized persons; and that Christian marriage symbolizes the union of Christ with the Church—an inseparable and permanent bond. As a Sacrament, the Church believes that it is her duty to safeguard and protect marriage, even as she assumes the duty of jurisdiction over Baptism and all other Sacraments. This dutiful concern about the Sacrament of marriage has for the past nineteen centuries impelled the Church to employ the technique of marriage counseling to help effect stable, successful marriages by premarital counsel and to arrest the early signs of family disintegration by postmarital guidance. Further, she has ever been solicitous that good marriages be improved and perfected and to this end has lent her counsel and facilities. The recent statement of Pope Pius XII that Catholics "with fatigue and patience employ all possible means" to stem family decline clearly implies the traditional position of the Church in matters marital.

Nor is Marriage Counseling merely advised. The Church has through its Canon Laws made it imperative upon the 14,501 resident pastors in our country to give such counsel prior to marriage. These, in turn, are assisted in this work of counseling by most of the 42,970 priests in the nation. Due to the clergy's training in the religio-moral-psychological aspects of marriage as well as in pastoral psychology, and due to the rapport which Catholic couples have ever, as a rule, enjoyed with their clergy, the latter have traditionally been resorted to for assistance and counsel in marital affairs. The vast network of Catholic Charities agencies with their family welfare activities in most of the 125 dioceses of the United States have and continue to offer the counsel of trained social workers to couples in distress. Each of the 125 dioceses in the nation has its own matrimonial court where counsel is given before legal action is initiated. In one such diocesan court as many as 2,000 reconciliations of aggrieved couples have been effected in a given year. An emerging tendency is the growth of marriage counseling agencies in the dioceses associated with but not a part of the court structure. The Pre-Cana and Cana Conference Movement, an adult educational venture in Catholic circles, finds its 1,000 priest-conductors in constant demand for personal marriage counseling, as well as its associated psychiatrists, doctors, and marriage specialists. Catholic educational institutions, from the elementary school to the graduate schools, have always deemed it a duty to offer marriage counseling to their students and have provided facilities for the same. The various and numerous Catholic psychiatric, psychological, child care, and out-patient centers, clinics, and departments of hospitals find it necessary to implement other scientific aids given the client with marriage counseling. The Catholic University of America subsidized by the Bishops of the United States has, for the past several years, been engaged in imparting specialized training in marriage and family education and counseling. The nature of marriage counseling given in Catholic circles is best illustrated by a description of one of the most successful centers.[16]

Among members of the Jewish faith, throughout the centuries, it has been not only the custom but also the duty of the rabbi to expound to his congregation the laws concerning marriage and family life, and to instruct men and women in the observance and practice of these laws. It was not, however, until 1937 that the Central Conference of American Rabbis established the committee on "Marriage, the Family, and the Home" and formulated a program unanimously adopted by the Conference, which stated:

The need for counsel and guidance in marriage and family life is recognized by every student of the problem. Men and women need counsel and guidance not only during the early and always critical period of marriage, but also during the later and more dangerous years of marriage and family life. . . . We, therefore, urge the establishment of consultation centers within the synagogue or by the synagogue in co-operation with other groups.[17, 18]

---

[16] St. Michael's Hospital Family Clinic, Milwaukee, Wis., Sister Mary Regis, M.S., Director.
See Appendix B for a descriptive report of this service, pages 286-90.

[17] Cf. Chapter 3, footnote 2.

[18] Jewish Institute of Marriage and the Family, Synagogue House, 30 West 68th St., New York 23, N. Y., Rabbi Sidney E. Goldstein, Director.
See Appendix B for a descriptive report of this service, pages 290-91.

The need to implement these connections is gradually being met. In several seminaries, among them the Jewish Institute of Religion of New York, the Hebrew Union College of Cincinnati, and the Jewish Theological Seminary of New York, courses on marriage and family counseling, human relations, and pastoral psychiatry are being given. Both the boards of trustees and the faculties of the seminaries now recognize that candidates for the rabbinate must be equipped for marriage and family counseling, and that courses in this field must be included within the curricula.

In the fall of 1949, Rabbi Samuel Glasner, Chairman of the Committee on Marriage and the Home reported:

The Central Conference of American Rabbis does not itself conduct any marriage counseling services. However, we have repeatedly urged upon our members that they prepare themselves more adequately for this important aspect of the ministry. We have encouraged our seminaries to establish courses in "Pastoral Psychiatry" with special emphasis on family guidance. We have encouraged the Union of American Hebrew Congregations and the National Federation of Temple Sisterhoods, two of our lay congregational organizations, to publish materials in this field. We have distributed to our members materials and bibliographies on marriage counseling, have set up exhibits in this field at our annual meetings, and have brought to these meetings reports of related programs initiated by our colleagues.

The B'nai B'rith Hillel Foundations on some two hundred college campuses do a certain amount of marriage counseling and education for marriage as a regular part of the program scheduled for the students.

The Central Conference of American Rabbis is deeply and proudly conscious of the high standard of family life which has always been taught by Jewish tradition and adequately maintained in Jewish life practice. In order that this significant value may be preserved, it is important that our synagogues continue to provide suitable opportunities for education of our young people preparatory to marriage, for parent education, and for family counseling services. And we urge all rabbis to continue and expand upon their own activities and study in this important field.

Rabbi Reuben M. Katz, Chairman of the Committee on

Marriage and the Family of the Rabbinical Assembly, writes in March, 1951:

The following brief statement represents my own interpretation of the current situation in the field of marriage counseling within our movement. A large number of the men conduct premarital interviews and a number of synagogues have conducted institutes on marriage and the home. While these are individual ventures, they point to the growing awareness within our movement [of the need] for further exploration into this field.

The Rabbinical Assembly of America, at its last convention, created a national Committee on Marriage and the Family for the purpose of co-ordinating the activities of the Conservative rabbinate in the techniques and goals of marriage and family counseling procedure. The Committee has since been enlarged to a national Commission on Marriage and the Family representing both the rabbinate as well as the lay leaders within the Conservative Jewish movement as reflected in the United Synagogue of America and its auxiliary organizations, namely, the Women's League of America, the National Federation of Jewish Men's Clubs, and the Young People's League. It is hoped that we shall then be in a better position to publish literature, to conduct surveys, and to develop a philosophy towards marriage and family problems which will represent the Conservative movement in American Judaism.

Through the Federal Council of Churches of Christ in America, the Protestant churches of this country have proclaimed a deep interest in marriage counseling. This is indicated in the following statement prepared in 1948 by the Council for the National Conference of Family Life.[19]

Two or three decades ago among the Protestant group a few pioneering ministers began to counsel with all couples whom they married. Those ministers who have been helpful to their young people in giving some educational preparation and counseling for marriage create relationships of confidence which make it easier for these couples after marriage, in the presence of some difficulty, to go freely to their ministers for counseling. The attitude of the Federal Council of the Churches of Christ in America (which in 1950 became an affiliate of the

---

[19] Cf. Chapter 3, footnote 2.

National Council of Churches) on premarital counseling was presented in a booklet in 1948, which states:

The growth of interest in educational and spiritual preparation of young people for marriage, of which premarital counseling is a part, constitutes one of the most striking developments in church life in our time. Not only are many ministers putting educational preparation for marriage into their programs but they are weaving close ties between individual families and the larger family, the church. . . . In a peculiar way marriage is a responsibility of the clergy because the safeguarding of the ideals and values of family life is a part of their function.

According to the Commission on Marriage and the Home of the Federal Council (1949):

Because marriage counseling is a difficult and exacting art requiring special training, increasing numbers of ministers have sought such training where they could find it. They have turned to physicians, psychiatrists, psychologists, and social workers for aid and have received invaluable help in the understanding of family relationships and the techniques of counseling.

In a study of the catalogs of twenty-seven seminaries in 1950, it was found that help in counseling is offered in the catalogs of all but one of these schools (Wood, 1950). Along with many courses which would contribute indirectly to the minister's preparation for counseling there were four types of courses under the following categories: courses on counseling offered by twenty-four seminaries; courses dealing with the psychology of personal relationships offered by fifteen of these schools; courses on marriage and the family offered by fourteen of the schools; clinical courses or clinical experience contributing to the minister's ability to deal with individuals offered by eleven seminaries. Other courses not listed in the seminary catalogs are available in adjacent university curricula in many instances, and many theological students take advantage of such opportunities. In addition, help is given in summer institutes and in various types of ministers' conferences. The conclusion is that seminaries and universities and conferences are increasingly offering help in preparation for counseling, that a literature (books, pamphlets, and periodicals) of

58

real usefulness is growing up, that pastoral contacts offer the minister rich clinical material (ably reported by such writers as Russell Dicks) and that the various professions offer one another their findings.

Dr. L. F. Wood, Executive Director of the Commission through 1950, reports that "there are no marriage counseling services under the auspices of the Federal Council of Churches. The relationship of the Council to the counseling done in churches and especially by ministers in their pastoral relationship is a very general one. It promotes the idea, supplies some material, co-operates in conferences and training schools pertaining to family life and counseling, but the counseling work is actually done under local auspices, usually as a part of the pastoral work of the particular minister." Three reports of this type of locally sponsored service have been received.[20]

Social Hygiene

The American Social Hygiene Association was founded in 1913 as the national voluntary agency in the field of venereal diseases control. From the outset, states Mrs. Esther Sweeney, Director of Community Service, "it was recognized that contributing factors to the venereal diseases were sexual promiscuity and tolerated commercialized prostitution. Accordingly, the latter problem was treated as a matter requiring community action and the former as one requiring sound sex education."

Although at first, sex education tended to be largely factual and closely related to the VD problem, increasing emphasis was laid on development of sound attitudes toward the place of sex in life. With growing realization of the relationship between happy marital adjustment and problems of sexual promiscuity, several of the Association's affiliated organizations developed marriage counseling

---

[20] First Community Church, 1320 Cambridge Boulevard, Columbus 12, Ohio, Rev. Roy A. Burkhart; Marriage Consultation Center of the Community Church, 40 East 35th Street, New York, N. Y., Abraham Stone, M.D., Medical Director; Religio-Psychiatric Clinic at the Marble Collegiate Church, Fifth Avenue and 29th Street New York, N. Y., Rev. Norman Vincent Peale.

See Appendix B for descriptive reports of these three services, pages 291-97.

services either as demonstrations or as planned, continuing operations.

Currently local social hygiene societies are not encouraged by the national office to undertake this type of program, as it is believed to be more properly a function of the family casework agency. Of course, since local societies are autonomous, no attempt is made to control their activities in this area and it is realized that, where a Social Hygiene Society can employ an adequately trained staff in sufficient numbers and do a truly professional job in marriage counseling, there may be good reason for them to do so either as a demonstration or as an agreed upon supplementation to the work of a family agency.

According to Walter Clarke, M.D., the present Executive Director of the Association, "there are four Social Hygiene group-sponsored marriage counseling services that have been functioning among the longest in this country." [21]

University Education

There are interesting and important trends to be gleaned from scanning the history and development of the national groups whose relation to marriage counseling has been discussed so far. There is evidence that, whatever brought each group into being, its work eventually carried it into the field of family relations, and finally into a search for *causes* of apparent maladjustments. Study of these causes has brought a realization that within an unsatisfactory and conflicting marriage relationship is to be found the breeding ground for much of the pathology which each group has been attempting to allay. Out of this has come a growing emphasis on earlier efforts for promoting healthier marriages. No discipline has a readier chance for early emphasis than the field of education.

---

[21] Cincinnati Social Hygiene Society, 312 West Ninth Street, Cincinnati 2, Ohio, Roy E. Dickerson, Executive Secretary; Counseling Service, 316 Huntington Avenue, Boston 15, Mass., Lester W. Dearborn, Director; Family Relations Center, 2504 Jackson Street, San Francisco 15, Calif., Henry M. Grant, Executive Director; Counseling Service, Social Hygiene Society of the District of Columbia, 927 Fifteenth Street, N.W., Washington 5, D.C., Ray H. Everett, LL.B., Executive Secretary.

See Appendix B for descriptive reports of these four services, pages 297-304.

The public school system in some states has made splendid efforts at meeting this and other important student needs by installing school counselors on its staff (Cox, 1945). "The need for individual counseling in our schools has become more and more evident as parents and educators have increasingly concerned themselves with the personal as well as the mental and physical growth of children. A brilliant pupil may fail academically because of personal maladjustment; a myriad of pressures and conflicts existing within the individual or his environment may block the learning process. From this standpoint alone, a counseling service is needed. However, when we consider the larger objectives of education involving the emotional and social maturity of children, counseling becomes a must in a sound educational program." [22] The staff in this area of school work has developed in many places into recognized professional status with training requirements on the graduate level. Students in many colleges and universities also have some sort of personnel service available to them through their dean's office, their psychology clinic, or a bureau of student counsel. In connection with an outstanding center of this type [23] the Director, Dr. Carl Rogers, stated: "I do not like to write about our Center as though it were concerned, even in part, with marriage problems or with marital counseling. It is interested in people and tries to help people to deal with themselves. We do find that if a person comes to understand and accept himself, then he handles his relationships with his employer, his wife, his friends, in a better fashion. In this respect only are we doing marital counseling."

Concurrently with the courses on marriage and family relations now being offered in many schools and universities in this country, requests come from students for the opportunity to discuss their individual situation in a confidential interview with the teacher of the course or some other available and

---

[22] Unpublished report of the Subcommittee on School Counseling, Section on Counseling and Guidance, National Conference on Family Life, Washington, May 6-8, 1948. Used with permission.

[23] Counseling Center, University of Chicago, Chicago 37, Illinois, Carl Rogers, Ph.D., Director.
See Appendix B for a descriptive report of this service, pages 304-7.

suitably trained person. In a few institutions, in contrast to the focus expressed by Dr. Rogers, trained marriage counselors have been brought to the college campus and paid for through the dean's office for the express purpose of making adequate marriage counseling easily available, and without extra cost to enrolled members of the marriage course. More and more these various sources of individual help for students have become aware of the effect on students' lives and adjustment to work of questions concerning their relations to their parents (Benz, 1940), to dating, courtship, engagement and marriage (Groves, 1936). Counseling on such subjects has, therefore, become an important part of daily interviews in campus counseling services, and the setting up of specialized services with staff trained for this aspect of service has become more usual and accepted.[24]

REPORTS FROM FUNCTIONING SERVICES ARE SUMMARIZED

Study of the thirty-five detailed reports received from functioning services indicates that they were initiated originally under the nine types of auspices just described: child study, family service, interprofessional, law, planned parenthood,

---

[24] Counseling and Guidance Service of the Merrill-Palmer School, 71 Ferry Avenue, East, Detroit 2, Mich., Mrs. Clara Lyndon, M.S., Director; Family Life Division of the Department of General Studies, University of Minnesota, Minneapolis 14, Minn., Mrs. Dorothy T. Dyer, M.S., Director; Marriage Counseling Service, Florida State University, Tallahassee, Fla., Dean Johnson, Ph.D., Director; Marriage Counseling Service, Furman University, Greenville, S. C., Aaron L. Rutledge, Ph.D., Director of Personal Guidance; Marriage Counseling Service, School of Education, Pennsylvania State College, Burrows Building, State College, Pa., Clifford R. Adams, Ph.D., Director; Premarital Counseling Service, Stephens College, Columbia, Mo., Henry Bowman, Ph.D., Director; Marriage Counseling Services, Southern Methodist University, Dallas, Tex., Henry L. Pritchett, Ph.D., Director; Marriage Counseling Service, Utah State Agricultural College, Logan, Utah, C. Jay Skidmore, Ph.D., Director; Bureau of Student Counseling, University of Utah, Salt Lake City 1, Utah, Rex A. Skidmore, Ph.D., Director; Marriage Counseling Center, Ohio State University, Columbus 10, Ohio, Merton Oyler, Ph.D., Director.

See Appendix B for descriptive reports of these ten services, pages 307-25.

psychiatric, religious, social hygiene, and university education. Certain items in these reports presented very similar information from each service, other items indicated wide variation. The following sections summarize the information received in each report. Items in which information from each service duplicates that of the others are omitted from the detailed agency report in Appendix B.

Inception Date, History, Sponsoring Auspices, and Support

The earliest date of inception reported was two services opened in 1928. This was about seventy-five years after the first family welfare agencies offered aid to families in distress, but only a few years before these family agencies directed programs toward offering casework help with problems of personal and family adjustment. Prior to World War II nineteen marriage counseling services were opened, two were opened during the war, and thirteen additional services were initiated between 1945 and the end of 1950 (if the Counseling Service of the University of Chicago is omitted as atypical in focus from the other marriage counseling services quoted).

Certain trends are noticeable. No new services among those reporting have been sponsored by social hygiene associations since the four pioneer agencies initiated locally before 1930, three of which have continued to operate with one-man staffs. These agencies now carry a heavy client and group education load in comparison with agencies having larger staffs, but have offered no training facilities for counselors and little research. Of the other clinics started before World War II, two were under child study auspices, two were under family service, three under interprofessional, one legal, one planned parenthood, three religious, and three university. Of the fourteen services reporting, initiated after World War II, one was under family service, one interprofessional, three under planned parenthood, one psychiatric, and eight under university auspices. In the entire group the initial sponsoring auspices have continued the same except in one instance where a clinic, started under planned parenthood, has been taken over by the local family service agency, and in a very few other instances where there were some partial changes.

Support of these services has come through the sponsoring group. If this group is a member of the local community fund, as in most family services and social hygiene organizations, then sums are allocated from this source. Where the sponsoring group is not a member of the community fund, support is allocated from the sponsoring auspices supplemented by funds for services rendered. For instance, in the case of interprofessional auspices, sponsors raise funds through contributions, fees are collected for individual and group counseling and more recently, in the case of one in this classification, grants have been received from government and private foundations for in-service training and research. Where the sponsoring auspices are religious or medical, the local group is responsible for support; where a university, funds may be allocated from the department under which the service is run and/or other departments, or the general university budget. In certain of these instances it is of interest to realize that taxpayers' money is involved in either operating the service, the training facilities, and/or research.

Physical facilities were reported by every service to include a counseling room or rooms, furnishing privacy to counselor and client, in addition to some sort of waiting or reception room. Variation was indicated in the number of such rooms and the emphasis on informality. Some pamphlets or books were usually available, in some instances under lending library arrangements. Whether or not a receptionist was on hand in the waiting room seemed to depend quite naturally on the size of staff and budget. Most agencies urged that appointments be made in advance and listed stated hours during which their service was open. The amount of time available for appointments also varied with staff facilities from services open one, two, or more evenings weekly to family services with branches in several parts of the city open full-time. Many services mentioned the possibility of special evening or week-end appointments in addition to "nine to five" regular hours.

Staff Personnel

Reports indicate, as might be expected, that the early marriage counselors officiating in the pioneer services, except for physicians, often had little if any graduate academic background. These counselors were in the main persons who felt so strongly the importance of what they were trying to do that they did it conscientiously and to the best of their ability, in spite of low pay, criticism, and lack of security. Counseling training was on the job, unsupervised, and grew out of experience. This was hardly surprising since the term marriage counseling was hardly known in the early thirties, and there was no specific training in this specialty on the graduate level offered anywhere. Even in the family service associations at that time there were many staff members who had not completed a master's degree in social work.

As recognition of marriage counseling has grown professionally, requirements for staff personnel have become much more stringent. A few of the early pioneers have acquired suitable graduate degrees while continuing with their jobs. Reports from the services initiated since 1940 indicate that all staff personnel have a minimum of a master's degree and many have a Ph.D. or M.D. Psychiatrists are found in consultant or supervisory relation to the staff in the large majority of services. These findings are in accord with standards recommended in 1948 by the joint committee of the American Association of Marriage Counselors and the National Council on Family Relations, summarized as follows:

Standards for marriage counselors are presented in terms of academic training, professional experience and qualifications, and personal qualifications.

Academic training. Every marriage counselor shall have a graduate or professional degree from an approved institution as a minimum qualification. This degree shall be in one of the following fields: education, home economics, law, medicine, nursing, psychology, religion, social anthropology, social work, or sociology.

Whatever the field of major emphasis, there shall be included accredited training in: psychology of personality development and interpersonal relations; elements of psychiatry; human biology, including the fundamentals of sex anatomy, physiology, and genetics; sociology of marriage and the family; legal aspects of marriage and the family; counseling techniques.

Professional experience and qualifications. The candidate shall have had at least three years of recognized professional experience subsequent to obtaining his degree. In addition, he shall have had actual experience as a clinical assistant in marriage counseling under approved supervision.

A candidate's qualifications shall include: diagnostic skill in differentiating between the superficial and the deeper level types of maladjustment, and the ability to recognize when the latter type requires referral to other specialists; a scientific attitude toward individual variation and deviation, especially in the field of human sex behavior, and the ability to discuss sexual problems objectively.

Personal qualifications. The candidate shall possess personal and professional integrity in accordance with accepted ethical standards; the candidate shall have an attitude of interest, warmth, and kindness toward people, combined with a high degree of integration and emotional maturity; the personal experience of marriage and parenthood is a decided asset.[25]

There are few one-man services now and many have from three to twelve full-time staff personnel. Qualified married women counselors often work part-time (if their families are young) or full-time. Men, if part-time, often carry other job responsibilities, usually of a more remunerative nature. Salaries for the most part are within the range of the professions involved. Where the part-time counselor is in active and successful private practice in his or her own field, the counseling work is occasionally on a volunteer basis.

Clients

The client population in the clinics reporting varied from one to seven hundred individual clients yearly. Several services did not furnish yearly figures. The number of clients counseled did not seem to depend necessarily on the size of the counseling staff, as some of the one-counselor clinics reported as many or more clients than clinics with several staff members. However, the total *number of client interviews* held yearly and the amount of activities other than counseling, such as in-service

---

[25] Printed with permission from the chairman of the committee, Dr. Abraham Stone.

training and research in which the agency was involved, did seem to be related. The clients were about two-thirds women to one-third men in the large majority of services. University services reported more nearly a fifty-fifty division, and one community clinic claimed 63 per cent men. In age, quite naturally, clients ranged from eighteen to approximately fifty-five. Variation in proportion of age groups was noticeable, the university and certain community services, depending on their name, stated purpose, and emphasis, tending to attract more clients under twenty-five and in the premarital group. In regard to religious affiliation, about one-third of the services kept no records. Of the remaining, those that were supported and organized under specific religious auspices, Catholic, Jewish, or Protestant, served almost entirely their own religious groups, as would be expected. The nonsectarian agencies which kept records of religious affiliation served a majority of Protestants, percentages varying up to 85 per cent, Jews up to 51 per cent, and Catholics up to 29 per cent. The majority of clients from other than university services were of high school level. Two-thirds or more of the clients from several services were of college or postgraduate level.

Range of client problems or reasons given for seeking marriage counseling fell into two main groupings, premarital and postmarital. Premarital clients varied from two or three agencies which had none to as high as 90 per cent in a university service. Problems presented went through the gamut of personality immaturities and maladjustments.[26] Sexual difficulties of all kinds were listed in the unmarried and engaged as well as the married group. These included ignorance, fears, misinformation, various degrees of inadequacy in performance to impotence and frigidity, homosexuality and many variations. There were many situations connected with weaning from parental possessiveness, parental disapproval, choice of a mate, infidelity, separation, alcoholism, reconciliation, infertility, adoption, health, and interreligious or international marriages.

---

[26] It is realized that severe neurosis and psychosis are occasionally encountered by marriage counselors although not always recognized by psychiatrically untrained counselors.

Method and Philosophy of Counseling

Where statements were made, counseling methods were found to be eclectic for the most part, drawing upon the varied contributions of casework, psychiatry, and psychoanalysis. Only in a few instances was one definite school of thought impressed upon or followed by all staff members. Client-centered therapy, combined with an educational approach when indicated, seemed to be the most popular compromise. All services recognized the dangers of staff counselors going beyond the realm of counseling, and the need occasionally for psychiatric referral.

Source of Referral

Clients came to marriage counseling services through friends, relatives, professional individuals, and other organizations, agencies or religious sources; through self-knowledge resulting from attendance at classes in schools, colleges, churches, or other community groups; and through books and periodicals, or listings in the phone book. Among the agencies that had been open for a period of years, referrals came also through former clients. Proportions referred from any group of sources varied, as would be expected, according to the auspices under which the particular service functioned and the amount of recognition it received in its own community.

Fees

Wide variation is reported in this area. Some services set no fee. These included predominantly university supported services which charge nothing to students but sometimes charge other than students, church sponsored clinics available primarily to parishioners of the church, early social hygiene clinics in which the present fee practice reflects the prevalent customs of 1930, one community service partly fund and partly church supported, and a service under legal auspices supported by taxpayers' funds. In the fee charging services, interview costs are quoted on a sliding scale depending on the clients' economic situation, as low as fifty cents and as high as twenty-five dollars, with the majority from one to five dollars. In all probability, fees at this rate seldom cover cost of service.

Client Interview and Length of Contact

The large majority of reports state their customary counseling interview as lasting fifty minutes to one hour. Some mention first interviews and premarital interviews as being longer. A few clinics went over the hour usually, and one had experimented with three and four hour sessions. There was more variation reported in the total number of interviews per individual client than in any other item. Some services stated that most of their work was in one and two interview contacts, some averaged two to six, others, notably family service agencies, quoted weekly contacts lasting from months to years, and a few university services gave their range as one to one hundred and fifty interviews per client. Actually, information was not available from more than one or two services on the exact number of one, two, three, four, and more interviews per client in a given year. Only through such data could any actual facts be obtained as to *average* length of contact in premarital and postmarital counseling.

Educational Work

Only one of the reports stated no group educational activities. All others reported active programs of meetings with groups of young people, married couples, and parents. Many agencies came in contact with thousands of individuals yearly through this phase of their staff activity. A few were experimenting with group counseling and group therapy.

In-Service Training

Only a small proportion of the reporting services offered any in-service supervised training in marriage counseling. A few educational institutions offer this for graduate doctoral students of the department under which the marriage counseling service operates, who have met course and training qualifications of the department.[27] Two other university services accept

---

[27] For details see Chapter 3, footnote 7.

students for field work placement from the nearby school of social work. One service under interprofessional and one under psychiatric auspices offer in-service supervised training for persons with graduate degrees in related fields, previous professional experience, and intention of working actively in the future in marriage counseling.[28]

Research

About one-third of the services reported research projects, and a smaller number had active programs involving a substantial proportion of staff time and energy. A very few were carrying on research projects on government and private foundation grants.

MARRIAGE COUNSELING IN PRIVATE PRACTICE

It is obvious from the preceding survey that there are as yet a comparatively small number of nonprofit functioning clinics which report the focus of their service as consisting of marriage counseling. This is true even if the proportion of marriage counseling done in the 238 member agencies of the Family Service Association of America, from which we could not list reports, was recorded. The conclusion then seems in order that the majority of counseling on marriage adjustment is still being done as part of the daily routine private practice of members of the various professions.

In this connection a breakdown of the membership of the professional association in this field, the American Association of Marriage Counselors, is of interest. The list of active members [29] (not including associate and foreign corresponding members) at the end of 1950 showed the following distribution: 27 per cent are gynecologists, 17 per cent psychiatrists, 12½ per cent social workers, 12½ per cent sociologists, 10 per cent educators, 8½ per cent psychologists, 8½ per cent minis-

---

[28] For further details inquire of Marriage Council of Philadelphia and the Menninger Foundation, Topeka, Kan.

[29] Individuals who have applied for membership and who met requirements of professional background and clinical experience. For details write headquarters office (see Appendix A).

ters, 2 per cent general medicine, 2 per cent urologists. Of this membership only 21 per cent give full time, with no private practice, as staff members of such functioning services as are described in this chapter. Seventeen per cent spend part of their time as staff members of such services and part in private practice. A few members, 6 per cent, are known to have become so interested in marriage counseling that they have given up other aspects of their private practice and concentrate entirely in this specialty. However, the majority of the group of active members, 56 per cent, carry on their marriage counseling as part of their day-by-day professional practice.

SUMMARY

Functioning marriage counseling services in the contemporary United States were explored to ascertain, if possible, certain systematic information. It was discovered that marriage counseling was promoted mainly by nine national groups. Some of these focused their interest and activity in closely related fields, some emphasized parent-child and family relationships rather than marriage counseling, some spent their energies in interpreting the field, setting up professional standards and holding educational conferences, and some initiated and supported functioning clinics offering one or more of the following services: individual and group counseling, lending libraries, in-service training, and research.

Data reported by thirty-five services indicated the earliest clinics were set up between 1928 and 1938, two during the war, and a further number between 1945 and 1950, predominantly under university auspices. Considerable similarity was discovered in respect to type of physical facilities, age range of clients, problems presented, length of interview, sources of referral, and group educational work. There was considerable variation between services in connection with sponsoring auspices, support, number of staff and academic background, method and philosophy of counseling, length of client contact, in-service training facilities, and research programs.

A breakdown of the active membership of the American Association of Marriage Counselors (not including the affiliate, associate, and foreign corresponding members) shows that the majority practice marriage counseling as a daily part of private practice in their own specialty. The next largest group give full time to serving as staff members of functioning services, the next to serving part-time as staff members of functioning services, part-time in private practice. A very few have concentrated their private practice on marriage counseling.

5

Characteristics of
Clients of a Marriage Council

MATERIAL PRESENTED so far has been historical and concerned with background and environmental conditions believed to influence marriage counseling and functioning marriage counseling services. It seems appropriate next to analyze the case material in one such agency, Marriage Council of Philadelphia, in order to furnish a specific and detailed illustration of work in this field. This agency is interprofessionally sponsored and was initiated in 1932 [1] (see Appendix B).

THE DETERMINATION OF CASES TO BE STUDIED

It was necessary to have certain criteria in mind in determining the case material to be studied in order to draw general conclusions about who uses a counseling agency and why, and to attempt to ascertain the impact of war:

1. The cases should be a consecutive group in no way selected.

---

[1] Certain readers may wish more detailed information in connection with the mechanics of a functioning marriage counseling service. This material, originally planned as an appendix to this volume, was omitted because of space limitations. It included: interpretation leaflets, book lists from lending library, case record face sheet, fee scale for clients, in-service training requirements and course outline, office manual on personnel practices (including suggested salary scale), schedules useful in counseling. If there is sufficient demand, these can be made available in mimeographed form at cost. Send requests to Marriage Council of Philadelphia, 1422 Chestnut Street, Philadelphia 2, Pennsylvania.

2. The group should be sufficiently large to constitute a population in itself.

3. The connection of the cases with the agency should be completed as far as possible.

4. The group should be comparable for a period before and during the impact of war.

It was decided to examine at least twenty-five hundred consecutive cases, the last of which would have been seen as long as one year before the study was completed. As a result, data from all cases seen in Marriage Council of Philadelphia during the thirteen years between January 1, 1936, and December 31, 1949, were summarized and tabulated in Table 3, to give an over-all picture of the factors studied. As already indicated this group constitutes not a sample but an entire population of cases, sufficiently large to justify the expectation that percentages derived from it have fairly stable characteristics.

FORM IN WHICH MATERIAL WAS AVAILABLE AND ITEMS YIELDING INFORMATION

Case records kept routinely for all clients coming to Marriage Council of Philadelphia were made available to the author, who has counseled in the agency since its inception, by permission of the Board of Directors of the agency.

The fact that written records were kept was shared with any client who inquired. The client was assured that his situation would be treated confidentially. The agency has always considered carrying out this assurance essential to ethical performance. Records used in any research study from this agency do not divulge the personal situation of any one client in such a way as to reveal identity, and individual case material used in teaching, publications, or reports is always carefully disguised. If cases have a familiar sound (see Chapters 8 and 9), it is because many of the problems which come to a marriage or family agency represent situations often experienced and therefore familiar in type to many persons although varying in individual detail. Slightly over one-third of the cases checked were counseled by the author, the remainder by other staff members under the direct or general supervision of the author.

74

Material from the case records of the 2,559 consecutive cases yielded information on the following subjects which will be discussed in the order mentioned: (1) background and social factors pertaining to clients; (2) sources from which clients were referred to the agency; (3) the client's reason for coming to the agency for help. Table 3 depicts frequencies and per cents in these categories and their subdivisions.

Information on residence, age, religion, education, occupation, and marital status was obtained at the time of the client's first contact with the agency and refers only to his or her status on that date.[2] It was determined for the first ten years of agency work by statements of the clients made to the counselor during interview, either in answer to a question or spontaneously, and was recorded by the counselor on the face sheet of the client's record. Since 1943, when a research program was added to agency procedure (see Chapter 10, page 199), such information has been obtained by asking each client routinely to check a Background Schedule before seeing the counselor. This checked schedule was then given to the counselor and any unchecked item could be added. Additional material, such as further births or deaths in the family, changes in occupation or other status, was often forthcoming at later office contacts with the client. This supplementary material will not, however, be represented in this study.

Residence of Clients. The two thousand five hundred and fifty-nine consecutive clients who used the services of the Marriage Council of Philadelphia during the thirteen years, 1936–

---

[2] Cross reference to a client's partner is now kept routinely on the face sheet of each record although this was not done systematically in the earlier years. For instance, among the 390 clients seen in the year 1949 both partners were counseled in 63.5 per cent of the cases. In such instances each partner is counted individually as one of the "consecutive" clients studied. It is believed, although accurate comparisons are not possible, that the number of cases in which both partners have been counseled has increased considerably as the policy of the agency has increasingly accepted the importance of both partners participating.

1949, came predominantly from the Philadelphia area (77%). Where the clients lived is shown in the following table:

TABLE 2

WHERE MARRIAGE COUNCIL CLIENTS LIVE

			Frequency	Percent
Total Philadelphia area.............................			1968	77
Philadelphia, Pa.....................	1457	57%		
Suburbs of Philadelphia, Pa...........	422	17%		
(taken as those towns near Philadelphia listed in the suburban telephone directory)				
Camden, N. J., and environs.........	89	3%		
(e.g. Collingswood, N.J., Merchant-ville, N.J., etc.)				
At school or college in Philadelphia area...............			179	7
Pennsylvania, other than the Philadelphia area.........			116	5
New Jersey (other than Camden and environs) and Delaware			128	5
Other states..			113	4
(Including: New York, Maryland, North Carolina, and District of Columbia)				
Unknown...			55	2
Total...			2559	100

Sex of Clients. Table 3 shows that approximately two-thirds (68%) of the total consecutive clients were women, one-third (32%) were men. Yearly intake showed a gradual decrease in the proportion of women clients following the impact of war from 82 per cent in 1940 to 62 per cent in 1949. Men clients increased proportionately from a low of 18 per cent in 1937 and 1940 to 38 per cent in 1949.[3]

Age of Clients. This is shown in Table 3 in six age groupings. The group, twenty-one to twenty-five years of age, contained the largest proportion of clients, averaging 33 per cent of the total group. It reached the maximum, 50 per cent of total intake, in 1940 at the time the first selective service bill was introduced, then declined through the war years, rising again somewhat following demobilization.

The next largest group, twenty-six to thirty years of age,

---

[3] Because of space limitations it was not possible to include graphs on yearly intake in each category discussed. This material is on file at Philadelphia Marriage Council.

TABLE 3

DISTRIBUTION OF TOTAL CLIENT POPULATION
BEFORE, DURING, AND AFTER WORLD WAR II

	Category	Before Selective Service (1–1–36 to 7–1–40)		After Selective Service (7–1–40 to 12–31–44)		After Demobili-zation (1–1–45 to 12–31–49)		Totals	
		Freq.	%	Freq.	%	Freq.	%	Freq.	%
Sex	Men	106	23	139	25	560	37	805	32
	Women	363	77	425	75	966	63	1754	68
Age	16–20	38	8	71	13	162	11	271	11
	21–25	189	40	207	37	450	29	846	33
	26–30	117	25	115	21	343	23	575	22
	31–35	53	12	57	10	230	15	340	13
	36–40	34	7	58	10	150	10	242	9
	41 plus	32	7	51	9	163	11	246	10
	Unknown	6	1	5	0	28	1	39	2
Religion	Protestant	251	54	347	62	909	60	1507	59
	Jewish	146	31	136	24	352	23	634	25
	Catholic	54	11	57	10	202	13	313	12
	Unknown	13	3	14	2	45	1	72	3
	Other	5	1	10	2	18	3	33	1
Education	Grammar School	67	14	48	8	77	5	192	8
	High School	239	51	229	41	557	37	1025	40
	College	104	22	225	40	708	46	1037	41
	College plus	33	7	37	7	134	9	204	8
	Unknown	26	6	25	4	50	3	101	4
Marital Status	Single	35	7	48	9	139	9	222	9
	Engaged	198	42	168	30	381	25	747	29
	Married	228	49	341	60	945	62	1514	59
	Sep. or Div.	4	1	7	1	53	3	64	3
	Unknown	4	1	0	0	8	1	12	0
Number of Years Married	Less than one	52	23	91	27	114	11	257	16
	1–5	71	31	113	33	380	38	564	36
	6–10	32	14	65	19	235	24	332	21
	11 plus	51	22	63	18	234	23	348	22
	Unknown	22	10	9	3	43	4	74	5
Sources of Referral	Private Indiv.	163	35	187	33	534	35	884	34
	Prof. Indiv.	88	19	114	20	290	19	492	20
	Agencies	136	29	113	20	166	11	415	16
	Educ. Ser.	70	15	142	25	425	28	637	27
	Other	12	2	8	2	111	7	131	3
Reasons for Coming	General Prep. for Mar.	181	39	153	27	255	17	589	23
	Specific Premarital	57	11	63	11	289	19	409	16
	Total Premarital	238	50	216	38	544	36	998	39
	General Postmarital	169	36	261	46	542	35	972	38
	Specific Postmarital	68	14	88	11	440	29	596	23
	Total Postmarital	237	50	351	62	982	64	1568	61

averaged 22 per cent of the total and varied little throughout the years except for a gradual falling off during the war years. The four groups made up of clients under twenty, thirty-one to thirty-five, thirty-six to forty, and forty-one and over have remained almost constant before, during, and after World War II with an average, respectively, of 11 per cent, 13 per cent, 9 per cent, and 10 per cent of total intake. However, the group under twenty rose slightly during the war and the group thirty-one to thirty-five years of age showed a slight increase after demobilization.

Religion. In terms of religious affiliation,[4] Table 3 shows that Protestants have been consistently the largest in number, averaging 59 per cent, or more than half, of total intake. The Jewish group has averaged one-quarter of the total, 25 per cent, and the Catholic 12 per cent. One per cent belonged to other affiliations and 3 per cent were unknown. Little variation in any of these groups is apparent through the years with the exception of 1938 and 1945 when the proportion of Protestants increased appreciably and Jews decreased, and in 1939 when a reverse change took place.

Mixed Marriages. Table 4 gives a breakdown of the religious affiliation of the married clients and their partners in the first 1,033 of the total consecutive cases. It indicates that in this group 73 per cent were known to have marriage partners of the same religious affiliation as themselves—42 per cent Protestant, 23 per cent Jewish, 8 per cent Catholic. Ten per cent of the group were married to persons of different religions from themselves.

Fourteen Jews, 2 per cent of the total married group, were known to be married to Protestants, and thirty-two Catholics, 6 per cent of the total married group, had Protestant mates. Half of one per cent of the Catholics of the group were married to Jews. There were, however, an appreciable number of marriages in each religious group, 17 per cent in all, in which the affiliation of the partners is unknown.

---

[4] Religious affiliation of clients was determined by their own statement to the counselor or by their checking of Background Schedule.

It would be of interest to know the per cent of the total number of Protestants, of Jews, and of Catholics who were married to partners of other religious affiliations. Unfortunately our sample is so small that figures might not reflect true proportions and therefore are not pursued. However, this subject

TABLE 4

MIXED MARRIAGES*

	Protestant	Jewish	Catholic	Other	Unknown
Protestant	238 *42%*				
Jewish	14 *2%*	131 *23%*			
Catholic	32 *6%*	3 *0.5%*	43 *8%*		
Other	5 *1%*	2 *0.4%*	1 *0.2%*	6 *1%*	
Unknown	56 *10%*	16 *3%*	8 *1%*	3 *0.5%*	11 *2%*

* Frequencies are shown by upper numbers in cells, percentages by lower numbers, based on total number of 569 married clients.

holds interesting possibilities (Baber, 1937), particularly in reference to types of problems brought by each group, and the differences or similarities between groups (Merton, 1941), (Slater, 1947).

Education. The percentage of clients of different educational levels by yearly intake is shown in Chart I. Clients with high school education were consistently the largest group un-

CHART I

EDUCATION OF CLIENTS

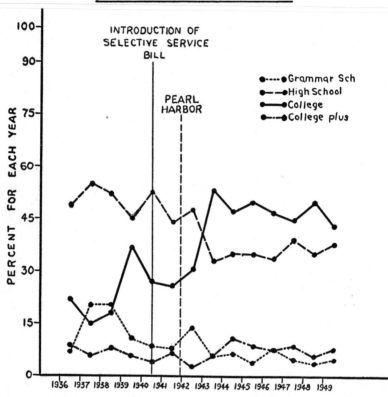

til after the war began. They decreased steadily from as high as 53 per cent in 1940 to 38 per cent in 1949, averaging 40 per cent for the thirteen years studied. The group with college education increased greatly from 22 per cent in 1936 to 47 per cent in 1944, remaining almost as high following the war and bringing the average for the thirteen-year period to 41 per cent of total intake or 49 per cent if clients with more than college are included. At the postgraduate level, although only 8 per cent of the total proportion of clients, the group has remained very constant through the thirteen years. It is of interest that there have been as many clients with postgraduate education as those with grammar school or less education—8 per cent of total intake. The educational status was unknown in 4 per cent of the cases.

Marital Status. This is shown by per cent of yearly intake in Chart II. The largest group has consistently been the married clients, averaging 59 per cent or over half of total intake. The proportion of married clients rose precipitously during the war to 68 per cent and continued almost as high after demobilization. The second largest group has consistently been the engaged clients, averaging 29 per cent of total intake through the thirteen years, but decreasing steadily from 38 per cent in 1940 to 23 per cent in 1949. The group of single persons has averaged 9 per cent of the total group, varying very little through the years. Clients who have been separated or divorced prior to seeking help at Marriage Council were a small group increasing slightly after the war and averaging 3 per cent of total intake.

The striking shift which occurs after July 1, 1940, in the proportions of engaged and married clients, indicating a considerable decrease in the premarital and a similar increase in the married group, will be discussed in Chapter 11, "The Impact of Mobilization and War."

Number of Years Married. The married clients, as shown in Table 3, varied from an average of 52 per cent who had been married not more than five years to 5 per cent who had been married over twenty-one years. The number of clients married under one year averaged 16 per cent of those married, rising to a high of 39 per cent when selective service went into effect; thereafter this group fell steadily throughout the war years, averaging only 11 per cent in the postwar period. The group married from one to five years increased from 24 per cent in 1936 to 48 per cent in 1943 dropping to an average of 38 per cent after demobilization.

The fact that over half of all married clients come for counseling within the first five years of marriage has a certain social significance in that, according to authorities in the field, the probabilities of divorce are conspicuously high during the first three years of marriage, being 10 per cent of marriages in the first year, with a gradual decline after the fourth year. About two-thirds of all divorces come before the tenth year of marriage (Burgess and Locke, 1945, p. 634), (Nimkoff, 1947, p. 632).

CHART II

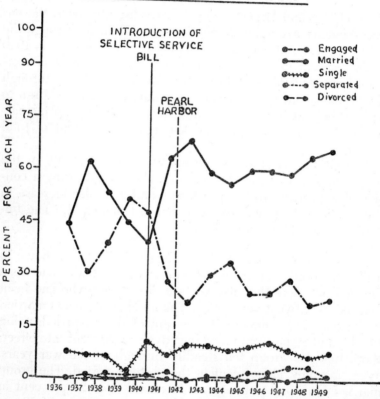

The next largest group, those married from six to ten years, averaged 21 per cent of total intake. It increased gradually from 13 per cent in 1936 to 26 per cent in 1949. The group married over ten years averaged 22 per cent of total intake and has remained fairly constant, showing only a slight drop during the war years. The length of time married of 5 per cent of the group was unknown.

The sources through which clients heard about and came to Marriage Council of Philadelphia are shown in Table 3 in four main divisions—private individuals, professional individuals, agencies, and educational sources. Clients who came to Marriage Council through *private individuals,* i.e., former clients, self knowledge, relatives, and acquaintances, have been constantly the largest division, 34 per cent of total intake, increasing from 18 per cent in 1936 to 38 per cent in 1949.

Educational sources of referral accounted for 27 per cent. Nearly one-half of this division came from college classes, slightly over one-half from community lectures and group discussions, and from articles and books. The source of referral of 3 per cent of the clients was unknown.

It is of interest that many referrals listed under educational sources came as a result of reading or hearing about such a service through courses, and are in essence self-referrals. Thus 61 per cent of the total intake came through private or lay persons, indicating appreciable interest on the part of the general public in finding and using a marriage counseling service.

Professional persons referred 20 per cent. Divisions in this group show that physicians were responsible for referring one-half, ministers, teachers, lawyers, and other professional individuals the other half. Only 16 per cent of the total cases came as a result of referral from *community services.* Social agencies, including hospitals and legal aid service, made up over one-half of this division and maternal health centers slightly less than half.

Clients' reasons for coming to Marriage Council for help were classified under two main groupings—(1) clients who came before marriage, and (2) clients who came after mar-

83

riage. These groups were further subdivided under headings suggested by the statements found on the face sheets of the records. (See Table 3 and Chart III.)

CHART III

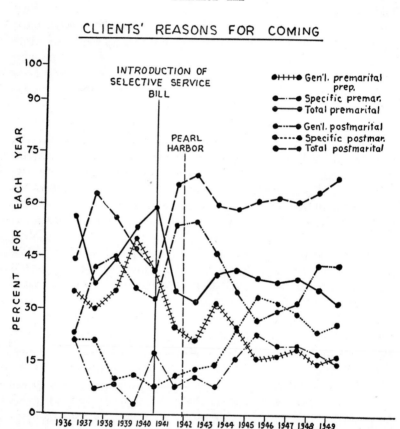

Clients who sought help before marriage. This group (already discussed under marital status, page 80) averaged more than one-third (39%), of the total cases seen during the thirteen-year period, falling from 56 per cent in 1936 to 33 per cent in 1949. It seemed to separate rather naturally into two subdivisions:

1. *Engaged clients who came for general personalized premarital preparation or "education" for marriage* accounted for 23 per cent of the total group of clients. Interviews with these clients usually included discussion of emotional and physical sharing in marriage, particularly as these processes involved past and present feelings and the behavior of the persons seeking counseling. Discussion of sexual matters was usually part of these interviews but seldom the focal point; therefore sex problems are not given a separate classification here. The general premarital preparation group constituted 35 per cent of the total in 1936, rose to 50 per cent in 1939, followed by a steady decrease during war to an average of 17 per cent in the postwar years.

2. *Unmarried clients who came for help about a specific situation* constituted 16 per cent of the total group of clients, varying little during thirteen years. Included in this classification are difficult parent relationships (weaning problems), desire to be more attractive, choice of a partner, engagement problems, questions of inheritance, sexual difficulties, illegitimate pregnancy, and a few diffuse personality problems.

Clients who came for help after marriage. This group averaged 61 per cent of the total cases, increasing from 44 per cent in 1936 to 68 per cent in 1949. It was classified into two main subdivisions:

1. *Clients having problems of general postmarital adjustment* averaged 38 per cent of the total group, varying little through the years. Individuals in this classification often had had difficulties over a period of years which indicated personality immaturities and disturbances. Their problems were apt to be diffuse and their use of marriage counseling either abortive because they did not really want to work on changing their marriage or, if they did take hold of counseling, their contact continued for many interviews over a period of months. Married clients giving sexual difficulties as their reason for coming constituted 15 per cent of the total group [5] and are

---

[5] Where sexual difficulties are persistent after counseling and medical complications have been eliminated they are considered as expressions of total personality involvement and as symptoms of neurosis.

85

included in this general classification. They reached a low of 14 per cent in 1939 just before mobilization began, from which the percentage more than doubled by 1941 to 35 per cent.

2. *Married clients wanting help in specific situations* averaged 13 per cent of total intake. This group included questions of health and preparation for parenthood (5%), consideration of separation or divorce (10%), reconciliation or adjustment after divorce (2%), difficult parent and in-laws relationships (2%), budget or financial problems, housing and war separation, or reunion (6%). This subdivision fell somewhat from 1939 to 1943 and then rose again to 27 per cent in 1949.

SUMMARY

Material presented in this chapter completes in the main the descriptive aspect of the study. It indicates that the clients of Marriage Council of Philadelphia between 1936 and 1949 were more apt to be young women than men, of Protestant religious affiliation, between twenty-one and thirty years of age, who lived in or near Philadelphia. The majority had high school or some college education and were either engaged or married under five years. They were more apt to be referred by a personal acquaintance or educational source than a professional person or agency, and were more apt to come for help shortly after marriage than before. If they came before marriage it was predominantly to use the general preparation-for-marriage service rather than because of specific or general problems. After marriage they were more apt to give general adjustment as their reason for coming for counseling rather than specific or sexual difficulties, or because separation or divorce was being contemplated.

6

A Comparison
of Men and Women Clients

I<small>N ORDER</small> to determine systematically whether there were differences between men and women clients in respect to the categories discussed in Chapter 5, data on the 245 men clients who came to Marriage Council between January 1, 1936, and December 31, 1944, were compared with data on the 788 women clients who came during the same period. See Table 5.

RELIABILITY OF DIFFERENCES

Examination of the contents of Table 5 discloses that the percentages contained in the column for men are closely similar to the percentages contained in the column for women in the large majority of categories. In those instances where differences were particularly apparent (from 5 to 20%), a series of statistical tests (Chi-square)[1] were applied in order to discern whether these differences were sufficiently large to be dependable.

The statistical tests enabled us to conclude with confidence that the following percentage differences are sufficiently large to be regarded as not due to chance: the larger percentage of

[1] The Chi-square test enables conclusions to be formed as to whether association apparent between two variables is sufficiently marked to be statistically reliable. The test does not measure amount of association but only whether the amount present is sufficiently large not to be accounted for by chance. In the present terms the Chi-squares are all 2X2 contingency tables in which the column distinction was based on the number of men and the number of women clients while the row distinction was based upon the variable under examination.

All statistical tests in this chapter and Chapter 11 are in the files at Marriage Council of Philadelphia.

TABLE 5

POPULATION OF 1,033 CLIENTS SHOWING SEX DIFFERENCES
JANUARY 1, 1936, TO DECEMBER 31, 1944

Category	Men		Women		Total
	Freq.	%	Freq.	%	%
Age					
16–20	11	*5*	98	*12*	11
21–25	72	*29*	324	*42*	38
26–30	67	*27*	165	*21*	22
31–35	38	*16*	72	*9*	11
36–40	28	*11*	64	*8*	9
41–	25	*10*	58	*7*	8
Unknown	4	*2*	7	*1*	1
	245	100%	788	100%	100%
Religion					
Protestant	143	*58*	455	*58*	58
Jewish	63	*26*	219	*28*	27
Catholic	24	*10*	87	*11*	11
Other	4	*2*	11	*1*	1
Unknown	11	*4*	16	*2*	3
	245	100%	788	100%	100%
Education					
Grammar School	21	*9*	94	*12*	11
High School	87	*35*	381	*48*	45
College	100	*41*	229	*29*	32
College plus	29	*12*	41	*5*	7
Unknown	8	*3*	43	*6*	5
	245	100%	788	100%	100%
Marital Status					
Single	20	*8*	63	*8*	8
Engaged	83	*34*	283	*36*	35
Married	140	*57*	429	*54*	55
Separated	1	*0.5*	4	*0.5*	1
Divorced	1	*0.5*	5	*1*	1
Unknown	0	*0*	4	*0.5*	0
	245	100%	788	100%	100%
No. of years married					
Less than one	34	*24*	109	*26*	25
1–5	56	*40*	128	*30*	32
6–10	23	*16*	74	*17*	17
11–15	8	*6*	43	*10*	9
16–20	4	*3*	36	*8*	7
21–25	3	*2*	8	*2*	2
26–	2	*2*	10	*2*	2
Unknown	10	*7*	21	*5*	6
	140	100%	429	100%	100%

TABLE 5—*Continued*

Category	Men		Women		Total
	Freq.	%	Freq.	%	%
Source of Referral					
Former client	47	19	64	8	11
Own knowledge	26	11	67	8	9
Other individuals	19	8	127	16	14
Lawyer	1	1	6	1	1
Doctor	22	9	61	8	8
Minister	8	3	32	4	4
Teacher	4	2	8	1	1
Other prof. ind.	11	4	49	6	6
Social agencies	13	6	48	6	6
Maternal health centers	20	8	133	17	15
Hospital	7	3	20	2	2
Legal Aid Society	2	1	6	1	1
College course	17	7	83	11	10
Talks	12	5	37	5	4
Articles	8	3	27	3	3
Books	6	2	2	0.5	1
Telephone book	6	2	14	2	2
Other	16	6	4	0.5	2
	245	100%	788	100%	100%
Reason for coming					
PREMARITAL					
Diffic. fam. sit.	2	1	11	1	1
Consid. engagement	8	3	30	4	4
Illegitimate preg.	4	2	15	2	2
Advice re others	2	1	6	1	1
Other premarital	13	5	29	3	4
Total specific premarital	29	12	91	11	12
Gen'l premar. prep.	74	30	260	33	32
Total premarital	103	42	351	44	44
POSTMARITAL					
Gen'l marital adjust.	43	18	121	15	16
Sex problems	42	17	166	21	20
Consid. div. or sep.	17	7	41	5	5
Total gen'l marital	102	42	328	41	41
Health, illness, contr.	18	7	48	6	6
Desire for reconcil.	3	1	9	1	1
Problems due to war	5	2	7	1.	1
Other marital probs.	1	1	10	1	1
Prob. follow. div. or sep.	0	0	6	1	1
Advice re others	7	3	27	4	3
Diffic. family sit.	6	2	9	1	2
Total specific marital	40	16	116	15	15
Total postmarital	142	58	444	56	56
	245	100%	795	100%	100%

women in the sixteen-to-twenty-year-old group and the larger percentage of men over twenty-six years of age; the larger percentage of women having grammar school and high school education, and the larger percentage of men with college or post-graduate education; the larger percentage of men married between one and five years and the larger percentage of women married for over eleven years; the larger percentage of women referred to Marriage Council from other agencies and institutions and the larger percentage of men referred by former clients. Among the agency referrals the larger percentage referred from maternal health centers is probably significant.

These data indicate that a significantly larger proportion of the men clients who came to Marriage Council during the period studied were (1) older, better educated, (2) if married, married for a shorter time, (3) probably less apt to be referred through institutions and more apt to come through former clients, than the women. Conversely, a significantly larger propportion of women clients were (1) younger, (2) less educated, (3) if married, they were married for a longer time when they sought help, and (4) more apt to be referred through community agencies, than the men clients.

The data give no reason to conclude that the religious affiliation, the marital status, referral from professional and educational sources, and, of particular interest, *the kinds of problems* for which the services of Marriage Council were sought were different for the men and women clients.

THE SEX DIFFERENCES ARE INTERPRETED

In considering the differences and similarities found in the data for men and women clients, relevant material will be introduced in attempting to interpret the facts. It is recognized that these interpretations are speculative, intuitive, and almost certainly provocative. Readers will undoubtedly react with their own speculations. Differences found in these data will be discussed first.

Sex Differentials

The most obvious difference—that between the number of men and the number of women who applied for services of

Marriage Council—was so great that it was accepted without testing its significance. It is a matter, however, of considerable social importance that deserves serious exploration. The fact that three-quarters of the clients between 1936 and 1945 were women and one-quarter men is either easily acceptable or startling, depending on individual reaction. We advance the following four suggestions in partial explanation.

1. *Women have more flexible use of free time than men.* This is self-evident for the unemployed single woman. Employment figures for women show that in spite of increases of working wives from 4.6 per 100 in 1890 to 15.2 in 1940, still only about one in seven married women was gainfully employed at the beginning of World War II. Although this proportion rose considerably by 1950, fewer married women than men were working outside the home (Women's Bureau, 1946). Although the majority of married women in this country are responsible for housework and child rearing and although these tasks require longer hours than a paid job, nevertheless these occupations as a rule give more flexibility in time off and therefore more opportunity to utilize marriage counseling (Young, ed., 1947).

2. *Women have less hesitation than men in seeking help.* They sometimes are inclined toward dependence and so may turn to an agency or counselor as a parent substitute. Men are considered in our culture to be the more powerful, responsible, and better trained of the two sexes. Their status in the social order is superior—a fact borne out by wage scales, educational and job opportunities, the use of the male pronoun in our language as representative of the whole people, by laws regarding property rights, etc. Therefore it seems logical that it would be more difficult both culturally and personally for the male to admit areas of ignorance, difficulty, failure, or defeat within his personal life and to be deterred from seeking help by "masculine pride" (defined by some experts as a compulsion to appear independent and self-sufficient in spite of a desire to find a kindly parent figure in the counselor). As exemplifying the impress of this caste mold and the greater spontaneity or lesser self-consciousness of the sex that is not placed so conspicuously

in the forefront of leadership, ask any family who first suggests approaching a policeman for directions and is willing to do so. This phenomenon applies to the unmarried as well as to the married.

3. *Women have to make more adjustments in modern life than men.* Some sociologists have made this claim in relation to the more privileged and educated group of society (Foster and Wilson, 1942). This seems to be borne out by the fact that more women than men patients actually were registered in private mental hospitals (Truesdell, 1947), and that according to general verbal statements more are found among office patients of psychiatrists in private practice. Women's conflicts are often focused on marriage (Mudd, 1947) whereas in reality they are often dependent upon many elements of cultural change which affect their value, as human beings, to themselves and to others. Our social order has not as yet accepted the concept that would eliminate a considerable amount of conflict for many women of today, namely, that one way of using women's abilities to the full, to enable them to feel and be of full value, is to train them for creative jobs *and* domestic activities and let them do both on part time instead of on an either-or arrangement (Beard, 1946), (Lundburg and Farnham, 1947), (Kluckhohn, 1950). Considerable data have been presented by contemporary writers which bear upon this point (Buck, 1941), (Deutsch, 1945), (Drinker, 1948), (Guest, 1943), (McBride, 1947), (Mead, 1949), (Young, ed., 1947).

4. *Women have more at stake in marriage.* For the majority of American women marriage with children is still the goal, the career, and the all-consuming venture of life (Duvall and Hill, 1945). In addition, at least partial economic security often goes with marriage. Men, on the other hand, are brought up with chief emphasis on training for active jobs or careers. To earn their way is essential to living. In addition they expect, along with 90 per cent of the population, to marry. Therefore, although marriage is important to men, it is seldom their chief goal and is usually contingent on the ability to provide for a wife and family.

These conjectures are advanced in partial explanation of the fact that three times as many women as men used Marriage Council during the years of this study.

Age Differential

Related data support the hypothesis that men clients at a marriage council would be expected to be older than the women.

The median age at which men married in 1940, twenty-five to twenty-nine years in the United States, is higher than that for women, twenty-one to twenty-five years. (See Table 6.) The average man of twenty-five marries a woman of twenty-two, and so on up and down the scale. Although the age at which people marry varies considerably according to the status of the man involved, increasing as the socioeconomic index is raised, nevertheless the man remains consistently older (Hunt, 1940). Girls who marry farm laborers do so on the average at slightly over eighteen, those who marry skilled workers average nineteen and one-half years of age; girls whose husbands are in business are usually between twenty and twenty-one years old when they marry; and girls who choose professional men gen-

TABLE 6

MARRIAGE PROSPECTS OF SINGLE MEN AND WOMEN*

Age in Years	Pct. Who Marry Within Year		Age in Years	Pct. Who Marry Within Year	
	Male	Female		Male	Female
15	0.1	1.0	28	17.1	11.7
16	0.3	2.4	29	16.8	10.7
17	0.9	4.5	30	15.9	9.6
18	1.9	8.5	31	13.1	8.5
19	4.2	12.0	32	11.7	7.7
20	6.7	15.5	33	10.5	6.8
21	9.4	18.2	34	9.3	5.9
22	12.5	20.8	35	8.2	4.9
23	15.3	21.3	36	7.2	4.4
24	15.9	20.9	37	6.3	3.9
25	17.0	18.9	38	5.5	3.5
26	17.3	16.0	39	4.9	3.0
27	17.3	13.3	40	4.5	2.7

* *Sixteenth Census of the United States: 1940*, Vol. IV, Part 4, p. 248, U. S. Department of Commerce, Bureau of the Census, Washington, D.C., 1943.

erally do not marry until they are between twenty-three and twenty-four [2] (National Resources Committee, 1938).

As clients who use Marriage Council come for help in preparation for or adjustment in marriage are predominantly in the business or professional group, these data support the expectation that there would be preportionately fewer men clients under twenty-five and proportionately more over twenty-five years of age.

Further exploration of this age differential in marriage is of interest (Parsons, 1942). Socioeconomic factors are conceded to be the main cause. Men in our culture have been held responsible socially and legally as the breadwinners for the family unit whether or not it included children. It has been the custom, therefore, for men to be equipped as breadwinners through experience or education or both, spending years preparing themselves in this way, before marriage is possible. This is, of course, particularly true for the professional group.

Early studies indicated that marriages of very young couples lowered the chance of marital happiness (Kirkpatrick, 1937). Later studies raised the question whether emotional age (maturity) was not the important factor in these marriages rather than chronological age (Burgess and Cottrell, 1939), (Cottrell, 1942), (Kelly, 1941), (Terman, 1938). A recent monograph (Monahan, 1951) presents contradictory evidence leading to the conclusion that no clear interpretation seems possible. According to Bossard (1933), "about one-tenth of all men marry women of their own age; another tenth marry women who are older, although in nine out of ten of these cases the difference is less than six years."

It seems probable that new mores may lessen the age differential between men and women at marriage. These mores are consistent with the gradual emancipation of women and their greater participation in the economic life of the community during the last century. As it is no longer considered peculiar for a young woman to go to college, so it is becoming less "queer or abnormal" to find working wives above the economic

---

[2] The average age at marriage of 1,175 Cornell graduates was twenty-eight and a half years, the women averaging twenty-seven and the men twenty-nine years (Anderson, 1950).

subsistence level. As already mentioned, the percentage of married women working increased 10.6 per 100 in the fifty years before 1940 (Burgess and Locke, 1945). Especially since World War II young couples are sharing the responsibility for their economic needs by arranging for both partners to work for a period after marriage. This arrangement makes marriage possible before the man has finished his training. The median age at first marriage, for all men who ever marry, dropped from 26.1 to 23.8 years between 1890 and 1947. For women the drop was less noticeable, from 22.0 in 1890 to 20.5 in the same period (K. Davis, 1950). Conceivably, it may continue to drop in the future. This sharing of practical responsibilities is becoming a reality largely because of economic pressure, because of the far-reaching knowledge of adequate methods of child spacing, and because of the gradual acceptance of women in a competitive society as employable citizens outside of the home.

Marriage at a younger age for men and to women their own age or even older might conceivably lessen conflicts in certain areas of our living, notably the sexual. The findings of Kinsey and his co-workers (Kinsey, Pomeroy, and Martin, 1947) seem to indicate that sexual activity is at its height in the average American male between the age of sixteen and twenty-five and considerably later for the woman. However, this activity decreases after forty at approximately the same rate for both sexes. Because mores in the United States put great stress on monogamy and in the educated groups on abstinence from premarital intercourse it would seem that marriage for men at an earlier age and with women the same age or older rather than younger might conceivably lessen certain areas of conflict for both males and females. It might also increase interest on the part of the average male in what a woman is and feels, rather than according to the current custom of valuing her primarily on the basis of how glamorous she looks.

This concept of glamor would seem to be closely related to the unreal or fantasy approach to marriage promoted so aptly by the commercial ventures which profit most highly from it. Few advertisements lead to the belief that women have glamor, with its concomitant sexual appeal, much beyond twenty-five years of age. How many short stories in the popular periodicals depict their heroines with other than the sexual allure of youth, beauty, and modish apparel?

The suggested age arrangement would increase also the span of married partnership considerably, as men have a shorter life expectancy than women (Metropolitan Life Insurance Co. Bulletins, 1940–48). At present the average wife outlives her husband approximately five years. This period of widowhood, in addition to the obvious problems of economic support and loneliness, also presents privation in the sexual life of the healthy wife who has been well adjusted to this aspect of her marriage.[3] Marriage by partners of the same age or by men with women older than themselves would modify this situation substantially.

Educational Differentials

Why are the men who come to Marriage Council better educated than women? Related data support the hypothesis that men clients of Marriage Council would be expected to have more education than women clients.

Attendance in 1943 at educational institutions in the Philadelphia area indicates that the percentage of girls and boys is nearly the same until the age of fourteen. After that males take the lead. At sixteen and seventeen years of age, 74.3 per cent of the male population and 71.6 per cent of the female population were attending school. At eighteen and nineteen years when college work usually begins this ratio changes to 24.7 per cent of males and 19.5 per cent of females, and at twenty-four and twenty-five years, the time of graduate education, there are over twice as many males, 5.9 per cent as compared to 2.5 per cent females.[4] If these figures are compared with figures in Table 3 which show that 49 per cent of the total 2,559 clients who have come to Marriage Council have some, all, or more than college education, it seems logical to expect a

---

[3] It is to be hoped that a book or pamphlet containing practical and helpful consideration of this problem of readjustment for women may be written shortly by an understanding and suitably trained and experienced professional person.

[4] Figures taken from *Sixteenth Census of the United States: 1940,* Vol. IV, Part 4, p. 248, U.S. Department of Commerce, Bureau of the Census, Washington, D.C., 1943.

higher proportion of more educated men than women in the series of cases studied at Marriage Council.

Differences in Length of Time Married

Why should a larger percentage of the men than of the women clients have used Marriage Council in the first five years of married life, and why should a larger percentage of the women than of the men clients have used it after ten years of married life? It might be postulated that in early marriage the men clients had more problems or felt their problems more keenly, considered their status more at stake than did their wives and therefore felt more pressure to do something about it. It might be postulated also that after ten years of marriage the wives had more problems, or had reached a saturation point, or were more desperate, or felt their status and security more threatened. Data in this study can contribute little beyond the facts in the situations reported. As has already been mentioned, further studies now under way at Marriage Council and elsewhere may contribute further knowledge against which these hypotheses may be tested. Certain suppositions, however, suggested by clinical material in the case records of these clients may be of interest in support of the above facts. The situation of the man married between one and five years is considered first:

1. Men recently married have a great deal at stake in making a go of their marriage. They have taken the initiative in deciding to marry and therefore failure in the marital adjustment would seem to connote poor judgment in their choice of a mate. Pride in their own investment is at stake.

2. Many employers frown upon marital discord which brings unsavory rumors and, possibly, unpleasant publicity.

3. In cases of separation (Ayrinhar, H. A., 1949) or divorce, the children are not often assigned to the care of the father. The courts and public opinion recognize his difficulty or inability to continue adequate daily care for the child and the man resents this threatened loss (Alexander, 1948), (Drown, 1936–49).

4. If separation or divorce is considered, the man resents the

97

economic responsibility of alimony and support orders for a wife and children from whom he is separated. This may seem especially partisan when no return in lodging, housekeeping facilities, and sexual outlet is allowed him (Thorman, 1947), (Lichtenberger, 1931). If his income is small and he is a responsible type of person, such orders make remarriage and new children financially difficult and in some instances almost out of the question.

These conditions indicate definite advantages to the young husband in making his marriage work.

Next we consider the situation of the women married over ten years. The following concepts may be postulated:

1. Older women are more threatened than their husbands by family breakup because of various conditions in our culture (Bergler, 1948), (Bradway, 1938). Chances of remarriage for older women are much less than those of older men (Bossard, 1933), (Ciocco, 1940). With the loss of youth, "glamor," in terms of modern American culture, disappears, and the sex appeal so important at present in attracting the male is supposedly lessened. It is conceivable that Kinsey's material may gradually change this apparently erroneous culturally imposed concept.

2. Opportunity for self-support is poor for the older married woman—especially if she has not been gainfully employed while functioning as a housewife (Women's Bureau, 1946).

3. The older woman is more apt to feel useless and lonely than the employed older man. Her children, if she has any, have left home and there is not enough to keep her busy in routine housework. Often she has built up few patterns of activity outside her home to fill her time and interest in a manner equivalent to her husband's job.

4. The physiological effects of the female climacteric are often misunderstood by both men and women (Hartman, 1948). Erroneous folklore reflects the belief that, along with the cessation of menstruation, sexual pleasure for the female lessens or ceases, whereas men supposedly continue their erotic activities with little impairment. When the man's enthusiasm, according to this false concept, is met by the female who is unresponsive, due to her physical climacteric, the ardor of the male is dimin-

ished and he quite naturally turns to be refreshed and invigorated through the "allure" of a younger woman who has (supposedly) full command of her sexual powers.

Actually, clinical material indicates that many members of both sexes have considerable anxiety in connection with holding the interest of their partners because of the natural lessening in the frequency of their own sexual desires and responsiveness. This anxiety often comes at a time when they feel physically fatigued, and actually have less energy—women because of temporary glandular unbalance, men often because of extra pressures and responsibilities from their work. Sexual potency is regarded as a barometer of manhood and vitality and men are extremely reluctant to admit that it declines as early as is often actually the case (Stokes, 1951). If wives are not aware of the natural gradual diminishing of activity, the effects of fatigue and other psychological factors which may cause this change in their husbands, they are apt to feel slighted and unloved and to develop strong feelings of inferiority, none of which, of course, help in their relationship to their husbands. Husbands, in turn, are inclined to joke about the attractiveness of young women in general or even to give subtle hints that their interests have been diverted elsewhere. If the wife accepts these defensive threats at face value she becomes at first upset and later suspicious. To save face or prove her attractiveness or bolster her feelings of inadequacy (her ego needs) she too may turn to someone else.[5]

At this point something usually happens to the marriage. Either partner or both may have enough insight to realize that their marriage is basically satisfying and be content with a temporary flirtation elsewhere. Or this pattern may be continued, and the relationship between the partners becomes further impaired. In this case feelings that the marriage is threatened easily develop. If, however, the husband is convinced that his wife is the sole cause of his loss of sexual interest, he may resort to relations with another woman or a series of other women in an effort to prove his sexual adequacy. Because such relations

---

[5] The author is indebted to Mrs. Harriet Moss for some of the ideas developed in this and the ensuing paragraph.

can be sporadic, he feels they can be regulated more easily to his needs than his home contacts in which the nightly possibilities may be embarrassing. When the marriage continues under such conditions, the wife usually feels unhappy and rejected; if she can weather the situation, she often regains her husband's companionship and a comparatively satisfying relationship is revived. If the situation results in divorce the chances are that the husband will remarry, with the same fundamental crisis unsolved and probably with a younger wife whose needs are more at variance with his own than those of the divorced wife.

Given an interested and co-operative partner, women are not only quite capable of orgastic response after menopause but often more eager for sexual activity than formerly because there need be no fear of unwanted pregnancy or consideration of child spacing. A few men and women continue sexual activity (with diminished frequency) until death. One psychoanalyst advances the hypothesis that impotence for either sex at any age is due primarily to unconscious hostilities, fears, and anxieties, rather than physiological processes. Clinical examples certainly indicate difficulties for the sexually responsive woman who is well adjusted to a sexually active man somewhat older than herself whose sexual desire is waning due to the various factors already discussed. A woman in such a situation may find herself with the same problems as the young husband whose desire is greater than that of his even younger wife.

It is interesting to conjecture whether this complex rejection, frustration, and anxiety-producing behavior experienced within the personal interrelationship of marriage may not be projected by the individuals who undergo it into the national and international scene, and so contribute to the type of aggressive behavior which is threatening society (Chisholm, 1949), (Saul, 1949), (Appel, 1950).

Differences in Source of Referral

Why were more men than women referred by former clients and more women than men referred from agencies?

1. Three-quarters of Marriage Council clients were women. Often, therefore, the first contact of the agency with the marriage was through the woman, either as the fiancée or wife. If

the partner came for counseling he was apt to come to Marriage Council later because of what he heard about the service from his partner, because he also wanted to work on the situation, or because of constructive changes in the marriage which he thought were related to coming to Marriage Council.

2. The difference in the number of men and women referred from other agencies or institutions was largely accounted for in the subdivision of referrals by maternal health centers. It seems obvious, as these centers in Philadelphia see almost 100 per cent women patients, that it is much more likely that women should be referred through their auspices than men.

AREAS OF SIMILARITY

The categories in which there appear to be no significant differences between the sexes are greater in number than those in which significant differences appeared. That there was no reason to believe the proportion of men and women seeking help from each religious group was different seems to imply that the influence of religious affiliations was similar on each sex. Nearly similar proportions of men and women were found in the single, engaged, married, and separated or divorced groups. This is of interest in itself, but perhaps of especial importance when added to the fact that the reasons given by the men and women clients for coming for counseling were almost identical. These findings present substantial evidence, within the population studied, to support the hypothesis that men and women who come for marriage counseling, contrary to popularly held opinion, do present very similar reasons for seeking help in spite of significant differences in age, education, length of time married when they sought help, and certain sources of referral.

SUMMARY

This chapter has presented separate analysis of the findings for all men and for all women clients in a population of 1,033 clients. Where noticeable percentage differences were apparent in the categories studied, the Chi-square statistical technique was applied to test the reliability of the difference. Significant differences were found in eleven instances, and probably in one additional category. There was no reason to believe the

101

groups were different in the other categories studied. These results warrant the conclusion that a significantly larger proportion of the men clients who came to Marriage Council during the period studied were (1) older, (2) more educated, (3) if married, married for a shorter time, and (4) more apt to be referred through former clients than the women. Conversely, a significantly larger proportion of women clients were (1) younger, (2) less educated, (3) and if married, they were married for a longer time when they sought help, and (4) more apt to be referred through community agencies than the men clients.

The data also enable us to conclude that religious affiliation, marital status, referral from professional and educational sources, and, of particular interest, the reasons given by the clients for seeking the services of Marriage Council, did not represent differences between the men and the women clients.

A number of hypotheses were advanced and related material introduced and discussed in an attempt at interpretation of the findings.

It was recognized throughout that the data presented contained such a small group of men that conclusions in some of the subdivisions can be suggestive only. Related material drawn upon in support of the hypotheses presented and many of the suggestions advanced must remain in the realm of conjecture until further knowledge is advanced.

7

The Selective Characteristics of Marriage Council Population

*I*T NOW SEEMS of interest to compare the Marriage Council clients in sex, age, religion, education, and marital status with figures both from Philadelphia, where 84 per cent of the first 1,033 clients lived, and from the United States.[1] This discussion should illustrate, in the areas examined, the special characteristics of the Marriage Council sample, bearing in mind, of course, changes in the composition of the local population, changes in the agency, and factors within the client group and its needs. Figures on the Philadelphia population of the type needed for yearly comparison with this group were available, in the majority of instances, for one year only. This year, therefore, was used as a basis for discussion. It is realized that this method cannot answer many of the questions of selectivity in connection with clients using such an agency, nor is it deemed our function to undertake such exploration.

Sex of Clients

The proportions of men and women in the general population of Philadelphia and the United States, in 1940, were approximately equal,[2] whereas there were three times as many

---

[1] The reader should note that in Chapter 5 the total client population of 2,599 cases was under discussion. In Chapters 6 and 7 the first 1,033 clients only are the basis for the data.

[2] Figures taken from *Sixteenth Census of the United States: 1940*, Vol. IV, Part 4, p. 248, U.S. Department of Commerce, Bureau of the Census, Washington, D.C., 1943.

women clients in the Marriage Council sample as men clients. Factors influencing this differential have already been discussed in the last chapter (pp. 91, 92).

Age of Clients

A comparison of the percentage distribution of the population of Philadelphia and the United States in different age and sex groupings, with approximately the same age and sex groupings in Marriage Council intake, is summarized in Table 7.

Comparisons noted in Table 7 appear suggestive. In the

TABLE 7

A COMPARISON OF PERCENTAGE AGE GROUPINGS FROM FIFTEEN TO FIFTY-FIVE IN MARRIAGE COUNCIL, PHILADELPHIA, AND UNITED STATES POPULATIONS*

Ages	Marriage Council			Philadelphia†			United States†		
	Men	Women	Total	Men	Women	Total	Men	Women	Total
16–20	5	12	*11*	14	13	*14*	16	16	*16*
21–25	29	42	*38*	14	15	*14*	14	15	*15*
26–30	27	21	*22*	14	14	*14*	14	14	*14*
31–35	16	9	*11*	13	13	*13*	13	13	*13*
36–40	11	8	*9*	12	13	*12*	12	12	*12*
41–55	10	7	*8*	33	32	*33*	31	30	*30*
Unknown	2	1	*1*						

* Based on 1,033 consecutive clients of Marriage Council (Table 5) and *Sixteenth Census of the United States: 1940*, Vol. IV, Part 4, p. 248, U. S. Department of Commerce, Bureau of the Census, Washington, D.C., 1943.
† Age groupings are one year younger throughout, i.e., 15–19 instead of 16–20.

sample of Marriage Council clients studied, the proportion found in the age group sixteen to twenty is slightly less than in the population at large, with a greater disparity between the men than the women. In the group twenty-one to twenty-five there is a considerably higher proportion of Marriage Council clients to those in the community of the same age, with the proportion of women still greater than men. However, in the age group twenty-six to thirty, although there is still a larger proportion of Marriage Council clients to persons of the same age in the community, the proportion of men clients now exceeds the proportion of women clients. From thirty-one to forty years of age there is little difference proportionately between Marriage Council clients and the general population, although again the proportion of men exceeds women at Marriage Council. However, from forty-one to fifty-five we find in contrast to the twenty-to-thirty-year-old group a much smaller proportion of clients using Marriage Council than in the general population, with the sexes about equally represented. These comparisons suggest that Marriage Council serves the age group in the general population in which the largest number of marriages are taking place or have taken place within five years, with more women proportionately than men in the younger age bracket, but more men than women proportionately in the age bracket twenty-six to forty.[3]

Religion of Clients

Table 8 gives the most recent information available at the time of writing on the distribution of the religious affiliation of the population of Philadelphia and the United States. Table 5 indicated that of the first Marriage Council clients 58 per cent represented themselves as Protestants whereas only 17 per cent were so designated in the population of Philadelphia and 21 per cent in the United States. Twenty-seven per cent claimed their Jewish affiliation in Marriage Council intake whereas 15 per cent were so recorded in the Philadelphia area and 4 per cent in the country at large. Eleven per cent of Marriage Council clients recorded Roman Catholic affiliation in contrast to 26 per cent as listed in Philadelphia and 15 per cent in the United States.

Before attempting to discuss these percentages it should be

---

[3] Material on age of clients just presented seems to indicate that Marriage Council of Philadelphia is fulfilling its purpose in part at least. This purpose, as stated in 1932 when the agency was first opened, has held and been reiterated through the years—*"to help young married couples or those contemplating marriage* to a better understanding of common requisites for a happy married life, to help them avoid some of the causes of marital difficulties." Sixty per cent of Marriage Council clients are found in the age brackets 21-30, which closely approximate the ages of 19-33 during which the large majority of men and women in the U.S. marry (see Table 6).

noted that the religious census of 1936 includes only those individuals actually belonging to religious bodies having a membership of over 50,000. Nor is any information given as to the age of the members on which the census figures are based. The Roman Catholic Church by its method of contact with families confirms, as church members, children of its members at an earlier age than the Protestant groups and lists these children among its parishioners. The listed members of a Catholic parish in all probability therefore have a wider age span than do the listed members of the Protestant group. By the calculations used in the 1936 census, 39 per cent of the total population of Philadelphia and 59 per cent of the total population of the United States are completely unlisted, whereas only 3 per cent of Marriage Council clients are unclassified and 1 per cent are members of "other" religious groups. However, the age span of Marriage Council client population covers only the years between fifteen and approximately fifty-five. From the above remarks, it is obvious that these various figures and percentages quoted are not actually comparable and can only be suggestive.

In discussing the religious distribution of the 1,033 clients,

TABLE 8

DISTRIBUTION OF RELIGIOUS AFFILIATIONS IN THE POPULATION
ACCORDING TO THE 1936 RELIGIOUS CENSUS*

	Philadelphia		United States	
	Number	Per cent of Total Population	Number	Per cent of Total Population
Protestant............	333,000	17	26,700,000	21
Jewish...............	293,000	15	4,641,000	4
Roman Catholic.......	529,000	26	19,915,000	15
Other................	6,000	3	1,252,000	1
Total listed..........	1,161,000	61	52,508,000	41
Total unlisted........	770,334	39	79,161,000	59
Total population (1940 census)........	1,931,334	100	131,669,000	100

* *Religious Bodies, 1936*, Vol. I, United States Department of Commerce, Bureau of the Census, Washington, D.C.

attention should also be called to the fact that the schools, colleges, and community groups listed in Table 10, which approached Marriage Council with requests for lecturing and group leadership, represented entirely Protestant, Jewish, or nonsectarian institutions. The percentage of Roman Catholic students in such institutions is apt to be small. It is therefore obvious that many hundreds more Protesants and Jews knew at first hand or indirectly of the availability of such a counseling service than did Roman Catholic individuals.[4]

The agency itself has never imposed any limitations on the availability of its services to all religious groups and prefers to be useful and co-operative whenever possible to all groups. It is entirely probable, however, that many other reasons in addition to the few mentioned above influence the variation between the proportion of Marriage Council clients in the main religious groups and the population in the Philadelphia area and the United States.

Education of Clients

Education of clients is considered (Chart I) along with the educational attainment of the population in the Philadelphia area and the United States. Here the reader must know that the first 1,033 clients of Marriage Council's population (see Table 5) were between approximately eighteen and fifty-five, whereas the United States census figures are for the total pop-

---

[4] As has already been stated in Chapter 3, Marriage Council services are available to anyone who desires to use them regardless of race, creed, or national origin. It is the policy of the agency that, when the client raises questions of ethics or morality, he be referred to his minister, rabbi, or priest for guidance in the religious aspect of the problem. It is considered a necessary part of each counselor's background that he or she have at least general knowledge of the rulings of the major religious sects in so far as they affect marriage or the dissolving of marriage. When the behavior of a client who is an active member of a religious group is at variance with the teachings of his group, this is called to his or her attention by the counselor, and further discussion with a religious leader appropriate to the client is suggested. When the client so desires, a definite referral is made to a priest, rabbi, or minister in the client's neighborhood.

ulation over twenty years of age.[5] Within the limits of these contrasting groups we find that the proportion of clients coming to Marriage Council with grammar school education or less was 11 per cent, whereas 26 per cent of persons with this amount of education are recorded in the Philadelphia population and 25 per cent in the United States. Forty-five per cent of Marriage Council clients had high school education compared to 64 per cent in Philadelphia and the United States. Clients with some college education appear as 32 per cent in Marriage Council intake in contrast to 6 per cent in Philadelphia and 8 per cent in the United States. The average percentage of clients with more than college education in Marriage Council is 7 per cent, and 2 per cent in Philadelphia and the United States.

In making any comparison with general population figures it should be borne in mind that intake at a marriage council is necessarily controlled in part by the stated purpose of the agency—that is, if the functioning of the agency actually puts into effect its stated purpose. The purpose in Marriage Council of Philadelphia has always been focused on service to those about to be or recently married. For this reason articles and other general publicity have emphasized a service for young adults. Staff members have accepted requests for group counseling or teaching with young people not less than seventeen years of age or older (Gaskill and Mudd, 1950). To date there have been more requests, through which appreciable numbers of young people between seventeen and twenty-five have been reached by staff members of Marriage Council for "education for marriage," made by colleges in this area than by the high schools (see Table 10). Groups at the Y.W.C.A., Y.M.C.A., Y.M.H.A., churches, or clubs usually have a broader age span and may include more older and married persons. Thus the larger numbers of young people reached in group counseling have probably been in colleges. It seems reasonable, therefore, to suppose that a higher proportion of young persons with some college education than those with high school

---

[5] Figures taken from *Sixteenth Census of the United States: 1940*, Vol. IV, Part 4, p. 248, U.S. Department of Commerce, Bureau of the Census, Washington, D.C., 1943.

education only have been exposed first hand to the knowledge that a counseling service was available, and so were able to consider using it when their own marriages approached. In addition, other teachers in college have contact with young people more nearly at the average age of marriage than do high school teachers. These teachers are apt to discuss marriage and the family during various courses. They may refer students to such services when they are asked for help in problems of a personal nature which they do not have time to go into, or for which they may not feel equipped to undertake counseling (see Chapter 3, pp. 31-32). Perhaps because of the activity in this field in institutions of higher learning, one of the substantial sources of referral of clients to Marriage Council is college courses.

If the educational differential between the percentage of Marriage Council clients in the more educated groups and the population in Philadelphia and the United States is considered along with the facts that about one-third of Marriage Council's clients are engaged persons, and of the married about two-thirds have been married under five years, some evidence is advanced of a positive correlation between the amount of education and the use of measures purporting to offer preparation for marriage and service in the early stage of adjustment. It seems appropriate to postulate on the basis of these findings that as the educational level is raised, awareness increases of the need for and advantages accruing from adequate preparation for the job ahead as well as the desire to do a good job, and, if there should be difficulties, to do something about them at an early stage.

Marital Status of Clients

Marital status of clients in relation to the marital status of the population 15 years and older in 1940 shows the following: In Pennsylvania 59 per cent of men and 58.5 per cent of women 15 years of age and older are married. The Marriage Council population shows 57 per cent men and 54 per cent women as married, including the widowed. Pennsylvania shows 35.6 per cent of the male population over 15 years of age single and 29.7 per cent of the women. Marriage Council intake

TABLE 9

MARITAL STATUS

OF THE POPULATION FIFTEEN YEARS OLD AND OLDER*

	Pennsylvania		United States	
	Number	Per cent	Number	Per cent
Total men 15 plus...........	3,736,473	100	49,335,632	100
Single...................	1,330,989	35.6	16,376,595	33.2
Married................	2,207,727	59.1	30,191,087	61.2
Widowed...............	173,763	4.7	2,143,552	4.3
Divorced...............	23,994	0.6	624,398	1.3
Total women 15 plus†........	3,768,121	100	49,361,562	100
Single...................	1,119,812	29.7	12,751,772	25.8
Married................	2,201,633	58.4	30,087,135	61.0
Widowed...............	414,612	11.0	5,700,092	11.5
Divorced...............	32,064	0.9	822,563	1.7

* Figures taken from *Sixteenth Census of the United States: 1940*, Vol. IV, Part 4, p. 248, U.S. Department of Commerce, Bureau of the Census, Washington, D.C., 1943.

† Approximately 90% of the total population of men and women marry at some time in their lives.

shows 42 per cent single men and 44 per cent single women (lumping engaged with single). Pennsylvania shows slightly less than 1 per cent of each sex divorced and does not list separations. Marriage Council lists 1 per cent divorced and 1 per cent separated. Thus the marital status of clients using Marriage Council and that of the population at large in the Philadelphia area, within the limits of the material already mentioned in this chapter, appear to follow much the same pattern in the married and divorced groups,[6] but to have a proportionately higher percentage of single men and women.

[6] In a study of 1,326 Cornell graduates of the classes of 1919, 1920, 1921, 90% of the men and 87% of the women were living with their first spouse a quarter of a century later. Of the 10% of marriages terminated at that time, 4% ended in death and only 6% in divorce. In the general population, one marriage in every six that was contracted about the time these college graduates married broke down in divorce, and many others in separations. Separations were almost unknown in these university families. Remarriage occurred in 4% of those divorced and in 2% where death of the spouse occurred (Anderson, 1950).

The other major categories which were presented in Table 5 about Marriage Council clients cannot readily be compared to the general population.

SUMMARY

This chapter has discussed data available on 1,033 clients who came to Marriage Council of Philadelphia during 1936 to 1944 in relation to similar data in the 1940 census for the population of Philadelphia or Pennsylvania, the area from which these clients were in large part drawn. In addition, comparisons were made from the population of the United States. According to obtainable census data people who live in or near Philadelphia were predominantly white adults in 1936 with an equal ratio of men and women. They had grammar school or junior high school education. They were more apt not to be listed as members of any religious group, but if they were listed they were more apt to be members of the Roman Catholic than the Protestant or Jewish groups. If over fifteen years of age, they were more than twice as apt to be married as single and, if married, to be married under five years.

The clients who used Marriage Council facilities during this period seemed to be for the most part younger, more educated, more apt to be white women and members of a Protestant church, than the general population of Philadelphia and the United States. They were a little more apt to be married than single and, if married, to have been married for about the same length of time as the general population of Philadelphia.

This discussion indicates, within the limits of the data, the kind of sample which the clients of Marriage Council of Philadelphia represented in the local population and in the United States.

8

Case Histories of Clients,
Interview by Interview

Sᴛᴜᴀᴛɪᴏɴs brought to marriage and family services cover myriad problems in human relationships. As the counselor continues work with these he or she becomes closely attuned to the most minute emotional gradations which he must learn to understand.

The case illustrations in this and the next chapters have been chosen as representative of a cross section of clients who came to Marriage Council of Philadelphia during 1936 through 1949. An effort was made to choose cases which reflect the periods before, during, and after World War II. Situations fall into the main groupings of reasons for coming, as listed in Chapter 5, Chart III, and will be related also to the three general divisions of intake referred to in previous publications from this agency (Mudd, 1937), (Mudd, Freeman and Rose, 1941). Meticulous care has been used to remove the identifying particulars of person or place. If the reader believes he recognizes an individual client, it may be borne in mind that these situations are sufficiently common to have been experienced by many people.

In general the cases selected are those in which the client had more than one interview at the agency and in which some report was received from or about the client following counseling. The cases present a fairly comprehensive picture of the counseling process, both from the point of view of the client who brings his situation to the agency and of the counselor who is carrying on the service. Four cases are given in detail in this chapter, in form similar to the original case records, except as modified to protect the client's anonymity. These records demonstrate as clearly as possible the total process of marriage counseling in this agency, and the various aspects of a client's contact. They also represent different counseling techniques and styles of recording as used by four counselors. In Chapter 9 additional cases will be summarized as examples of various types of situations and of the subclassifications under clients' reasons for coming to the agency.

Many situations improve; others do not seem to improve but the client feels better; sometimes the client does not return or let the agency know what happens; sometimes neither the situation improves nor does the client feel better. Each situation is unique. Through becoming acquainted with the variety which appears in a counseling agency the reader will gain understanding of generalizations about the process of counseling.

CASE I

This case illustrates two ways in which premarital counseling can be used. The young man used Marriage Council first to clear up his feelings of anxiety and guilt in connection with a specific sexual problem which made him extremely uncomfortable as he began to consider marriage. Later Mr. A came with his fiancée to Marriage Council for "general" counseling in premarital preparation. Both partners later reported their good adjustment by means of the postmarital adjustment schedules sent them four months after marriage.

As already noted in Chapter 5, Chart III, persons coming to Marriage Council before marriage with a specific problem constitute 16 per cent of the total intake at the agency, persons coming for general premarital preparation 23 per cent. Mr. A's first visit would classify him in the specific problem group, his second visit and that of Miss B would fall in the general premarital preparation group.

Mr. A was about twenty-four and unmarried. He had grown up and received a high school degree in a foreign country and was working here as an apprentice engineer. Miss B, seen first seven months after Mr. A, was an American girl of twenty-one who had been through high school. Both were Protestant. A fee of $1.00 was paid for each interview.

Referred by: Self.

Reason for coming: Premarital interview after reading Dr. Clifford Adams' book, *How to Pick a Mate.*

Counselor's Impression of client: Mr. A was an unsophisticated country-type lad with a most pleasant personality. It was quite evident that it had taken considerable courage for him to come and discuss his problem, although as the interview proceeded, he gradually relaxed and was able to talk with ease.

First Interview—Mr. A: Upon entering the office, Mr. A said immediately that he came because he was anticipating marriage and was concerned as to whether masturbation since adolescence would have any bearing on his ability to make a satisfactory sexual adjustment. He had tried to secure information previously and learned of the Marriage Council through a book by Adams. While at first it was difficult for him to talk about it, he became more at ease as Counselor made him feel that the habit was nothing unique on his part and is a fairly common practice among both sexes. He then explained that he came from a farming district and had never received any sex instruction from his own parents. Consequently he never realized that masturbation would have any undesirable effect upon him later in life. Now that he is contemplating marriage, he had become extremely anxious and was greatly relieved when Counselor discussed some of the recent thinking on the subject to the effect that moderate masturbation practiced by normally sexed individuals who are not having coitus regularly, is not abnormal or unnatural, but merely the expression of a biological urge. In order to substantiate the discussion, he also read a chapter on masturbation in a sex manual while in the office and borrowed a book by Groves to take home.

After concluding this part of the interview, he seemed eager to talk about his forthcoming wedding and present situation. He was impressed by the opportunities in this part of the country and the high standard of living. He is working hard and looking forward to an early promotion. He has no relatives here and rooms in the home of a motherly widow.

Several months ago he became acquainted with a girl with whom he feels certain he is in love and wants to marry. Aside from his anxiety regarding his sexual adjustment, he felt sure that he could make a go of it as they seem to have similar ideals and standards,

114

enjoy the same forms of recreation, have many mutual friends and are of the same religion and similar family backgrounds. He has often visited her home and likes her parents. They are not actually engaged, although he has made her understand that he feels she is the one he desires to marry. Consequently it was agreed between them that they would not come to any definite decision until she returned from a vacation trip.

Meanwhile he has been thinking about sex matters and since he expects her to return in a few days, wanted to settle the question in his mind. If he should become engaged, he would like to have a premarital examination by a physician and thought his girl friend might like to do the same although he has never discussed it with her. Since Counselor felt he might need more reassurance concerning the problem of masturbation, she suggested sending him the name of a physician whom he could consult. Mr. A seemed to appreciate this but wanted to be assured that any correspondence would not bear the name of the Council for fear of being kidded.

Letter in, 10-19-37: Letter from Mr. A expressing appreciation of book and visit and asking referral to doctor.

Letter out, 10-23-37: Letter to Mr. A enclosing referral to Dr. C.

11-39-37 Close: Inasmuch as nothing further has been heard from Mr. A case is being closed. Counselor believes he did receive a certain amount of reassurance concerning his problem and believes he is the type of person who will readily return if he feels in need of further assistance. However, he seemed quite a self-reliant, capable young man, who may have received sufficient help to proceed on his own.

Medical Report, 2-27-38: Medical report received from Dr. C who saw Mr. A on 2-7-38. Examination negative. Additional remarks: "Greatly helped by interview at Marriage Council. Had some further questions about anatomy and physiology. Still anxious about 'confession' to his fiancée of his masturbation. She'll probably never ask! He shouldn't 'unload' to her!"

Telephone in, 4-8-38: Mr. A telephoned that he expects to be married 5-29-38 and would like to arrange for a premarital interview for fiancée. Mentioned how very much he was helped by Dr. C and since "consultation with him and previous interview with Counselor he no longer has any problem." However, he asked if Counselor would refrain from mentioning his former worry to fiancée as he has never discussed it with her and Dr. C did not think it necessary. Counselor assured him this would be held strictly confidential.

Case re-opened, 4-15-38

Impression of client: Miss B was very pretty and petite, shy and quiet. She appeared bright and intelligent.

Joint interview, second for Mr. A, first for Miss B: Mr. A brought his fiancée to office in the evening following their work. He seemed radiantly happy and almost overenthusiastic concerning their marriage. When Miss B spoke one could see that she had a very definite mind of her own.

As Miss B completed Background, Personality, and Engagement schedules,[1] over which she seemed quite meticulous, Mr. A related how everything was just about set for the wedding and reception, even to ordering flowers. They have also rented a furnished apartment which they are planning to redecorate. Mr. A seemed delighted that his parents and sister are coming before the wedding and was anxious to have everything arranged so that he and Miss B would have time to show them around.

When Counselor asked Miss B if she would like to talk with her alone, she thought not, stating that she and Mr. A have learned to discuss everything very freely, which was brought about by reviewing so many books on marriage together. In fact they have now started a library and have read and acquired some of the better-known books. Consequently they both felt pretty well prepared for marriage and thought they only needed further information on child spacing. Miss B felt extremely hesitant about having a premarital physical examination which Mr. A said was their only source of disagreement. While Miss B admitted that it might be helpful she said that she doubted whether she could ever bring herself to it, even by a woman physician. Moreover her mother is opposed to her having the hymen broken before marriage, which was another reason for her hesitation. Therefore she preferred to have Mr. A take care of things, at least during the honeymoon, after which she would consult a physician. They both felt that for financial reasons they must limit their family and preferred postponing having any children for at least a year during which Miss B would continue with her job. She apparently has a good position. Consequently Mr. A said he would take as much precaution as possible. Since Miss B had no family physician at present time and they both needed to have a blood test taken, they asked for the name of

---

[1] For explanation of schedules used routinely in connection with counseling see Chapter 10, "The Process of Counseling," sections on follow-up, on research, and on sex adjustment.

a physician, preferably a gynecologist in her locality whom Miss B might consult later.

In conclusion they both felt they did not have any other particular problem relating to marriage and expressed great appreciation for their interview at Marriage Council. As they departed they were very friendly and happy and readily agreed to complete further schedules or co-operate in any way possible.

Telephone out—collateral, 4-20-38: Telephoned County Medical Society and secured names of five gynecologists in her locality which were given to Miss B.

5-29-38: Mr. A and Miss B were married.

Report in, 6-12-38: Medical report in from Dr. C about Mrs. A. Everything normal. Estimate of patient's expected sexual adjustment—good. Advised as to method of child spacing suitable to Mrs. A.

Letter out—Mr. and Mrs. A, 10-18-38: Follow-up letter sent as planned to Mr. and Mrs. A after their marriage enclosing Marriage Adjustment A Schedules for both to check and return.

10-29-38: Adjustment A Schedules received from Mr. and Mrs. A. The schedules were checked after five months of marriage. They indicated both partners are extremely satisfied with husband's occupation and wife's occupation. They are living in their own quarters. Both get along very well with their parents and in-laws. They share responsibility for daily household tasks, buying of supplies and budgeting. They like household activities very much and participate together in ten different additional activities. They confide in each other about most things and are both satisfied with the amount of affection. Disagreements have been worked out between them in practically all areas by mutual give-and-take except that Mr. A checks a little disagreement about his mother, Mrs. A a little about her mother and considerable about her father-in-law. Neither checked any trait of themselves or spouse which caused any difficulty. Both rated their marriage very happy and believe that the marriage has been very happy for their spouse. They felt their love is much stronger now than before marriage.

3-15-39: Letter to Mr. and Mrs. A thanking them for checking schedules and asking whether they would be interested in making an appointment to discuss the B Schedule on sex adjustment. As no response, case closed.

It is apparent that there was definite value to Mr. A in consulting Marriage Council. In all probability he would have entered into marriage a more hesitant and insecure individual had he not had this counseling experience. The acceptance by the counselor of his problems and feelings and her factual explanation of what science knows about human behavior in this area gave this young man definite reassurance. Substantiation of counselor's verbal reassurance was furnished through use of reading. The offering of a medical referral was another source of confirmation helping Mr. A to get a firmer footing in the reality of his situation.

It is obvious that Mr. A received sufficient relief to proceed to discuss and make concrete marriage plans. His return with his fiancée for a general premarital exploratory talk gave them both an opportunity to survey attitudes and areas of sharing. The furnishing of another medical referral for obtaining the couple's blood tests was again a concrete service of the agency.

CASE II

Here we see how a couple already married and with a basically sound relationship may suffer through the years because of attitudes and misinformation leading to sexual maladjustment. (Fifteen per cent of total married clients seen gave problems of sexual adjustment as reason for coming.) The partners apparently were so ready psychologically to use help at the time they came to Marriage Council that a change in attitudes appeared quickly after the first counseling interview in which each released guilt and anxiety and expressed much feeling about earlier sex experiences both before and after marriage. Further counseling helped increase understanding of partner and parental relationships and aided each in cementing the new behavior into a constructive and persistent pattern. Throughout contacts with this couple, the counselor made active use of agency procedures which were accepted by both partners.

Mr. and Mrs. C were both Protestants in their early thirties. They had been married about seven years and had two small children. Mr. C earned a good living as a minor executive in industry.

Referred by: Article in popular magazine, through which Mr. C wrote the National Association for Mental Health and was referred to Marriage Council. (See Appendix A.)

Reason for coming: Wife's lack of satisfaction in sex relations.

Impression of client: Mr. C is tall, slim, quite good looking, well dressed, and appears somewhat older than his wife. His hair is graying and gives a distinguished appearance. He was obviously shy but seemed very eager to work on his problem.

Mrs. C is small and has a good figure. From the standpoint of features, she is homely but her face is fluid, expressive, and she makes the most of what she has by dressing simply but attractively. She was much more vocal than her husband but obviously distressed at having to be here.

First Interview—Mrs. C, 6-18-38: The C's seemed at a loss when asked if they would like to be seen by the Counselor alone or together, finally deciding to come together. Mr. C asked if Counselor wanted "background" information, or if she preferred that they start immediately to talk about their problem. Counselor thought it would be best to talk first about why they were here. Mr. C said their only difficulty was in the sexual area. The C's looked at each other and together decided it might be better to talk to Counselor alone. Mrs. C chose to be first. In a slow, deliberate manner Mrs. C launched into her story, forging ahead with dogged determinedness. She spoke intelligently and with what appeared to be a good bit of insight. Many superfluous gestures with her hands indicated her nervousness.

From the very start of marriage, physical difficulties interfered. Intercourse was unsatisfactory and painful to both. Since neither had had a premarital examination they consulted doctors and learned that each had a condition needing surgical care. Mr. C's treatment was long and serious.

About eight months after marriage Mrs. C had to have one ovary removed. Upon resumption of relations thereafter she was very fearful that again something might be wrong with her. Her husband was very patient and considerate and sex relations were "fairly satisfactory" although she did not experience orgasm. Her doctor had told her she shouldn't have children for a year and that year was an unhappy one for her. Mr. C had said before marriage that children were of no importance to him and she almost didn't marry him because of this.

During the next few years, Mrs. C was pregnant four times, each time having to wait a year before trying to conceive. Her first two miscarried at two months and the two others resulted in Caesarean births. She was in bed most of the time during these pregnancies and was allowed no intercourse. Mr. C was sick some of this time, too, and was worried about their economic situation. After the second baby the doctor tied her tubes and Mrs. C felt relieved that there need be no more children and was sure intercourse would now be all right. She has kept feeling that this trouble is all her fault as Mr. C has been extremely considerate.

The sexual difficulty came to a head nine months ago. Whenever Mr. C approached, Mrs. C realized she had some excuse—a headache, backache, indigestion, etc. She spoke to her sister, a social worker, who suggested she seek help. Part of the trouble is that Mr. C has orgasm almost immediately upon penetration. Her occasional orgasm takes so much effort. Following her period there is increased desire and particularly then is she left "up in the air" when unsatisfied. They tried intercourse frequently but it didn't make any difference in his ability to delay orgasm.

They decided together to do something about their difficulties. Mr. C went to a doctor, had a series of treatments and if anything he is worse. Counselor asked at this point if Mr. C is able to arouse her in any way. She has attained orgasm manually but wants to have it the "right" way. Counselor gave some explanation here briefly about the acceptability of manual caressing as a means of helping achieve orgasm. This was somewhat reassuring to the client.

Counselor commented that the C's had certainly been through a lot of physical difficulties. She wondered how they got along in general. Very well except for sex which is now beginning to tinge their whole relationship. "I no longer know how I feel about my husband. I wonder if I really love him as much as I should. I feel irritated most of the time about very small things. I think I might be irritated even if sex was all right." She almost hates Mr. C for arousing her and then leaving her unsatisfied. She cannot pretend any longer that she doesn't care. If they cannot have satisfactory intercourse, why should they have it at all? She thinks he insists so often in order to prove that he can be successful as a man. He puts so much pressure on her to reach a climax. Sex has never been fun to her but it could be. Mr. C doesn't really enjoy their relationship either. He complains that the satisfaction is purely physical and so brief that he knows there should be more in it for him too.

They have done little reading. After her first miscarriage a doctor said they were too considerate of each other and didn't encourage them to return to him. He blamed their physical difficulties and felt time would straighten them out. Because the doctor said nothing could be done, they allowed matters to drag on. Counselor asked how Mrs. C had been prepared for marriage. She said, "My own parents' attitudes upset me greatly. Mother's wrong sex attitude was relayed to me. She's a bitter woman who merely tolerates sex."

Premarital lovemaking with Mr. C was very satisfactory although they never had complete intimacy. She expected complete satisfaction in marriage and it was a great blow to find intercourse so painful. They married on a shoestring after waiting five years. Although Mr. C does well economically now his biggest difficulty is lack of confidence. They wouldn't be here if she hadn't finally blown up. She resents most his allowing this thing to go on indefinitely.

Counselor pointed out that Mr. C is getting some sexual satisfaction and Mrs. C is really the one who feels this thing more keenly. Therefore, wouldn't it be natural that she initiate this step? Perhaps it was hard for Mr. C to come here at all and it did show his concern. Mrs. C agreed, commenting again on her husband's considerateness, adding that many men would not care whether their wives were satisfied or not. She realized that it hurt a man's pride to admit not being able to satisfy his wife. She seemed to soften toward her husband after this discussion.

Mrs. C was anxious to read and bought Butterfield's pamphlet *Marriage and Sexual Harmony*. Counselor thought they might plan tentatively on six interviews, weekly, and another appointment was made. Counselor explained that research indicates many educated American women never experience orgasm but are able to get a great deal more from intercourse than Mrs. C now does. It would be hard for us to anticipate now what our ultimate goal would be.

First Interview—Mr. C, 6-18-38: Counselor realized it would not be easy for Mr. C to discuss something so personal with a woman but if he could get over his initial discomfort it might be helpful for him to see a woman. He admitted that he had been startled but was able to compose himself while waiting for his wife and is ready to go ahead. Where did Counselor want him to begin?

Counselor said she now knew of their physical difficulties from Mrs. C and they had indeed had a hard time of it. Perhaps Mr. C would like to talk about his reaction to intercourse after his operation. Recently there had been a slight irritation, and he consulted a urologist who treated him with catheterization and massage of the prostate. As a result he feels he has orgasm just as quickly or more so, and doesn't intend to return.

Counselor encouraged Mr. C to talk about premarital experiences. He was "slightly promiscuous," although never attempted relations with his fiancée. When he was satisfied by coitus—this wasn't always—it was a purely physical thing and he never considered whether the girl was satisfied or not although he thought some of the girls were. He gave serious thought to only one other girl before marriage, but his wife was more enjoyable and more intelligent.

Now Mr. C desires intercourse very frequently and is quickly aroused by his wife. Actually he is tired a good bit of the time, and then is indifferent. He works a full week and goes to school three nights. This is his fourth year of study and there are two more years. He is preparing himself "just in case a better opportunity presents itself."

Counselor commented that Mr. C seemed very ambitious and she could understand his being tired much of the time. Did he often find it hard to get to sleep? The only times are when his wife is out in the evening and he goes to bed without her. Then he falls into a kind of half sleep in which two dreams recur. In one he fears that someone, unidentifiable, is trying to enter the house and he gives him a fierce thrashing. In the other, he is having a beautifully satisfying sexual relationship, most frequently with his wife; only sometimes it is an unknown female. At first he said only that this second was a sexual fantasy and Counselor said perhaps he would like to talk about it another time. He seemed anxious to go ahead but found it difficult. Finally said that in the dream he is able to satisfy his wife by oral genital contact with her. She also satisfies him in this way. He consciously has wanted oral contact but she refuses. Counselor explained that oral play was sometimes a part of pre-coital play if both partners desire it. Mr. C was surprised, having thought it a form of perversion. Other women have had oral contact with him and he has liked it. Counselor asked if there had ever been contact with other boys when he was growing up or with men. Mr. C's immediate reaction was that he never had contact with other men—had never desired it but then he recalled an experience with another boy his age when he was twelve. They played with each other three or four times but stopped, thinking this was wrong.

Counselor felt Mr. C had been able to be quite frank, and recognized his willingness to work on his problem. He felt that it is not physical but is all in his mind and the trouble is mostly his fault as he has orgasm too quickly. Counselor said that rarely was any difficulty between two people the fault entirely of one of them. The important thing was to get to understand the feelings and attitudes of both partners in order to see how they played into this situation. Mr. C is very willing to return as often as necessary even though it will be difficult. Counselor asked that he read the Butterfield pamphlet too and he was anxious to do this. He asked if he and his wife should refrain from discussing their interviews with each other. Counselor thought this should be handled in whatever way was most comfortable for them. However, Counselor would not discuss Mrs. C's interview with him or vice versa. She wondered if he could cut down the frequency of intercourse for a few weeks to not more than twice weekly; in between times he might try to show his wife he could be affectionate and not insist on relations. He thought this was a good idea and he would try it.

Fee: Mr. C raised the matter of fee himself and selected a suitable figure. This will not, because of the depression, be easy.

Second Interview—Mr. C, 6-24-38: Mr. C came into the room looking quite different—much more cheerful and at ease. Counselor had a chance to say only "good evening" before Mr. C launched into about fifteen minutes of enthusiastic description of what had happened. He found the Butterfield book very enlightening. He felt the reading and the interview had enabled him to have satisfactory relations with his wife for the first time in their marriage. He grinned as he said he had been able to perform successfully three times in the past week. Although he realized from what Counselor said it might have been well to cut down, both he and his wife were so highly satisfied and so mutually desirous of relations that it seemed all right. Counselor commented that this was certainly so and she was very glad to hear his positive report. He only regrets that they couldn't have had such a good relationship before. "We have renewed our confidence in each other." He was no longer tense or irritable at work during the past week.

After Mr. C's report, he said of his own accord that he is afraid of his own enthusiasm about the improvement—he might again become too anxious and overdo the good thing that he now has. He first thought that he would come back and thank Counselor but would not need further help. He later decided it would be better to come back for awhile to insure lasting results. Counselor thought this showed remarkable insight, and agreed with Mr. C.

Some time was spent discussing oral contact, and Mr. C finally decided it was not important to him, since he has found regular intercourse satisfying. Mr. C thought that possibly learning such contact isn't wrong had done a great deal towards helping him enjoy relations with his wife.

Mr. C wanted more reading and Counselor loaned him another of the helpful sex manuals now available. He asked how there can be contact with the clitoris during penetration. Counselor thought this was something the Manual might help explain. Also he might find it well to experiment with various positions until they find ones that are comfortable and make contact possible.

The remaining few minutes Mr. C used to talk about how scared he was when he first saw Counselor and how he determined doggedly to go ahead even though Counselor was a woman. He feels extremely hopeful now and made another appointment.

Second Interview—Mrs. C, 6-30-38: Again Mrs. C spoke in a deliberate, halting manner as if weighing each word. Said she is going to have to alter her mental attitude a lot. Both she and her husband have been guilty of ignorance, "I was greatly influenced by mother who thought that anyone who enjoyed sex was abnormal. She made it seem nasty." Her mother told her about an aunt who always had intercourse twice the same night with her husband, "which was no better than being an animal." In her parents' home things were all right on the surface until she was nineteen. Then her parents went through a very bad time and Mrs. C was the only one of five children at home. There was a continual outpouring from her mother about everything bad in the marriage and deriding the father. Last spring when Mrs. C began to break away from her mother she incurred severe criticism from a sister. She feels that she need now answer to neither her mother nor sister. Her prime responsibility is to her husband and children.

Seeing sexual difficulty behind her parents' unhappiness made Mrs. C panicky about what would happen to her own marriage. This feeling in addition to the pressuring about intercourse she was getting from her husband was about to drive her crazy. The only time she and Mr. C could discuss things was when they went to bed and because she feared his request for relations whenever they were in bed, she was too blocked to be able to talk freely. For the first time now in her married life she really is able to anticipate going to bed. The release at the time of their first successful intercourse was terrific and she was relaxed for the first time in many years. She used to feel that if she made an intellectual search for the proper mechanical aspects of sex, this would detract all the more and remove whatever mystery there should be. She analyzed out loud details of their sexual experience before marriage and since visiting Marriage Council, wondering what she can do to keep the new improvement lasting.

Mrs. C considers her relationship to her mother of prime importance. She tried through the years to give her mother the emotional support the latter didn't get from the father. She realized that her own home was suffering as a result and she was largely successful in severing this dependence on her. When this finally happened her husband said they had lived entirely too close to her mother and she realized for the first time that he was concerned. He's such an easy-going guy. She never knows when he is annoyed and often wishes he could blow off steam more. She feels sad that they had to have nine years of frustration when things could have been so fine. Counselor reminded her that the first break with her mother came very recently and the help that Mrs. C has recently received might not have been acceptable earlier. She readily understood this idea and appeared relieved. Although now she and her mother have patched things up on the surface, she is not secure enough in the new relationship with her husband to see too much of her mother. Mrs. C's early childhood was very happy; her relationship with her mother was excellent then (Strauss, 1946), (Taylor, 1942).

Mrs. C said that from now on her husband would come first. She hopes that by attaining a normal attitude toward sex, she can develop the right attitude in all phases of her marriage. Her husband has always had an inferiority complex and she has aggravated it particularly in her former attitude toward him sexually. She has always wanted him to be free to come to her with his feelings and perhaps now he will.

Counselor commented that Mrs. C seemed to have come a long way in her thinking and apparently had been able to do a lot herself towards improving the relationship. She was as agreeable as her husband had been regarding future appointments and thought she would like to go a bit farther in her discussion about her family and the part they have played in her adult adjustment.

Third Interview—Mrs. C, 7-7-38: Even though intercourse was infrequent this past week, Mrs. C said it is wonderful to know that she can be in her husband's arms at night and just relax and there will be intercourse only if both desire it. Looking back, she supposes she exaggerated the frequence before they came here. Because she didn't want it, no matter how often it was, it was too much for her. She has seen such a remarkable change too in her husband and realizes now that he did not enjoy their relations before either. He is almost a different person. If he is tired now he just wants to go to sleep without having any sense of urgency about sex. Mrs. C still doesn't understand what happened to make this change.

At this point Counselor asked which of them took the initiative to write to the National Association for Mental Health. Mrs. C. thought her husband had written for information. She had gotten him to the point where he too realized something had to be done. Counselor commented on there being a right psychological time for seeking and accepting help. Mrs. C thought this quite true. Counselor added that there must have been something in her approach to the problem when she discussed it with her husband that was more positive than negative and the apparently good basic relationship between them couldn't be overlooked.

Mrs. C has realized more and more through her contact here that she really does have a good marriage. She never had the idea that if things couldn't be worked out she would walk out on the marriage. Counselor gave some commendation here and then said that the break with her mother seemed important in this too. Mrs. C thought it was of prime importance and recounted feeling that she would have to consider her husband first, since her mother had been so unreasonable. Counselor asked if this was the first time she had felt she had to choose between her husband and her mother. She thought about this for awhile and guessed it was. She feels disloyal in that she has no desire now to see her mother. She thinks her mother may be jealous and resentful and feels if the children's marriages broke up they would come to her.

Counselor said that when children begin to observe members of the family objectively and realistically they are bound to come in for a jolt and to experience doubts as to their ability to be loyal—which was exactly what Mrs. C had been saying. Mrs. C could accept this and is worried now about whether she is capable of loyalty to anyone, even her husband should he fail her in some way. Counselor pointed out that because we see the weaknesses in those close to us, we don't have to. overlook their good points. One is truly grown up who can be aware of strengths and weaknesses and accept people for what they are—not just glorified versions of them. Mrs. C felt she was wrong to be aware of flaws in her mother's character and Counselor drew an analogy of the high school student who blindly worships a teacher, suggesting that this is not a mature relationship, because the worshiper can not see his idol as a human being. Mrs. C was enthusiastic, thought she was just growing up late and perhaps in time she would be more comfortable with her mother. She guessed she had to work harder on some of these feelings and try to see things clearly for herself. The major part of the job is now up to her.

Counselor wondered how Mrs. C wanted to handle future appointments. Mrs. C would be very busy in the next week and thought it best not to come in for awhile as that would give her a chance to see how some of the things we talked of are going. She hastened to add that she still wants to see Counselor, however, as she feels pretty much in the middle of things. She almost reeled going out of the interviewing room, and said these interviews stir her up a great deal emotionally. She takes away so much to think about and she thinks they have done her so much good.

Third Interview—Mr. C, 7-8-38: Mr. C didn't quite know how to begin tonight. He feels quite comfortable about the physical relationship now and isn't worried any more that it will regress. When things worked out this past week so that there couldn't be much contact between them, he wasn't disturbed. Now when he is tired he just wants to go to sleep.

Counselor wondered then if there were any other areas in the marriage that Mr. C would like to talk about. He mentioned his feelings for the children. When they act like wild Indians, he finds them very trying. Counselor questioned the amount of time Mr. C has to spend with the boys. Mr. C realized that he has less time at home than the average father and therefore the children make demands for his undivided attention. Also when he is home, his desire for relaxation is so great that the children easily become annoyances. Counselor stated that his feelings are not unnatural but, since he uses much of his spare time for study he cannot be very close with the children during that period. Mr. C had never looked at it that way but supposed it meant deciding what was most important and making sacrifices for it. He feels he can easily be lost at his work and should have this extra training to fall back on.

Then with some difficulty, Mr. C guessed that all of his life he has had an "inferiority complex" and worries a lot to himself. He lacks ability to sell himself and his ideas. Counselor suggested they look at his record. Had he gotten any recognition on his job? Were his superiors dissatisfied? What is his wife's attitude toward him? As he looks back he sees what he has accomplished and is amazed.

Counselor encouraged Mr. C to talk about his background. He mentioned his brother who had been desperately ill. He felt it only fair that the brother get most of the parental attention. He was on his own since sixteen but never minded. His parents never held up the brother as an example or did anything he can think of to make him feel inferior. He wondered if he were able eventually to understand reasons for his inferiority, was there anything he could do about it? Counselor thought this might be something they could work on for awhile and find out. Was anything now particularly disturbing to Mr. C? He gets upset about little things and can let off steam about them but the big things don't seem to annoy him. He realizes his need for more push and self-confidence. Counselor asked if this was really his own feelings or had someone else suggested these things to him? He said it was his own feelings entirely and he would be grateful if Counselor could help. As the time was up arrangements were made for another appointment in a few weeks.

Telephone call in, 8-4-38: Mrs. C called. One of her children is ill and she can not keep her appointment today. She will call when she feels free. She arranged an appointment for Mr. C on 8-19.

Telephone call in, 8-19-38: Mr. C called. He had a bad cold and could not come in. Counselor wondered how things were going with them. He feels that the sexual adjustment for which they originally came here is satisfactory and that he doesn't need another appointment at the moment.

Counselor wondered about the other matter he had raised in his last interview and he said he would like to give that some more thought on his own—he really hasn't been thinking about it lately—and perhaps will call when he is more ready to work on it. Counselor said she would leave this entirely to him and was glad to hear that he was satisfied otherwise.

Counselor's Closing Note. 9-28-38. Case closed. From the tone of the last 'phone conversations with the C's, it is apparent that this contact is at an end. Counselor thinks they are both sufficiently in tune with the agency to return for future help if indicated. This is one of those situations where the hoped-for change seems to come miraculously and almost too quickly. However, there were certain factors functioning even before the couple came here. First, the break with Mrs. C's mother, when *she chose* her husband in preference to the mother was a step in drawing them closer together. Secondly, both these people are capable of warm and deep feeling for each other and have their mutual interests in mind. They had been actually aware of the need for help several months before coming to Marriage Council, as indicated by the date of writing to the National Association for Mental Health. By the time they got to counseling both were eager and ready for help to the extent that they were willing to be very revealing of themselves even though this was painful. This case is less complicated than might appear from a first statement of the problem and its duration, because there were misconceptions about sex. Through re-education, reading, and frank discussion the C's were able to understand many things in a new light and be freed of some of their inhibitions. Of great importance is the fact that the poor sexual adjustment was not complicated by other areas of difficulty in the marriage or by severe personality problems in either partner.

5-39: Counselor learned indirectly through a personal friend who lives in the C's community and has been friendly with Mrs. C since childhood that she and her husband have joined a group to which the C's belong. She commented on how well liked the C's are by other members and how well they seem to get along. Mentioned a few things about Mrs. C's family which bore out very strongly what Mrs. C had said in her interviws.

10-30-39: At a meeting where other caseworkers were present, a worker for a children's service spoke to Counselor about the C's. This worker is a friend of Mrs. C's sister. Through this contact, Mrs. C asked the worker about resources for children in her own community. She mentioned her contact at Marriage Council in this conversation and how it had helped her to understand how to use caseworkers. Felt she had gotten a great deal of help here which had continued. The worker seemed to feel Mrs. C clearly understood that it was possible to get help in many different areas and also saw the value of getting it when difficulty was just beginning.

It is apparent that by divesting the sexual behavior of this couple of right and wrong connotations, the counselor helped both partners to a healthier attitude. As in Case I the counselor's point of view was reinforced by the reading done by Mr. and Mrs. C. The counselor tied in Mrs. C's insight in connection with her mother's approach and her own way of doing things and helped her to evaluate her relationship to both husband and mother more realistically. In turn, Mr. C also came to see himself and his accomplishments in a truer light, thereby enabling him to let up on his drive to prove himself constantly the successful male. The understanding relationship furnished by the counselor set the stage for both Mr. and Mrs. C to work out a situation which had been more a side-tracking of a good marriage than the explosion of a poor one.

CASE III

Mr. and Mrs. D are older than the average Marriage Council clients and had been married for a longer time before trying to do something about their difficulties. Mrs. D felt her way toward getting help by first seeking assistance for her daughter who was upset over a decision about marriage in war time (4 per cent of total intake was for "advice in regard to other persons"), and later seeking it for herself. Although her marriage was apparently badly deteriorated when Mrs. D got to Marriage Council (38 per cent of total intake involved general postmarital adjustment, see Table 3), much change took place between the partners as a result of Mrs. D's six interviews and Mr. D's one. This counseling contact came at a time when Mrs. D was desperate and her husband most unhappy. Basically these two people needed and wanted each other. Their use of the counseling relationship enabled them to remould their own daily living so as to find some satisfaction and comfort from each other and from marriage.

Mr. and Mrs. D were past middle age, Mr. D being four years older than his wife. Both were Protestants and college graduates. There were three children, two daughters twenty-three and eighteen, and a son eleven. Mr. D had a business position with a salary of $7,000; Mrs. D was a housewife.

Referred by: Own knowledge of Marriage Council.

Reason for coming: Desire to get adequate help for daughter who was having difficulty deciding whether or not to marry a man she had been going with since the beginning of war.

Impression of client: Mrs. D was an earnest, refined woman, intelligent and reserved in manner.

8-11-43: First contact with agency: Mrs. D telephoned and talked with Counselor about the situation of her daughter who was considering breaking up with the man she had been planning to marry for two years. Mrs. D felt he was a nice fellow but temperamentally quite unsuited for her daughter. She thought him nervous, unstable and badly adjusted, and felt they both brought out the worst in each other. The man had been pressing her daughter to marry and finally issued an ultimatum that a date was to be set before he was sent overseas "or else." Mrs. D rather hopefully seemed to think this was the "or else." She said her daughter had a terrific need for help and guidance in connection with her relationships with men. Perhaps particularly due to the uncertainties of war, she got involved without using proper judgment. Counselor spoke of our willingness to see the daughter should she wish to come in.

8-26-43: Letter from Mrs. D enclosing check (for membership in Marriage Council [2]). She reported that her daughter had not desired an interview. She has announced her engagement but they do not plan marriage until he is discharged. Mrs. D then asked if she could talk with someone on the staff about some matters that have been worrying her about herself.

8-29-43: Counselor replied thanking Mrs. D for the check and suggesting she call for an appointment at her convenience, mentioning Mrs. Z as the Counselor she may work with.

9-15-43: Case closed.

11-25-44: Case reopened.

First Interview—Mrs. D, 11-25-44: It took Mrs. D about twenty minutes to fill out the schedules and when she came into the office Counselor wondered if filling them out had not been quite a hurdle for her. Mrs. D said uncertainly that the real hurdle had been to get here. She looked ready to cry. She explained that she was unwell and needed a maid to help with the housework and that her marriage was just impossible. She hoped that Counselor would be able to tell her what she could do to adjust to her husband so life would be more tolerable. As it is she has gotten to the end of her rope. She was pretty annoyed with her husband in every area of their life, particularly because of his interest in their car on which, from her account, he did seem to work furiously. He then demands that the family appreciate all his work. She made detailed references to former squabbles they have had.

She contrasted herself as a refined woman to her husband whom she characterized as vulgar. He constantly embarrassed her and she could not stand up for herself because of her dislike of scenes. She was very startled when I asked her why not, and now she moved with humor and sweetness to say perhaps she had not stood up enough for herself. She described the way she retreats from Mr. D by withdrawing into herself.

---

[2] For a discussion of means of support for Marriage Council of Philadelphia see Appendix B, pp. 268-70.

I said it would sound as if she had gotten into a hole and pulled the top in over her and maybe our job was to help her get out. By now the time was practically up and we used the remaining few minutes around Mrs. D's decision to continue here for a few more interviews. She made an appointtment in ten days' time.

Fee: The fee presented quite a difficulty since Mrs. D had no idea of her husband's income. She did not think she could discuss this with him but because we have a sliding scale and needed to know her income before we could set the fee, Mrs. D decided she could ask him. We also discussed briefly how Mr. D could be involved in what we were doing.

Mrs. D was given *The Happy Family* to read.

Second Interview—Mrs. D, 12-9-44: Mrs. D arrived ten minutes early and looked much happier than she had last week. She expressed a great deal of discomfort at being here but said it had done her a lot of good to come last week; she had gotten a maid and had even answered her husband back once. Her face was very mischievous as she recounted this and her other little stories of times when she answered Mr. D back. She was awfully pleased with herself and when I went along with her on what she had done she told me that she had been thinking over a remark that I had made last week as to why she worried about the past. It had made her think more about the present and she realized that a lot of her trouble was her own sense of inadequacy.

We explored this briefly. Mrs. D had said earlier that when her husband had found that she had come here he had asked if she were getting a divorce. She had been so overcome by this conclusion of Mr. D's that she had not been able to cope with it at all. I said it was my feeling that we were trying together to find a way to make her marriage work and that I had no sense of her really wanting a divorce. At my use of the word "divorce" Mrs. D gave me a look of terror.

We went on to discuss, but inconclusively, the possibility of Mr. D having an interview here. Mrs. D decided that she herself wanted to continue no matter what her husband did. We planned two more interviews at this point with the idea of an evaluation when they were over.

Mrs. D said she had gotten a lot out of *The Happy Family* and I suggested she read *Discovering Ourselves*. Mrs. D had been able to ask her husband about his income and was a little surprised that he had told her directly. The fee worked out at $6.00 a visit which

Mrs. D felt was fair, but she also felt that she would have to use her interviews sparingly.

Schedules—12-9-44: Mrs. D brought back the Engagement and Marriage A schedules today, filled out. She is having so much difficulty in the interviews that I felt it inadvisable to give her the B schedule on sexual adjustment until she could express her negative feeling more directly.

Third Interview—Mrs. D, 12-20-44: When Mrs. D came into the office she stalled along, talking in a social kind of chitchat for the first ten minutes. Then with some help from me she was able to get into the interview by telling how puzzled she is to find herself coming to Marriage Council and being very much helped by the interviews. She looked at me gayly and said "you know I am feeling very well now." She recounted a conversation with her husband that she had had a few years ago in which he had compared himself to a mountain and the other people in his life to a river which had to flow around him while he did not move. Mrs. D said with spirit that her husband did not realize that the river could change its course if the mountain was too unyielding.

From this she recited several instances of the past week which formerly would have led to trouble between herself and her husband. She had answered him back directly and to her surprise that had ended the matter. Mrs. D was delighted at the way things were going between them and her attitude was that of a mischievous child.

Just at the end of the time she told me that her blood pressure is normal now. She was inclined to give me the entire credit for this in spite of the fact she is having medical treatment.

Mrs. D also has been able to manage her household much more easily. Her doctor had told her that she should play more and we discussed the kind of activity she would like. When our time was nearly up I suggested that we fill out the sex schedule. The D's haven't had intercourse for the past four years and it had been "tapering off for a long time." Mrs. D's reason for this was that she could not stand her husband's attitude towards her during the sexual act but she felt that if they could work their other problems out that they could work this one out too. She almost always had orgasm but she achieved this by fantasying that she was having intercourse with another man.

Mrs. D brought up the next appointment and said that she had not been able to ask her husband to come in but she would like to have the time saved and if he would not come in she would keep the appointment herself.

1-2-45: Letter received from Mrs. D saying that Mr. D will keep the appointment on 1-3-45. He had made the comment that he had no marital troubles, it was all one to him if his marriage broke up or didn't break up.

First Interview—Mr. D, 1-3-45: Mr. D is a dignified man dressed in a worn suit. In manner he was defensive and guarded and spent most of the interview protecting himself against anything I might say. I imagine this was in part his natural pattern of meeting a strange and threatening situation and in part due to his fear at finding himself here. Though he did not express any negative feeling directly himself, whenever I brought up the possibility that he might not like something, he agreed directly and charmingly.

Mr. D was ten minutes early for his appointment. I brought him immediately into my office and had him fill out the schedules while I sat reading. He looked like a sheepish school boy who was expecting to be chastised, but as we talked a little about the schedules he began to relax and I had the feeling that when he was through he was feeling rather at home. At least he could tell me that he had been wondering what it would be like to come here. His own idea had been that I would put him through the third degree or just tell him how wrong he was. This was more theoretical, it turned out, than from anything his wife had told him about her visits here.

He now told me quite defensively that he had no marital troubles at the present time though things had been very difficult several years ago but since then he has taken measures to protect himself. When I showed an interest he described a quarrel which had ended with his wife telling him that she wanted a divorce, so he had deliberately cut himself off from her and his children so that he would not be hurt should she leave him. He did not care now whether she stayed or left. I said gently that I found that very hard to believe. He came right back at me and said he told me I would cross-question him.

He then said how much his wife had improved recently and gave specific details about her conduct. The only thing she has not done that he would like is to do more entertaining but he felt that this was not as important as he had thought it to be. Somewhere in here he made reference to my having called him a liar. When I said I did not recollect having said anything like that, adding that maybe what I said did sound that way to him, Mr. D had a very good time trying to quibble with me. I told him directly that I did not get any feeling that he had anything he really wanted to talk over with me. Mr. D agreed that he felt just that way. He stood up to go (as the time was up) and said, "That's all, it's been just a diversion for my spare time." I said gently if a time should come when he wanted to come here for other reasons I would be very glad to see him.

1-6-45: Mrs. D telephoned and asked for an appointment today if possible. She told the office secretary that she was sure I would want to see her now that I had seen her husband and decided that she wanted to come at the one available time though it would mean being late for dinner.

Fourth Interview—Mrs. D, 1-6-45: Mrs. D had on a bright green sweater and scarf and a lapel ornament. In spite of her brave and cheerful trappings she looked scared to death and was almost trembling. Her husband hadn't told her a thing about his interview here which she felt was very strange because she was used to long and vituperative accounts of his activities. She hesitated and looked at me trustingly and said her husband had referred to me as "that woman." I laughed and said I had been called a lot worse things than that. Mrs. D laughed too and somehow gathered the courage to quote her husband further after assuring me that her husband's tone had been quite kindly, in contrast with his usual tone.

He had told her, "That woman certainly gets herself into boxes." He thought a cross-questioning would have been helpful after I had told him that I found something he said hard to believe.

He had also told her that he had told me he had no marital troubles—and these were all of the things he said about his interview. I gussed that Mrs. D wondered what had gone on. She was "curious as a cat," but realized I might not be able to tell her. I told her Mr. D had given me permission to use any of his material and that I felt she should know his quotations from the interview were extremely accurate. I here told her his account of the quarrel they had had several years ago when she had told him she was going to get a divorce. We explored this together, I suggesting that I felt Mr. D was really very much in love with her and part of his actions were to spare himself future pain. Mrs. D exclaimed, "And I have come to someone else to learn that he loves me." Then quickly she said, "I wonder if he has not told me that and I did not hear it."

She said that all the compliments he gave her had stings in their tails and now she began to think that maybe she had paid too much

135

attention to the stings and not quite enough attention to the other parts of his remarks. We explored this for a long time with Mrs. D becoming more and more appreciative of her husband as we went along.

From here she gave a vivid description of their management of finances and the elaborate way they settle accounts at the end of the month. Mrs. D was quite sure that Mr. D must have gotten something from the interview or he would not have forgotten to collect the money from her which she had offered him to pay for the interview. Then she asked in a little voice, "Did he say I have improved?" When I said I had had the feeling that he was very appreciative of all the things she had been doing recently, Mrs. D cheered up and briefly looked like a young girl.

She described the good times she had had on a visit dancing and being beaued around by the husband of one of her friends. From this she moved to saying that she was going to reorganize her household routine so that in the very near future she could do some entertaining for Mr. D which he so much enjoys.

She told me how much she had gotten from the book and we discussed it at length. She said how interesting and fascinating it was to come here and work on a relationship. She had never known anything like it. She ended the hour with a hilarious account of Mr. D's afternoon naps which he always excuses because of some illness that he imagines he has recently contracted. Then she giggled and said he had not needed a nap after he had been here but instead had gone out and called up a friend and gone off with him. She was very pleased that he had had this bit of fun and felt that somehow during the interview here he had gotten "relief."

She now remarked that he had started to tell her about the visit but that they had been interrupted by one of the children so he had not continued. Now she again began to talk about how much she was getting from seeing me and said she wanted to make another appointment. When I got out the calendar she found that two weeks was too far away and made an appointment for eleven days from now.

Fifth Interview—Mrs. D, 1-17-45: Mrs. D was about seven minutes early. There was an air of calmness and gentleness about her which I thought indicated that she had gotten hold of something. This feeling of mine was confirmed by her first words: "I think I have turned a corner of some kind." I wondered how the world seemed to her from around the corner, was it the same as always or were the sign posts changed? Mrs. D's eyes twinkled and she said quite seriously that it was like seeing the same world from a different point of the compass.

She went on to say how different things had looked to her during the past week. She and her husband are getting along very well which Mrs. D sort of took for granted but she was extremely surprised at her recent insight into the marriages of her two most intimate friends. She had considered these marriages extremely successful and without difficulties, only to find recently when she talked to these women that neither of them was as happy as she now is and both had problems that were quite appalling. We chatted about this for some time and I was interested that Mrs. D had referred both of these women to us. She hoped that they would be able to get as much help as she had. She made a fleeting reference again to the help she was sure her husband had gotten. She said he was much softer and gentler with her than he had been for a long time and the children had noticed the difference in their relationship. She quoted her son as saying, "You are acting like parents now."

From here she went on to talk about her daughter because of whom she had originally contacted Marriage Council. She said she was still very worried over her and explored her relationship with her. She now told me that recently she has done quite a bit of entertaining for her husband as she had decided that she had done too much entertaining for the children and had been neglecting him. She remarked on her new feeling about not needing to make too much fuss over guests.

I think more than anything else in the interview the above pointed up to me what Mrs. D has accomplished in her visits here. I ventured to comment to this effect. Mrs. D looked at me trustingly and asked how much longer she would need to come here with all she had done. I recognized how well she had used our services and said a little about the value of a planned ending, leaving the decision to Mrs. D. She thought she would want two more appointments, one in two weeks, then another the following month, for she did not really feel that "things had jelled yet."

Sixth Interview—Mrs. D, 1-29-45: Mrs. D was wearing the same suit that she has worn for the last three times, but her blouse and accessories were varied in color and she had on a good deal of lip-stick, so altogether she looked very gay. She started with a long description of her relationship with her youngest child, a son, about whom she feels very guilty. I said relatively little at this point and Mrs. D was able to decide by herself that she was prepared to work it out now that things between herself and her husband have cleared up.

She was rather thoughtful for a minute and said, "You know I think I turned my corner very soon after coming here." She went on to describe the schedule that she had filled out which asked questions about areas of disagreement between herself and her husband. She said she had always thought that they lived on different planets and when she filled it out there it was in black and white that they liked most of the same things and disagreed on relatively few.

She went on to describe their life together at the present time. I found out that they are sharing the same room and have had intercourse frequently. Mrs. D said frankly that her husband's actions in bed are much more friendly. She was still somewhat surprised about this and even more surprised that she could sleep in the same bed with him. In a burst she said that coming here had been such a big help. She gave me a meaningful glance and said, "I am so much better psychologically and physically."

There had been so much evidence of being through in what Mrs. D had said up to this point that I wondered if perhaps she felt that she was through with this place. Mrs. D did feel this way but said she had one question to ask me—was she bossy? I said frankly that I had never thought of her as a bossy person but I had thought that it was very hard for her to do the thing that said no to another person. Mrs. D worked on this pretty hard relating it to her early training and then decided that it was silly still to be doing things the way she had been brought up to do when she was a girl.

I said I really felt that she had gotten from us by now the thing that she had come to get and I wondered if she wanted to carry out her plan to come in for another interview next month. Mrs. D could tell me directly that she did not want to come again unless some new problem arose. She looked at me and laughed and said in a burst, "Well we never had our fight," and quoted back to me something I had said in her first hour about how she seemed to be trying to fight with me. I said that after she had left I had realized that what I had said to her had probably terrified her. Her eyes got big at the words terrified and I laughed and said, "Here I go using exaggerated words again with you." Mrs. D laughed and said, "Here I go being upset again." I felt that the implication of this last remark showed clearly the change in attitude that Mrs. D had made in her visits here though I did not share this with her since I felt it might be a threat to her.

I guessed that Mrs. D had made up her mind not to fight with me and so maybe in a way we had our fight after all. Mrs. D giggled and indicated that this was what had happened. At the door she was a little tremulous about leaving but reaffirmed her feeling that she could carry on without our help.

2-28-45: Mr. and Mrs. D's case closed.

10-15-48: Mr. and Mrs. D, their elder daughter and her husband (the man referred to in interview one) were all seen together by chance at a community function by a staff member of the agency. They spoke in a friendly fashion and gave the impression of being comfortable and relaxed in their relationship with each other.

In the case just described we see a woman who used her interviews largely to clarify her behavior in relation to her husband. She first was helped to accept her own negative feelings and impulses and to realize their legitimacy. Following this she was able to express them with her husband, whereupon an immediate improvement in the relationship of the D's ensued. She learned with the help of the counselor to appraise both her own and her husband's actions and was able to utilize this increased understanding. The fact that there was a total improvement reported, inclusive of a renewal of sexual relations after four years abstinence, indicates the extent to which this woman became unblocked and able to communicate and share. It is obvious that she was ready to use help of this kind. The acceptance of her defences, which were very high at first, enabled her to proceed into the permissive atmosphere in which she could face and accept and then change herself. The one contact with the husband apparently reassured him to some extent as to what his wife was doing at Marriage Council and helped him to accept and go along with the changes which he welcomed.

CASE IV

The fourth case in this series represents apparently hopeless personality difficulties. Many such find their way to marriage councils. Although counseling cannot hope to effect deepseated personality changes, it can sometimes bring about amelioration of behavior on the part of neurotic individuals so that their mutual adjustment in marriage is vastly improved. It is obvious that in the following situation we have two neurotic

139

people whose marriage in many ways plays into their neuroses. The friction had, however, become intolerable, and though neither partner could assume responsibility for the state of affairs they were able to move sufficiently to make the combination work, for the time being, at any rate.

The case is presented partly in summarized form and partly in detail to furnish a picture of how the counseling proceeded.

The Referral: Mr. and Mrs. E were referred to the agency in December 1949 by a psychiatrist to whom they had gone several weeks previously. The psychiatrist gave as his reason for the referral that each partner considered the other one the candidate for treatment. He had suggested that one of them consult another psychiatrist while he treated the other but this was unacceptable. The referral to Marriage Council was in the hope that by focusing on their desire to keep the marriage together each would progress to the point of seeing his own need for help.

Background Information: Mr. E was a large, serious-looking, white, Protestant man of thirty-one. He was a college graduate, had served extensively in the Army during the war and was employed as an engineer. Mrs. E, a very pretty, neat blonde, also a college graduate, had worked as a teacher prior to and at the beginning of their marriage which had taken place in the fall of 1943. They had one child, a girl of five who had not been too cordially welcomed by either parent.

The Treatment Period: Mr. and Mrs. E came to the agency together but preferred to be seen separately. Both continued in treatment for three months having eight interviews each at approximately weekly intervals. There was one joint interview in addition after each client had had two individual ones. At the conclusion of the contact Mr. E stated that he believed his wife had changed 90 per cent and he 10 per cent which, in Counselor's opinion, was a pretty accurate estimate.

Summary of Contacts with Mr. E: Mr. E began by complaining of "maximum incompatibility" and by picturing his wife as a virtual psychotic who had long periods of depression wherein she was irritable, slept almost around the clock, and was highly inconsistent in her handling of their child. His language in discussing his wife was vivid, vituperative, and at times so metaphorical that it was difficult to understand. He felt dominated by Mrs. E and considered that she despised him. In spite of all this he maintained his own love for her and a strong desire to keep the marriage going provided his wife could improve. They had had a lengthy and companionable premarital relationship which he felt had given no indication of his wife's mental difficulties. He expressed tremendous hostility towards his mother-in-law and frequently likened his wife to her. His own early life had been unhappy due to a broken home and he had been raised by distant relatives. What he wanted from the agency was to learn how to subdue his wife and how to become more forceful himself. Neither partner considered it possible to reason with the other.

Mr. E thought of himself as easy-going, an impression definitely not gained by Counselor nor confirmed by his wife's description of his behavior at home. He actually held several jobs and frequently worked till late at night. Mrs. E mentioned his having frequent and violent nightmares and spoke of excessive sexual demands. Neither of these facets was ever mentioned by Mr. E who talked about himself very little and spent a major part of his time venting his hostility against his wife and then swinging ambivalently to a brief mention of her virtues and his love for her. His dependence on her was obvious.

He was helped to see his use of language as a weapon against his wife and he gradually began to assert himself in a less vindictive and more relaxed fashion. He showed considerable warmth and friendliness towards the end of his contact in marked contrast to his almost brutal coldness at first. This was observed by his wife as well as by Counselor. He also came to recognize his own need to "grow up" though he could yield no further introspections. The contact with Mr. E was terminated comfortably when it was felt that he had used the service as much as he was able to at this time. Although Counselor believed that his immaturity and excessive hostility indicated a need for psychotherapy he was both unready and unwilling for this. It was thought that even so he could function more adequately as a result of his work at Marriage Council.

Summary of Contacts with Mrs. E. In a fashion similar to her husband's, Mrs. E began her eight interviews by laying on him the onus for their constant quarrels. In the first two interviews she expressed the desire to move out of the marriage and it was not till the joint interview which followed that there was any glimmer of her real desire to make a go of the situation. Her insights were much greater than her husband's and she came very soon to recognize some of the reasons for his behavior. Being a narcissistic person she was more willing to talk about herself than was he. She began to understand her own behavior patterns, realizing the causes and effects of her "selfishness." As this process progressed she was obviously more attractive and less cold in appearance, a fact noted by the office receptionist as well. She was able to deny her husband sexual relations occasionally without using this as a weapon and substituted real companionship in ways to which he soon responded.

The treatment came to a comfortable and logical conclusion with marked improvement in the relationship noted by both partners. At a follow-up a month after the end of the formal contact Mrs. E reported a continued trend toward mutual tolerance and understanding and a warmer feeling for one another. It seems quite possible that the E's will retain some of their gains.

The interviews taken from Mrs. E's record are the 2nd, 6th, and 7th. All other interviews are briefly summarized below to help in orienting the material.

First Interview: Discussed husband's difficulties at length—his resentments, hatreds, suspicions, tantrums, and nightmares. She handled them by getting mad. Described their fraternal relationship before marriage. Sex now the best part of their marriage. Convinced that Mr. E needs psychiatric care and has tried to get him into this. Resents his dependence on her and emotional demands. Feels he is a poor father. Can find nothing positive in the marriage and not ·anxious to keep it together except for child's sake. Spoke of resentment of child because of the limitation on her activities and the fact that she cannot work now. Is at Marriage Council to work things out one way or other.

Second Interview: After asking if Counselor had called the psychiatrist she said that she had come to her own conclusion and that is that she is going to leave. Does not want any part of it now. Mentioned that they had talked last night and this morning. Even if both were to get psychiatric care she still would not stay. Mr. E is threatening her again, is violent, and is determined to make it work. As far as she is concerned the whole thing is completely dead. He thinks he loves her but she doesn't know whether he does or not.

Spoke of his consulting business and the fact that she has to take calls for it. At first she was home seven days with a small child. She absolutely had to go out and take the child with her occasionally for a few minutes to get some air. Became upset and felt hampered and got very nervous. Finally told Mr. E she would take calls only certain hours of the day which he didn't like. Finally he got an operator's service for $12 a month which she considers very reasonable. For a while this was all right then he decided to economize by cutting out this service. Mrs. E thought he was kidding and couldn't believe he would do such a thing. She told him she couldn't do this and he maintained she was selfish. She has had very little actually and has had no clothes except those that have been given her until the last couple of months when Mr. E has finally given her $3 a week for herself. As far as working out any kind of a budget, she maintains there is no reasoning with him.

Counselor brought up the fact of Mr. E's difficult background and inquired if Mrs. E had ever given him any special solicitude because of that. She said she had thought of it but hadn't done it because it wouldn't have been sincere. It is a principle with her and she feels respect only for a man who can stand on his own feet. Feels sorry for Mr. E but does not respect him, in fact, has a great deal of disgust for him. Counselor wondered if perhaps he did not measure up to what she had thought he would be. She said this was true, that her parents had overemphasized, perhaps, the niceties of life. There was no crudeness in their language or actions and both her parents were high up in the financial and social scale. In reply to Counselor's question about her family's feelings about the marriage, she said her mother was pleased at the beginning. Her father was not alive at the time. After a while her mother did not like Mr. E.

She had been very careful at the beginning of their marriage to appear very nice at all times and in the mornings would always get up early to make up her face and fix her hair to appear attractive at breakfast. Instead of the wife letting herself go in their situation the tables were turned and Mr. E would come to breakfast with his pajamas on and his hair rumpled and his teeth unbrushed. Mrs. E tried this but he didn't care. She is alert, reads editorials, current events, is up on what is going on in the musical and theatrical worlds. Mr. E doesn't know anything that's going on and when she mentions someone like Stokowski he doesn't know what she is talking about. In reply to Counselor's question as to what were the things they shared before marriage she said that mostly they used to go sailing and fishing. She feels she cannot have friends in because Mr. E embarrasses them and insults them. He is always making jokes about sex. Gave an example of the time when she had a girl friend over for the night and Mr. E began to fool with her and pretended he was going to attack her. Though Mrs. E knew he did not mean it seriously both she and the girl friend were humiliated. Counselor and Mrs. E then discussed the possible source of Mr. E's attitude toward sex and that he had had no real instruction whereas

143

she had had very good information from her mother. Mother had taught her that her virginity was her own responsibility. Told her that if she preserved it sex would be beautiful and if she didn't it would be ugly and left the whole decision as to what she would do entirely up to her. Mr. E, on the other hand, was pushed off by his mother to a clergyman who unfortunately did not handle the matter well.

Actually Mrs. E believes there is absolutely no meeting ground between herself and her husband. Spoke of her teaching and the decision she had made. Mr. E does not know of this. She has decided to go and stay with her mother for a while in Wilmington and do substitute teaching. After she has enough money to set up her own place she would try to get a full-time teaching job. In that set-up she could afford help to run an apartment and take care of her child when she could not be home. Eventually she wants a separate home for the child and herself so she could have as much time with her as possible. Some day her mother's house will be hers and she will have that security. She has not thought in terms of another marriage.

Although she would like to, she does not feel she can leave now because, if she did, she would be harassed and pestered and threatened, that is, if Mr. E means what he says. She is even now afraid for her life and that of the child. He feels that she has hurt him badly, that she has been scheming and malicious, and has even told her that at times he has felt like killing her. He wants to wait until one of them comes to the viewpoint of the other. She is staying in the marriage for the one reason only, to see if through coming to Marriage Council he can come to realize that the situation is hopeless. Counselor commented that in other words she expected Mr. E to come to her point of view, to which she agreed. She is definitely going to leave. Wants him to come around to her point of view because she thinks it would be much simpler and would relieve her of the fear of a court battle. Wanted to know about her legal status with the child and said she had already talked with a lawyer and would do so again to get all the information straight. Hopes that Mr. E will come to see that their situation is useless so he won't contest a divorce. Knows he is as anxious as is she to get things settled. Stated again, as had Mr. E, that something must be done quickly. Counselor pointed out again that this process could not be rushed. Wondered if Mrs. E thought a joint interview next week might be of some use. We decided we would wait until Mr. E had his interview on Wednesday. She paid her fee of $3 and made appointment for following week, then spent considerable time in the office before leaving, looking at various books on divorce and divorce laws.

Joint Interview: Both stated desire to fight for instead of against each other. Mrs. E less yielding than Mr. E and both stressing desire to maintain individualities. Mrs. E still unwilling to trust him and wouldn't put any future earnings into common fund. Discussion of anger and how they both handled it. Superficially, at least, very successful interview.

Third Interview: First real change in Mrs. E's attitude and appearance. Discussed at great length the reciprocally close attachment between her father and herself and how this has made adjustment to husband difficult. Recognized intellectual awareness but emotional inability to handle this. Spoke of mother's rigidity and own attempt to avoid acting similarly in relation to daughter. Feels Mr. E's relationship to child improving. Still skeptical about outcome of marriage; feels she must be at fault too but can't see beyond this yet. Counselor indicated again all this couldn't be rushed.

Fourth Interview: Reports great change in self. Realizes her withdrawal from Mr. E after early part of marriage which she considers a result of Mr. E's treatment of her. Compared Mr. E. to her mother of whom she is still afraid and at whom she is still angry for former restrictions. Is aware that she doesn't "go out" to people. Has come to understand many things objectively but for first time questions value of continuing in treatment. Counselor indicated she felt it worthwhile to continue.

Fifth Interview: Told of greater concern over Mr. E this past week than over herself. Is now waiting for him to change too. Discussed his immaturity and shelving of responsibility on to her. Spoke of her love for him being selfish and sexual and her bewilderment at the resurgence of these positive feelings. Told of a highly successful discussion they had shared. Is now impatient to have things settled.

Sixth Interview: Mrs. E appeared looking much more relaxed and prettier than any time before which was noted also by office receptionist. Opened the interview by saying, "Last week things have been much better. However, there have been other upheavals before followed by periods of improvements which lasted only a short while." In reply to Counselor's question she said there was a difference in the betterment of this period. She has been trying to work on the angle of her mistakes, thinks it is true that she has been

145

in the wrong many times but believes Mr. E to have been the cause of much of this. Brought up fact of being self-centered and feels at first in marriage she was not this way although she had been so prior to the marriage. Discussed relationship with father and the amount he had centered on her. In reply to Counselor's question about friendships while growing up said this had always been a problem as there were very few of whom her mother would approve. Mother was a social climber and Mrs. E reacted against this. Realizes now her lack of friends was bad.

Went on to complain of times when Mr. E showed lack of consideration of her as justifying her self-interest. Gave specific examples from the time of her pregnancy. Had fainted once while washing dishes and Mr. E could hardly wait till she was on her feet again as he disliked washing them. He had done things which she believed harmful to her over her protests, such as having intercourse immediately preceding the delivery of the baby. Counselor agreed this must have been very difficult. Told of another recent episode when Mr. E had been rude to her friend but she was able to handle this not by getting mad, as she had always done previously but discussed it with him later, explaining her feelings of anger. She also told him that their whole relationship was a vicious circle, which frightened him and he initiated talking this over. Feels his attitude toward her is based on fear which she does not consider wholesome. Spoke of her own meticulousness, fostered by her upbringing, which is in direct opposition to Mr. E's way of doing. This, however, has been something she has been able to work out and each has accepted the differences in the other. There is a change, however, in their relationship and she finds herself turning toward him. The other morning when she was all upset because everything had gone wrong she asked him to sit down with her and have a cup of coffee. Mr. E responded to this, much to her surprise. She wonders what she thought she was going to get by this as she had never before tried to enlist his co-operation when she was upset.

Counselor pointed out that she was including him when she did this, and that in order to receive you have to give, which was what she was doing. She wonders why she should think he will respond. Counselor indicated that the important thing was that she was going out to him. She mentioned another incident—to Mr. E sex is like eating dinner, something he has to have every day. The other night she asked him for a "night off" as she was very tired and wondered if he would not just as soon sit down with her in the kitchen over a cup of coffee. He was delighted with this and they had a very pleasant time. She cannot understand why she did this, as before she simply would have said "no" to him. Counselor and Mrs. E discussed Mr. E's need for love and the fact that he was getting this from her by her offer and that in his constant demand for sexual relations he was seeking love. Mrs. E is very much pleased with this development and also surprised.

The question of tapering off the contact was brought up and this is something we shall discuss next week. She is concerned about Mr. E's contacts and Counselor pointed out that this was something Mr. E and Counselor would have to handle. Appointment made for following week and fee of $3 paid.

Seventh Interview: With some embarrassment Mrs. E reported feeling guilty because she talked so much last week and perhaps Counselor hated to tell her. When pressed as to why she felt this way she said she was here to learn but that she actually had things on her mind today. She is anxious to know more about the problem of identification and just exactly what would have been a normal development for her in relation to her father, also what can she do about it now in order to straighten things out. Counselor answered her question by discussing first a healthy psycho-sexual development, and secondly, by indicating that her need for and use of therapy would depend upon how adequately and comfortably she was now functioning. Counselor asked if she felt her tie-up with her father was interfering in her present relationship. Mrs. E believes not; realized the situation in the second year of her marriage and feels she has been able to handle it.

Her big question now is where to go from here, and how much of her husband's vulgarity and crudeness she can stand. Would it be necessary for her to have psychiatric help in order to accept this? Counselor questioned why she felt it was her problem rather than Mr. E's. Unless things change Mrs. E does not believe they can continue to live together. His crudity disgusts her. Before marriage Mr. E had been very inhibited and she knows he was afraid of women; believes he had no intercourse before marriage—at least, that is what he said. Gave as an example of his timidity with her that after a companionship of eight years he was afraid once of coming closer to her than twenty feet. Following their marriage all this changed suddenly and there was nothing but "sex, sex, sex." This is fine in its place but Mrs. E considers the pendulum to have swung too far.

She believes Mr. E has improved during the last month and that they both have gained from the experience here but also that both are becoming dependent on Counselor. Counselor agreed with this and indicated that that was why a tapering off for both of them had been suggested at their last interviews, pointing out that this would be one way also of finding out if the changes undergone by both Mr. and Mrs. E were at all permanent. Mr. E demands of her constant assurance that everything is going to continue to be OK but she feels unable to give it. Counselor agreed that she was in no position to do so but pointed out the importance of giving Mr. E something to hold on to. She is of the opinion that nothing is really going to do Mr. E any good except psychiatric treatment, and went into considerable detail, describing his sleeping patterns. He ascribes his difficulty to night work and since he has changed to earlier hours there has been a lessening of his difficulties but not a complete stoppage of them. His pattern is to wake up suddenly, after the first half-hour of sleep, cursing and swearing in a great rage. In his dream someone has always done something to make him angry. It is a definite pattern and alternates occasionally with another dream —a choking one which also has fury connected with it. Mrs. E is actually afraid of him at these times.

In general the situation is now livable in comparison with what it was before, but she is unwilling to commit herself to permanent personal changes without the condition of his changing also. Counselor pointed out that if Mrs. E felt this way real changes had not taken place within her. She knows now that she understands Mr. E and their entire set-up better and that she can move in either direction. In discussing her ability to "give out" to Mr. E she feels that at the beginning of their marriage she did this but stopped because of her fear of losing her own identity and self-respect. Her giving in to him was bad. Counselor pointed out the difference between a feeling of warmth which comes from a person and a giving-in process. In reply to Counselor's question as to what she was afraid of she cited their sex life from the beginning of their marriage on. She erected no barriers at the start and Mr. E wanted sex all day and all night. After the child was born and she used a diaphragm it became more difficult for her to have intercourse so frequently, as she did not feel she should wear it all the time. Even following the child's birth they had intercourse three times a day—at breakfast, lunch, and dinner—and three times every night. She finally persuaded him to cut down to once a day and three times a night, later to twice a night, and most recently, until just before their difficulties which brought them here, once a night. Since coming here intercourse is now a question more or less of mutual desire for it. Actually, she was able to adjust to the foregoing situation without resentment and believes she has her husband to thank for awakening sex desire in her. This all was given as an example of her giving in to Mr. E and its not doing any good inasmuch as his demands continued to be excessive. Counselor pointed out that both in this and in the examples she gave last week of sharing situations with Mr. E that the important thing was not in the sharing itself, but the feeling she got across with it. She understood this.

We then discussed the question of further appointments, Mrs. E wanting to know again what assurance she could have about the effect of her work here. Counselor indicated again that we could give no definite answer on this, suggesting that time would show if any gains had been consolidated. Counselor also expressed the opinion that both Mr. and Mrs. E had used this experience constructively. It was decided to meet again in two weeks. Any further plans would be made at that time. Fee of $3 paid.

Eighth Interview: Mrs. E had not missed coming in the intervening week as much as she had expected. The relationship between the E's has continued to improve and she is anxious to know what happened during the treatment process. Can't quite understand her own positive feelings toward Mr. E but they exist. Decision made to conclude the contact after discussion wherein Mrs. E wanted to use her continuing as a means to keep husband in treatment.

Follow up, one month later: Mrs. E came in to participate in the research program of the agency by filling out a special schedule. Everything is still going well and Mrs. E described herself as actually happy now. The E's are moving out to the country, a move which has pleased Mr. E especially. The decision was mutual and was based in part on their finding a satisfactory school for the child. There have been some difficult experiences in the past month—Mr. E had an automobile accident and Mrs. E's mother is sick and will need some special care but, for the first time, according to Mrs. E, each partner has shown real understanding of and sympathy for the other one.

The mere fact that each partner had put real effort into working for the marriage undoubtedly had great meaning for both and indicated a unity of purpose which was a cementing factor. No one would question that this is a neurotic marriage, but Mrs. E's increased understanding and lowering of her barriers against Mr. E, plus the diminution of his hostility because he has had an outlet for it, will help preserve it temporarily at least.

SUMMARY

Four cases have been presented in detail to illustrate not only varying types of problems but also how these are handled by different counselors within the counseling situation.

In the first case a specific difficulty prior to marriage brought the client to the agency where general premarital counseling was also shared by his fiancée. Many young people just in this way avail themselves of the opportunity to release guilt and anxiety prior to marriage and subsequently to add to their readiness for this new experience-to-be by discussing other adjustment factors and acquiring information and medical assistance.

The second case is a striking example of how a problem that is focused on sexual adjustment, even though there were many additional complications, can respond successfully on the counseling level. The last two cases concern more general marital maladjustment. In the first of these two situations more profound changes took place than in the second, where deep-seated personality problems were a larger factor. Even with such a handicap in some instances counseling is able to ameliorate the marital discord although fundamental problems may remain essentially untouched.

We see the results of the marriage counseling accomplished through many techniques. Catharsis is practically universal, and reassurance plays an important role when used appropriately, and in that use lies the skill of the case worker. Exploration of many facets of a problem furnishes the client with the opportunity to evaluate his difficulties more realistically. Insight, if achieved by the client and provided it is not solely intellectual, is a valuable tool. All these processes are present plus the most important service of all rendered by the counselor's merely being an impartial, more experienced, interested, and kindly agent in relationship to whom an individual may have the opportunity of working out his problem himself.

9

Further Case Histories in Which Counseling Helps and Fails

To provide a further cross-section of situations brought by clients for help to Marriage Council, sixteen additional cases are here summarized. These illustrate many of the different types of problems listed in "clients' reasons for coming for marriage counseling." See Chapter 5, Chart III. They follow the same general order, i.e., specific premarital problems, general preparation for marriage, and postmarital adjustments. The counseling processes were similar to those used in the cases more fully reported in the preceding chapter. The first nine of these cases were handled during the period of World War II, the other seven in subsequent years. Differences among cases are sufficiently great that no two are ever actually identical. We become better prepared to meet the unknown, however, as we become acquainted with a variety of situations.

We have purposely included cases in which counseling could be considered to have failed. It is important to realize that such cases are a definite part of this agency's work, and probably of the work of other agencies doing marriage counseling. It is difficult to determine whether these failures are due to lack of skill on the part of the counselor, to inability or unreadiness on the part of the client to use the assistance offered, to the limitations of the processes of counseling, or to a combination of these factors. Systematic evaluation of the results of work at this agency with a method of known reliability (Preston, Mudd, Peltz and Froscher, 1950) is now under way under United States Public Health Service grant.

Reported preliminary findings from a small group of 76 cases revealed that 7 per cent showed retrogression during the counseling, 32 per cent showed no movement (change), 58 per cent showed positive movement or improvement during counseling, and in 3 per cent there were insufficient data to judge (Mudd and Preston, 1950).

CASES SEEN DURING WORLD WAR II

CASE I

Miss F is a nineteen-year-old unmarried high school girl who heard of Marriage Council through group talks on health and human relations at her school given by a staff member of the agency. She sought an interview following an incident in her life about which she had intense feelings of guilt, fear, and disloyalty. She was afraid to talk of the matter with her family. Her case would be classified as a specific premarital problem, a type which constituted 11 per cent of total intake during the war.

Miss F was an unsophisticated, attractive, simply dressed young girl, very tearful and distraught. She explained she had gone for the weekend to visit friends of her family who had a son recently graduated from her school. This boy was home on his last furlough before being shipped to Germany. The boy had felt apprehensive and lonely at going overseas and wanted to feel close to someone. "Necking" led to a "soul kiss," which led to much more than she had "any idea of getting involved in. I gave in after a struggle. Neither of us felt badly at the time. It was our first experience." After returning home she had had pains in the stomach and "felt queer" when she got up in the morning. The more she felt this way, the more worried she got, as it seemed like the symptoms she had heard that women felt when pregnant. She had had these pains until she had talked with her schoolmate and came in here. The family had not known of her worry. She had been through some terrible weeks.

The Counselor recognized understandingly and sympathetically the suffering Miss F had gone through alone and how deeply disturbing this must have been. The fact that Miss F's monthly period, although delayed, had come on after she made the appointment at Marriage Council was discussed, the Counselor commenting on the way fear and anxiety often affected menstrual regularity. It was emphasized that what had happened had not been at the fertile period in the month and that with a normal menstrual period just completed, the possibility of pregnancy, so feared by Miss F, was practically eliminated. Following the discussion Miss F visibly relaxed and looked greatly relieved. She was then able to tell the Counselor that she was engaged to another boy away for a year in the Pacific. He was now twenty. She knew that he would feel "just terrible" about what had happened. She didn't know whether she should tell him when he got home, or what. She knew she could not do it through the mail.

The Counselor and Miss F discussed ways of handling feelings of guilt, what were real obligations to people we loved, of fairness, of the relief of telling, of the carrying of individual responsibility, and of the practical aspects of the situation. Miss F felt sure that no one else would ever know, and that, since physically she was all right, the incident was over and closed, except for her feelings about it.

The Counselor suggested that as her fiancé would not be home for over six months and that she had already decided the situation should not be handled in writing, it would not be necessary to make a decision now as to what she should do when her fiancé returned. Time often helped such matters, and her feelings might be different later. If the matter came up naturally, the Counselor felt Miss F would know how to handle it so that it would disturb her fiancé and herself in the least possible way.

Miss F was made to feel welcome to return if uncomfortable feelings continued. The curing powers of sharing feelings with another person were reiterated. Mention was made by the Counselor of Miss F talking with her priest and of Marriage Council's desire to co-operate in every way possible in urging her to do this if she desired. She said the interview had been a tremendous relief and that it was wonderful to know that there was such a place to which girls could come with their troubles.

No further appointments were asked for by Miss F in the next six months and because of the type of situation, Counselor made no follow-up.

CASE II

Mr. G was seen in the pre-World War II era but he is typical in peace or war of the group of clients in whom Marriage Council is the most interested from the point of view of good

mental hygiene. This group used the agency for general premarital preparation and often seemed to represent intelligence,
strength, optimism, and the will to do. They constituted 23 per
cent of total intake.

Mr. G was twenty-three and in professional school when he first
came to Marriage Council. He wanted to learn about marriage
counseling methods and philosophy on his own account, and in
order to suggest sources of help for young married friends in another
city who were having severe difficulties. He was told something of
how the agency functions and given material from the office lending
library. He was also given names for his friends of both a counseling
service and individual psychiatrists in the city in question.

Nine months later Mr. G made an appointment for himself and
his fiancée. He was now engaged and wanted to discuss the various
aspects of adequate preparation for marriage. Both young people
filled schedules before seeing Counselor. They felt their information to be fairly complete in physiological matters, a fact authenti-
cated by later discussion. After ten minutes or so together with the
Counselor, they were seen separately. Attitudes and feelings toward
present physical sharing and sexual experiences as they grew up
were discussed frankly and easily with each partner alone. Opportunity was given for each to raise questions and mention past
experiences confidentially. It was suggested that they read the
Butterfield pamphlet separately or together and return for further
interviews if new questions occurred.

Mr. G and Miss H were then seen again together. Mr. G wondered whether it would be a good thing for his future wife to have
some sort of a job. She was used to working under pressure at college and didn't know just what she wanted to do now. Roles of marriage partners were discussed in their interchangeability, feelings
of adequacy and mutual respect, ways of bolstering each other,
means of talking over hurt feelings constructively, and causes of
oversensitivity. The need for each partner to share in plans, decisions, and responsibilities was explored. Mother and father influences and identifications were also mentioned. Mr. G realized that
he wished to understand better the emotional and psychological
reactions and differences between the sexes. These were discussed,
after which Mr. G requested supplementary reading for the summer
period. Several appropriate books were suggested by Counselor
from the lending library. The importance of premarital medical examination for both partners was stressed and an appointment made

154

by them subsequently with a reliable physician. A fee of $4.00 was paid for the interview and use of lending library.

In the fall of the same year Mr. G sent a contribution of $10.00 "for help received from books and counseling." He was now married but as war had broken out he was volunteering for active duty. His wife thought she might be interested in training herself for counseling. She would like to talk to counselor about suitable graduate courses.

A year later Mr. G, on furlough, called Counselor asking for referral suggestions for a friend who wanted good vocational guidance. These were given him. He reported he and his wife were getting along famously. He felt they had worked through any misunderstandings and differences during engagement and had established such a sound give-and-take relationship that they would be able to carry on with confidence in spite of war and would be able to weather any new differences which might result from the war.

After his discharge in 1944, Mr. and Mrs. G took an active part in a Youth Conference organized by Marriage Council. Mr. G and his wife presented themselves to the group as persons who had found much comfort in using the premarital service. Five years after this Mr. G phoned Counselor that he and his wife now have three fine children, one a newly arrived baby. He asked about a good pediatrician, as his own family physician had recently died. He was given several suggestions for sources of expert pediatric care and the name of one of Marriage Council's sponsors, a professor of pediatrics. He was told of the referral service of the Philadelphia County Medical Society.

Subsequent reports from other sources indicated Mr. G to be taking a leading part in civic affairs. The marriage was apparently very satisfactory to both partners.

War brought many nationalities together and led to some marriages which otherwise never would have taken place. In some instances the differences and responsibilities involved in international alliances, added to other anxiety-producing factors in the world of war adjustments, aided in precipitating acute symptoms of distress.

CASE III

In the case of the next young couple we see such factors at work; we also see courage, inner resilience, and persistent strength win out over the inherent emotional and environmental complications. Specific premarital problems were 11 per cent of total intake during war.

Mr. J was referred to Marriage Council by a psychiatrist. He was thirty-two, the son of middle income Jewish parents. He had done well at college and held a fair job before war broke out. During his four years of frustrating and isolated overseas service, Mr. J had fallen in love with a girl whom he had asked to marry him. After he had returned to this country and been discharged, plans were made by him and his family for his fiancée to visit and then stay on to marry. It was at this point that Mr. J developed acute anxiety symptoms and finally went to a psychiatrist.

The psychiatrist saw him six times and then talked to Counselor at Marriage Council, suggesting that Mr. J be seen at Marriage Council as well as occasionally by him. The psychiatrist told Counselor "he felt Mr. J had a serious condition and was subject to extreme depression periodically." He felt some question as to what marriage would do to Mr. J. There was a possibility that it might precipitate more acute depression. There was, however, an equally grave responsibility in making any such statement to either Mr. J, his parents, or fiancée, because if anyone were to forbid marriage this factor in itself might be a precipitating cause for a more acute mental depression. Dr. X felt it important for Mr. J to get all the help he could from Marriage Council as well as from him.

The Counselor accepted the case with the understanding that she would work with Mr. J on his feelings, hopes, goals, etc., in connection with *his fiancée and his marriage;* the psychiatrist would continue to work with him as the need arose in connection with his depression and would keep a supervisory relation to the whole case. It was also agreed that counselor would see Miss K and work with her, focusing on the marriage.

Mr. J and Miss K came in together for their first appointment and were seen separately by counselor. Mr. J was seen three times in the next two weeks and Miss K twice. In his interviews, Mr. J discussed in detail with Counselor his questions about Miss K—her differences from him in background and personality, and her similarities; his obligation to her to carry through with their plans since his fiancée had left her home and country and was here as a stranger waiting to be married. He talked of his parents' marriage, his relation to his father and mother and to his older brother who was already married and had not had a good relationship to his mother since marriage. He considered his work and how it might be affected by the new interruptions and responsibilities, and his own ideal of marriage and its meaning to him. His attitude toward affection, sharing and sexual expression was explored and found to be apparently very normal and natural.

After these interviews Mr. J, on his own initiative, took steps to work out the practical details of the wedding which he had been postponing indefinitely. He bought an engagement ring, chose a best man, and set the actual date.

When in his third interview, Mr. J discussed his periodic depressions and it became clear the wedding date was set, Counselor recommended to him that he see his psychiatrist again. Counselor reported her contacts with Mr. J to the psychiatrist.

Miss K had two interviews. She was young, vital, warm, and healthy in attitude and physique. She had a practical, realistic, as well as idealistic view of marriage and its responsibilities as well as joys. She was anxious and ready for physical sharing. She used her interview time to explore her feelings about the possible effects of her fiancé's depressions on their marriage and later on children. She tried to gain deeper understanding of her responsibility in this matter and how best she might help. She then answered counselor's questions about her parents' marriage, her relation to her own father and mother, her feelings about living in a new country, her in-laws, her fiancé's work, and the way she herself would have to live and work. She gladly accepted referral for premarital physical examination and wished to discuss the temporary postponing of children because of her fiancé's emotional as well as economic condition.

Counselor reported her interviews with Miss K to Mr. J's psychiatrist. He felt it unnecessary for him to see Miss K because of the helpful and adjusted person she seemed to be. Following these conferences, Dr. X felt that if no acute depression developed, Mr. J would be able to go through with the wedding and that this would be an advantage to both young persons.

A report received a month later from the psychiatrist stated Mr. J's family had written him that the marriage had taken place and everyone seemed well and happy; Mrs. J also wrote counselor. "Both J and I want to thank you for your good wishes for our future, and for all the help you gave us, which has helped to give that future such a sure foundation. J has been so full of life lately, without a trace of his former depression, that I cannot help believing that he has discovered the secret of his rightful happiness."

Four months after marriage the routine follow-up material was sent to Mr. and Mrs. J and returned. This indicated an excellent beginning adjustment. They subsequently came to the office for the routine postmarital interview on sex adjustment. This showed a participating, full, and mutually satisfying relationship. Other areas of the marriage were explored and although there were minor adjustments to be made, both partners independently reported they were able to work these out, and did not feel that they constituted problems. Both also reported only occasional and mild feelings of depression on Mr. J's part—"nothing like before." As Mr. J put it, "Marriage makes one hold on to one's self more than when one lives alone. It is fine."

Mrs. J took books from the lending library on mother and baby care and said they were hoping to have a child soon. A year later Mr. J wrote of the arrival of a fine healthy boy and sent a membership contribution to Marriage Council. "We do greatly appreciate the work you are doing."

Reports received after another two years indicated Mr. and Mrs. J, his job, the child, and the marriage all to be in splendid shape.

The value of a corollary service to the psychiatrist is apparent in this case. The interviews with Mr. J made it possible for him to feel out his reactions to the responsibilities and limits of a marriage relationship, with an understanding and sympathetic and objective person who personally had nothing at stake in his decisions and brought no pressures. In particular, these feelings and reactions were explored as they reflected on his job, his attitudes towards his parents, and his former affectional experiences. In the interviews with the fiancée the Counselor was able to assay the soundness of the girl's emotional balance and her healthy outlook. The reassurance implicity given these young people by the exploration and acceptance of their attitudes was undoubtedly a strong support as they moved into the marriage.

CASE IV

Some families were affected acutely by the time limitations and pressures of war—feelings familiar in one form or another to almost every family in the country. The results of these conditions as reflected in Mr. L's reactions and in lesser degree in those of his wife were not manifestations of abnormality but were what may be expected in intelligent, sensitive persons subjected to abnormal life conditions. Sexual difficulties increased 9 per cent in the married clients after July 1, 1940.

Mrs. L and her husband, who was waiting to be called to the Army, were a young couple who came to Marriage Council together. They had looked forward to their marriage and loved each other dearly, but their honeymoon was a disillusionment. They thought people who loved each other just naturally found it easy to express their love, especially when they were intelligent and well informed. They had read books and thought they understood all there was to know about marital relationships. But when they experienced difficulty they thought something was wrong.

Mr. and Mrs. L have become tense, Mr. L does not want to express any kind of affection because he is so unhappy over the fact that they could not have perfection. They both want very much to have only the happiest remembrances of their brief marriage. Instead it has given them nothing but heartache.

Counselor discussed with this eager and open-minded couple, first together and then in separate interviews, the effect that the urgency and the desire for immediate fulfillment were having on them. In their need for putting a whole lifetime of experience in a few months, they were being blocked in the enjoyment of what already existed in their relationship. Clarifying what could be expected in the first months of marriage was a real help to both. Counselor felt that they went away with more regard for what they had already achieved in their relationship and the possibility of enjoying what they had now. A letter received several weeks later told of much more comfortable and satisfactory experience. "We feel very grateful that there was such a place for us to come to."

This is an excellent example of the responsibility of a marital counseling service to supply information that will aid young people who are simply unskilled in some of the arts of adjustment to gain perspective and reassurance in their basic ability to reach their goal eventually.

CASE V

War served to form or crystallize problems of long standing in some family situations and in certain instances precipitated constructive action. This case came within the 1 per cent of problems of married persons classified as "other."

Mrs. M came to Marriage Council for help in adopting a child. She and her husband had been married for over eight years and had considered adoption at several points in their marriage but could never quite make up their minds. It was interesting that she came to Marriage Council less than a month after her husband's discharge. She gave as one of the reasons for wanting a baby as soon as possible her husband's feeling, developed in the Pacific, of the importance of children in a marriage to enable his country to carry on.

The counselor was able to discuss with this intelligent couple the coming of a child into a family, the usual emotional reactions for the man and wife, some of the practical changes, special problems of adoption and finally to refer them to a reliable adoption agency.

Reports received a year later told of a beloved son finally in their home and plans already underway for a baby sister. A Christmas card to Counselor after three years showed a cheerful family group with two healthy looking youngsters. A little note stated, "We still remember how you helped us to have courage to get started. We never regretted it, even during the measles! We are sending one of our close friends to you with a different problem."

CASE VI

This case presents a type of situation not uncommon during war in which the pressure and urgency to experience "everything" before separation seemed to eliminate thoughtful criteria for mate selection and permanent values. Such situations usually got to Marriage Council only after trouble had crystallized. They dealt with emotionally exhausting, frustrating and, from the point of view of society, barren relationships which probably would not mature into constructive, enduring marriages in any era. Six per cent of total intake during the war were considering divorce or separation.

Mr. and Mrs. N were married in 1943 after knowing each other only a few weeks. During the first months of their marriage they made an adjustment which was satisfactory to Mr. N and apparently to his wife. They established a modest home. The furniture was not yet paid for when Mr. N was inducted into the Army. Mrs. N, who was pregnant, returned to her family, putting the furniture in storage.

Mr. N remained in this country for two years and came home on three long furloughs. He enjoyed the baby and established a good relationship with his in-laws who hadn't cared too much for him previously. In between times, Mrs. N wrote him such pathetic letters about how much she missed him that he often had to cry. Then he was sent overseas. "When you are away from home all you do is dream about what it is like and what you'll have when you get home. I've been in the Pacific for two years, I've dreamed for two years; two years is too long to dream."

He was returned to America in October, 1945, and immediately given a five-day furlough. On the third day his wife asked him for a divorce. She gave as her reason that she'd nearly gone crazy when he first went away, and then had become so used to working things out alone that there was now no place for him in her life. He spent the remaining two days of the furlough wooing her, and returned to camp feeling that everything would be all right. A week later he was released from the Army and returned to Philadelphia only to be told in the first hour he was home that his wife had seen a lawyer. She had been told she had no grounds for a divorce unless she lied. She followed this by asking him to move out of the house; her parents asked him to remain.

At this point, Mr. N, deeply disturbed, went to the Veteran's Information Service which referred him to Marriage Council. He was so confused he didn't know what to do. He was able to work through a great deal of his feelings of disappointment and maltreatment with the Counselor and to come to the conclusion that what he needed most at this time was legal advice. He was referred to the Legal Aid Society.

An appointment was offered the following week for him and his wife, which Mr. N accepted. It was, he said, the first hope that he'd had. However, when the day arrived, Mrs. N would not come, and he kept the appointment alone. In this hour he began to face the fact that his wife didn't love him and that he needed to go on alone.

He began to plan his life—what he'd do about living arrangements, job, friends and recreation—in other words to begin to get a real hold of the reality of his problem.

CASE VII

The following is an example of a married couple who had enough basic compatibility, plus the will to do something about it, to win out over their difficulties and the complexities of the era. Sixteen per cent of total intake during the war were general marital adjustment.

PFC and Mrs. O came to Marriage Council when he was in Philadelphia on furlough. They were a young couple with a three-months-old baby. Their reason for coming was that they were getting along so poorly sexually and in other ways that they didn't know how they could get along once he was released from the Army. Their concern about the future and what they discussed in their interview made it appear unlikely that they would have come had V-J Day not taken place and had not his discharge from the Army seemed imminent. "When you have seen your mates blown to bits in the sky," he said, "men who have never seen their own children, you owe it to them to have children and take good care of them."

During his furlough, they each came to Marriage Council once a week, at first to work on the problem that they had with his parents. Then they began to see their difficulties in terms of their adjustment to each other. PFC O began to find any number of qualities to admire in Mrs. O instead of harping on her lack of education, while Mrs. O was able to see that she was "too sensitive" and too demanding. At the end of the furlough a plan was worked out for Mrs. O to continue to come in once a week and Mr. O to come in once every two weeks. (He was stationed nearby and was able to obtain weekend passes.)

They carried out this plan and follow-up reports showed that they made a good start in laying a firm foundation for their marriage. Their sexual adjustment improved as their general bickerings and misunderstandings decreased and a spirit of comfortableness and optimism grew between them.

CASE VIII

This case indicates how differently individuals react to prolonged grind and deprivation, and mobilize their resources for release from an "unbearable" situation. Marital problems related to health as a reason for coming to the agency constituted 4 per cent and problems focused by clients on war 2 per cent of total intake after the impact of war.

Mr. and Mrs. P were referred by the Social Service Department of one of the large city hospitals. Mr. P, who had recently been drafted into the Army, was a likable and fairly intelligent young man with a foreign accent. Mrs. P was a rather pouty, cheaply dressed young woman with a none too pleasant manner. She described herself as ill and nervous most of the time now. She was not interested in her friends and did not feel well enough to hold a position although the physicians could find no physical pathology to account for her symptoms.

Mr. P had been so worried about his wife that he had contacted the Red Cross Home Service and been granted special leave. His wife hoped for his permanent discharge on account of her ill health. Mr. P seemed to understand that Mrs. P's condition might be due to worry about his military duty and the fact that she was lonely and had too little to do. He said that he did not wish to leave the Army, but that he was continually harassed by telephone calls, telegrams, and letters from a sick wife.

Mrs. P returned for further visits and poured forth her grievances, complaints, and unhappiness at her "undeserved" hard luck. She gradually gave up her idea of getting her husband released from the service. It was hoped that through counseling she might eventually gain courage to face the separation and to take her place in the difficulties of the time. She continued to keep appointments for six weeks, after which she broke her contact and did not respond to a follow-up letter from the counselor. That she found temporary relief in a time of great stress is assumed, although the final outcome is not known.

In Marriage Council a few persons seek interviews who for various reasons, usually their early relations with one or both parents (Strauss, 1946), (Strecker, 1946), (Taylor, K., 1942), have so much general or unfocused hostility toward everyone and everything that they are often unable to use help of any kind. The prognosis for working with this type of person on a counseling level is certainly not good. At such an agency as Marriage Council, if early diagnosis were possible, it might be advisable to attempt to refer such persons for psychiatric help within the first few interviews. This type of case also raises problems in connection with the recognition of such factors in a premarital interview. Should the counselor take responsibility for questioning the advisability of marriage, or at least for recommending psychiatric consultation before the couple goes ahead, if either one or both partners have personality characteristics of this kind?

When such a person comes after marriage it is difficult to decide whether he can make use of counseling and achieve relief in the marriage if *the counseling is focused on the marriage relationship and the difficulties in the situation.* Certainly counselors can hardly take responsibility for withholding service to such a client with a marriage problem on the basis that the service will be of no help. At least this should not be done until the situation has been explored in several interviews. In such instances the counselor should seek consultation with a supervisory psychiatrist, and if psychiatric referral is advised by the psychiatrist then counseling skill should be focused on adequate interpretation of psychiatric treatment and of referral to such a source.

CASE IX

Although Mrs. Q was first seen before marriage, the fact that she did not return for a second interview made it impossible for the counselor to explore the questions she had about future adjustment or to discuss psychiatric referral. When Mrs. Q returned after marriage, the previous contacts and the attitudes which Mrs. Q showed made the counselor doubt that she could use counseling help and she had already seen more than one psychiatrist, apparently without benefit. However, as no one had worked intensively with her and her husband on the marital problem, it seemed worth while trying counseling with both of them. Although Mrs. Q was first seen in a war era, in all probability she would have had the same type of difficulties in a period of peace. This case was classified among the 16 per cent coming for general marital adjustment.

Miss Q was a college graduate of twenty-five who sought an interview at Marriage Council in 1942 following a marriage class at her college. Her problem was whether or not to marry a young service man against her parents' wishes (2 per cent of total intake during the impact of war are listed as family difficulty or war problems).

She presented herself as a person who had always been "unhappy," and never gotten along with her mother or father. Counselor felt she was very aggressive in her approach. She quoted her family doctor as agreeing with her that "marriage would help her adjustment."

The Counselor tried to interest Miss Q in a series of interviews to explore her desire for marriage, her relationship with her parents, the kind of mate she had selected, and what her goals were. Miss Q saw no reason for such an arrangement and apparently wished only for authoritative approval from, the counselor for her marriage plans. When this was not forthcoming she did not return for counseling. She wrote later that her wedding was, however, subsequently postponed when her father "threatened to leave home if she went through with her plans," and her mother became ill and underwent an operation.

After six months a postcard from the South told of Miss Q's marriage in spite of the fact that "both parents still disapproved." The couple were living near Mr. Q's military camp and offered to fill out all follow-up schedules from Marriage Council. These schedules were sent eight months after the wedding and returned by Mrs. Q who reported "difficulty resulting from the clashing of two strong personalities, lack of satisfaction with sexual adjustment, too little love making, and no orgasm." She was consulting a psychiatrist and being "psychoanalyzed" to find the difficulty.

Three years later Mrs. Q once more contacted Marriage Council and saw a second Counselor. At this point she was classified as having problems of general marital adjustment (16 per cent of total war intake). Mrs. Q was seen five times, twice before her husband came for his first interview; then each was seen once more two months afterwards. The Counselor felt that Mr. Q was probably a better adjusted person than Mrs. Q and had more real insight, but he was an unaggressive person in a very unhappy position, and there was little he could do unless Mrs. Q changed. He seemed dependent upon her and not interested in considering break-up of the marriage.

In her last interview Mrs. Q made it clear that she felt it impossible to change and still placed entire blame on Mr. Q. She rejected the idea of separation which was explored with her pretty actively because of the feelings on Counselor's part (unexpressed) that the marriage was a very neurotic one which was not going to improve. Mrs. Q considered separation as a possibility to the extent of making a tentative appointment for herself and Mr. Q to discuss it, but later wrote to cancel the appointment and instead sent Counselor a personal gift and invitation to visit them.

Counselor felt that Mrs. Q subconsciously recognized that she did not want to use Marriage Council services to improve her marriage nor could she use any help in giving up her immature and neurotic relationship with Mr. Q. Therefore, her gift was probably an attempt to salve her conscience at terminating her contact.

Five months after the last interview counselor met Mrs. Q quite accidentally on the street. Mrs. Q was cordial and stopped to speak.

She looked well and attractive and reported she was expecting a baby. She remarked, "It is funny that it happened just after you told us not to have a baby." (This was Mrs. Q's interpretation of a discussion in which the counselor explored with her the question of whether having a baby would improve their relationship.) She felt now that her reasons for having a baby were not sound and that the pregnancy had complicated things, but Mr. Q was pretty pleased and she believes would take a better attitude after the baby is born. At present, he irritated her by not helping enough with lifting, etc. She gave the impression of being more cheerful, relaxed, and able to accept her feelings towards her husband than in the past. However, Counselor realized from experience that this kind of change may take place in this type of woman during pregnancy, with former patterns reappearing sometimes even more intensely, after the birth of the child. Counselor wondered whether Mrs. Q's neurotic pattern and hostility would not again be reflected in her children.

A further word should be inserted here concerning agency responsibility in connection with Mr. Q should he have wished to continue counseling (for which at this time he did not seem to feel any need). Further exploration of his feelings and attitudes might have led Mr. Q to (1) a decision that nothing could be done and counseling was no use, (2) a change whereby he would feel sufficiently dissatisfied with his marriage to move out of it and seek something more satisfactory, (3) temporary relief through sharing his disappointments, resentments, and hostilities with the Counselor. Any of the three mentioned possibilities would have made Mr. Q acceptable for counseling had he wished to continue. In the third event it is conceivable that he might return to the agency for a few visits at yearly or even less frequent intervals as one means of strengthening himself for facing a somewhat dreary and continuingly unhappy marriage.

In this connection agency policy might be mentioned. When one partner in a marriage is tied to a neurotic person who really does not want to change (like Mrs. X), and will do nothing about it, or an emotionally ill or psychotic person who refuses psychiatric treatment and cannot be hospitalized, such a client can have a counseling interview occasionally in a "carrying" capacity. This would be done of course only after the case had been discussed with a supervisory psychiatrist and the "carrying" recommended.

POSTWAR CASES

We turn now from situations which came for marriage counseling during the war years, to examples of cases seen between 1945 and 1949. Again we start with the premarital group and continue with the married clients to illustrate several types of situations in which counseling seems of little avail, as well as several in which it seemed to help.

CASE X

This is an illustration of the type of assistance that can be valuable where there are seemingly insoluble family complications prior to marriage. In this instance the counselor helped Miss S to "grow up" and function on an adult level with her family.

Miss S, a young and talented musician, had been engaged for several weeks to a man of similar talents. Both were in their early twenties and were continuing with their respective studies in cities at some distance from each other. Miss S's mother raised violent objections to the forthcoming marriage as she felt she herself had made a mistake by marrying a gifted musician who had been unable to support his family adequately throughout the depression. The fact that the fiancé, Mr. T, was also preparing himself for public school teaching did not alter her opinion.

When Miss S came to Marriage Council her whole family was doing everything in their power to discourage her interest in Mr. T. Things had become so strained in the home that they were barely able to talk with one another. Miss S found it very hard to accept her family's objection to a musician when she herself had been given a fine musical education and was thus constantly in the company of musicians almost to the exclusion of people with different backgrounds and interests. Miss S and Mr. T had known each other during three years of college and had gone "steady" for over a year of that time. The family was unable to raise any objection to Mr. T except on the score of his profession.

After her first visit to the Council, Miss S brought a recent letter from her fiancé. It revealed him as a warm, understanding, and sympathetic person who appeared to have some insight into

167

what Miss S was undergoing. It was perhaps because of these qualities in him that she never felt as comfortable when dating others even before their engagement as when with Mr. T. When she came for counseling, however, she was so confused and torn between her loyalty to her family and her interest in her fiancé that she no longer knew if she loved him or should plan to marry him.

More than anything else Miss S needed to feel that there was someone "rooting" for her and Mr. T. She found this help in the counselor, an adult who was sympathetic to her problem of weaning from her family's domination as constructively as possible. Miss S worked out a plan to find living quarters through her school so that she could be relieved of the oppressive home atmosphere and be in a position to think things out better for herself without being constantly made to feel guilty. Through counseling she also understood more clearly the factors leading to parental objection of her choice of mate and became more sympathetic with rather than completely hostile to her mother. She determined to go ahead with the marriage, realizing that Mr. T had the qualities she desired in a husband. The couple are now married and living in a distant city.

CASE XI

This case is representative of the group of young clients who come to the agency in the hope of receiving specific information focused on the sexual aspects of their coming marriage. If the information requested by the client is not in accordance with the dictates of his religious group, this fact is called to his attention. It is suggested to such a client, if he or she is a Catholic, that he consult his priest or a Catholic agency.

Miss U, a third-year college student nineteen years of age, came to Marriage Council ten days before her wedding. Her fiancé also was a student and it was the desire of both to complete their education and establish a good economic adjustment before planning the family they both very much desired. Miss U had known of the agency through a marriage preparation course at college. Although very timid about discussing sexual matters, she gradually became more comfortable and explored thoroughly with the counselor the meanings of various terms and types of sexual procedures which heretofore had been obscure to her. She wished to consult a female physician for a physical examination and the names of several were suggested to her after she explained she did not wish to consult her family doctor.

She discussed also her relationship to a somewhat domineering mother from whom she had never received any sex information and her feelings towards her fiancé's family. She showed a realistic and mature attitude. Miss U went to the doctor for her physical examination, reporting that she was helped very much by her.

A year later she returned to the agency to discuss a minor problem in sexual adjustment. In the course of several interviews and with a return visit to the doctor whom she had consulted prior to her marriage, she and her husband were able to work out a more satisfactory adjustment. Other aspects of their relationship had occasioned no difficulties.

CASE XII

The following problem of impotence is one which is brought by clients to the agency periodically. If the wife in such a situation is adequate sexually, the situation is quite different than is common if both partners are essentially inadequate. The problem, as is well known, is exceedingly involved and one of the main questions concerns the amount of help that counseling can provide. To recognize the limits beyond which he or she should not go in this type of situation, as well as in others, is one of the counselor's prime responsibilities. It might be disastrous to stir up anxiety which could not be handled within the counseling situation. On the other hand, some clients referred often by physicians, have come to our agency with problems of both impotence and frigidity in which the counseling helped to overcome sexual difficulty. The following case illustrates the involved nature of such a problem. As both partners were too threatened by the possibility of sharing their real feelings with the counselor, they did not return after the first interviews. In our experience unless the relationship between counselor and client brings out the client's feelings, little change is apt to take place.

Mr. V, an attractive, well-educated man with an excellent position in an advertising agency came for help with his problem of impotence and premature ejaculation. He had recognized the nonphysical nature of the difficulty and after discussion with his wife had selected Marriage Council as the logical place to go. He had been having trouble ever since his marriage ten years before at which time he had been a virgin, although he had masturbated a great deal. This he continued to do following his marriage. His parents were reserved and conventional. His wife was from a similar background and was also well educated. They had four children to whom he was devoted. He was very worried about how hard his wife worked to maintain their standards; felt that they shared activities and attitudes and that other than their sexual adjustment everything was fine. He seemed to feel a certain amount of guilt at "hurting" his wife, and concern because she made many sacrifices. He wanted to work on the problem and made future appointments for both his wife and himself. Mrs. V had one interview only and ran a half-hour over her time. She was nervous and didactic. She intellectualized the situation pretty completely, "knew all the answers," believing that the trouble lay with her because she had tried to provide Mr. V's standards of behavior for him. She expressed a certain amount of concern over his periodic gambling which he had not mentioned. She believed she had acted in a parental role towards Mr. V which was wrong, and that now that they had faced this problem, and Mr. V had accepted his responsibility in it, they would be able to proceed satisfactorily. She saw no need to return to Marriage Council and felt that it had served its purpose with her husband by getting him started to do something.

Mr. V came in for one more appointment, repeating the exact sentiments that his wife had expressed. He indicated that they were sharing more intellectual stimulation and that they were working on the problem together and would have to work it out themselves.

Neither Mr. nor Mrs. V has been heard from since. The fundamental pattern of their relationship was apparent even in the three interviews. Mrs. V was controlling and aggressive and in acting the martyr, was pushing to maintain this pattern. She probably was very much threatened by the presence of a third person in relation to the marriage problems and influenced Mr. V in withdrawing from the contact. The intellectualized nature of the approach to their problem prevented them from acquiring any real help as the counselor was unable to break through this protecting shield to enable either partner to discuss his real feelings.

CASE XIII

Counseling the problem of homosexuality is a matter which comes but seldom to the attention of the agency, at least as a consciously recognized difficulty. Nevertheless, the counselor must be prepared for discussion of this topic. The following is a good example of the level of treatment deemed advisable within the jurisdiction of a case-work agency such as ours.

Mr. W came to Marriage Council complaining of so many things wrong with his marriage that he was contemplating leaving his wife. He criticized many of her characteristics. She, in turn, told in her interview of his immaturity, but seemed a good deal more accepting and understanding of him than he was of her. In his second interview he revealed that the real problem was his tendency toward homosexuality. Mr. W had been considered homosexual by his mother during his teens. Although he had had no homosexual relationship until he became very friendly with another man while he was away in military service, he was very fearful of this tendency in himself. The relationship had not been completely a sexual one but Mr. W felt tempted and this upset him so that he was unable to enjoy sex with his wife after his return. After discussing this quite freely and expressing his conflict and guilt about it, he claimed to feel much better.

Mr. W concentrated then on deciding whether to discuss this with Mrs. W. Although she had commented on some of Mr. W's characteristics she knew nothing of his conflict. He decided to tell her and afterwards both came in for a final interview. Part of this was joint at Mrs. W's suggestion and the counselor felt that the feeling between this couple was very good. Mrs. W had accepted the idea of his homosexuality very matter-of-factly and sympathetically, to his great relief. They talked it over together with the counselor, both from the point of view of what they could do to improve their own relationship and what Mr. W could do to improve his personal adjustment. There was no further question of separation. Mr. W had considerable insight but felt that he needed psychiatric help to understand himself better. After discussion of this the counselor encouraged him to seek help from one of the local clinics and a referral card was given him.

Both Mr. and Mrs. W impressed the counselor as fairly warm and intelligent people with strong feeling for each other in spite of their difficulties. Each seemed willing to put effort into the marriage and the counselor felt that counseling was useful in helping them to clear up misunderstandings which were blocking any improvement in their relationship. Mr. W seemed more guilty about his homosexuality than was warranted on the basis of the facts presented, a matter which the counselor discussed openly with him. In view of his own concern the counselor felt he could be helped by a psychiatrist.

A few months later Mr. W wrote that he and his wife had moved to another part of the country and were "slowly working out a better relationship." Mr. W said, "You helped us work things out so that we knew each other better." He still felt he needed help with his own personality and was seeking a psychiatrist. A list of resources was sent him.

CASE XIV

Here the case illustrates how a couple may seek marriage counseling in the hope of receiving help in actual separation. Although this may seem in contradiction to the purposes of a Marriage Council the important thing is for each partner to have a part in making a decision which is valid for both. If all other possibilities for working out a constructive relationship in the marriage have failed, as long as the partners share in the planning of the move the experience need not be a totally destructive one.

Mr. and Mrs. X came to the office together on the initiative of Mr. X who wished to establish a legal separation after a marriage of four years. The X's were seen separately. The marriage had been contracted during the war and Mr. X felt he had been pressured into it and that he only entered into it because of a need for security. Following his return from overseas he attempted to make a go of the relationship but he believed there was a basic incompatibility due in part to his wife's impulsiveness. He had recognized his own confusion to the extent that he had at one time sought psychiatric guidance which confirmed his own attitudes toward himself.

The fact that Mr. X did not want to have any children and that Mrs. X definitely did wish children, caused sufficient friction to create an acute situation one month prior to the couple's coming to Marriage Council. At that time Mr. X decided to proceed with a legal separation as he felt his business, a small store, was suffering from the distress he felt over his marriage. Mrs. X realized her husband's conflict but cared a great deal for him and wished to continue the relationship. During her interview she was able to come to grips with the reality of the situation and the fact that her husband was adamant in his feelings. Mr. X had been relieved that the counselor had not told him what to do nor had tried to hold him in the marriage. He seemed rigid and egotistical and gave evidence of underlying problems. Mrs. X appeared more mature than he and tried to approach the problem intelligently and maturely though she was quite upset.

Although both Mr. and Mrs. X had only one interview each both stated that it had helped and subsequent reports from Mrs. X indicated that, with her interview as a starting point, she had been able to move into acceptance of the separation forced upon her by her husband's decision.

CASE XV

This case affords an excellent illustration of the type of situation that plagues every agency and that is, for all intents and purposes, "hopeless." How to handle the client who comes solely to air his complaints and to project his difficulties, so that the time of the agency will not be wasted and so that something constructive, no matter how infinitesimal, may result is an unsolved problem.

Mrs. X came to the agency first after having gone for assistance for the youngest of her three children to a psychiatric clinic. She had been referred to Marriage Council because it was the belief of the social worker who saw her that nothing could be done for the vague complaints of the child until the marital problem had been somewhat disentangled. During her first two interviews she repeatedly aired the following grievances against her husband: that he found her repugnant to him; that he picked on the youngest child, a boy; that he had temper tantrums with violence directed against her and this child; that he exhibited not the slightest interest in her sexually; and that he was rude to her parents and insufficiently affectionate with them. The parents had always lived immediately next door to the X's who had been married for twelve years. The difficulties were of long standing and had existed almost since the beginning of the marriage. Mrs. X helped out her husband in his small clothing business and resented having to do this. After his first interview she was aggrieved that he had paid what she considered too high a fee.

Mr. X came in very willingly at his wife's suggestion and covered almost identical material to hers in his first two interviews. He recognized his inability to be a loving son-in-law and expressed almost dislike for his wife but no desire to sever the marriage ties chiefly because of his responsibility to the children. He felt he had

173

been high-pressured into the marriage by his wife. His own home had been a broken one due to the death of his mother when he was an infant. His relationship with his own father also had been poor. His sole desire was to be left alone. He would do his part as the economic support of the household but farther than that he did not wish to go. He had been an enlisted man in the Navy during the war and had liked that because he did not have to assume any responsibility.

As may have been expected Mrs. X spent the ensuing three interviews repeating the complaints of the first two. She wanted a definite verdict from the counselor as to what to do and how to understand her husband. It had been explained to her in the beginning that this was not the way that the agency could help, but she had been unable to accept this. The counselor discussed with Mrs. X the fact that there was no point in continuing the appointments unless she was willing to work on her own aspect of the adjustment. Apparently disturbed at the prospect of losing this outlet for her complaints she rather vigorously assumed some responsibility for the state of her family affairs. However, she did not resume her contact with the agency and the last that was heard was that she had applied a few months later for help from a child guidance clinic. Mr. X, as could also be expected, in his passive way did nothing further. In his three ensuing interviews he simply reiterated his desire to be left in peace and his inability to feel anything for his wife. He felt the fact that he had been corraled into marriage at all when he was so obviously unsuited for it, had been the great mistake.

The outlook for this type of situation is bleak. The marriage obviously contains satisfaction of sorts for both partners or they would not have tolerated such an unfavorable arrangement for so long. It is probable that Mrs. X will continue to go from one agency to another in the hope of having some solution presented to her. That the children in such a set-up are the chief sufferers is painfully apparent. Since neither partner is willing really to assume any real responsibility for his or her personality difficulties any type of treatment probably will fall on barren ground.

CASE XVI

There is a goodly number of problems of the "other woman" or the "other man" in the total case load at Marriage Council. The reasons for the existence of such situations are usually not far from the surface. Here is a case which illustrates how a reconciliation was effected through the services of Marriage Council following an estrangement on the score of the "other woman."

Mr. and Mrs. Y were referred to Marriage Council by a physician uncle of the bride. The couple, married for eighteen months, had separated four weeks before. Mr. Y had become interested in a young secretary at the office where he worked, a young girl whom he had known casually earlier in high school. He had been seeing Miss Z at office parties and his interest in her had been growing. Mrs. Y was aware of this and friction between the young couple increased to the point where they felt their marriage had been a mistake and Mrs. Y had gone to live with an older sister.

Although they had not been in touch with one another the Y's came to the office together and wished to be seen jointly. Within the first hour it became apparent that the difficulty between this couple had a sexual basis. They had been over-anxious to make a good adjustment and had read so extensively on the subject that they had worked too hard and too intellectually to make everything *perfect*. When complete success had not been forthcoming after a period of six months to a year the young husband became discouraged, blamed the trouble on his wife whom he accused of being frigid, and turned elsewhere for solace.

The Y's still loved one another very much and though it was hard for Mrs. Y to overlook the disloyalty of her husband and his turning toward another woman she recognized it for what it was—a symptom of their own troubles. After two joint interviews and one individual interview for each, the Y's had successfully evaluated the situation and seemed to have assimilated the implications emotionally. Through discussion of the way they had handled their sexual adjustment they were helped to be more relaxed in their approach. They reunited within a week of their last visit to Marriage Council and when last heard from were continuing to make a success of their relationship.

SUMMARY

The foregoing cases afford a view of the variety of situations appearing in the offices of a marriage counseling agency. Some of the problems first presented were specifically related to difficulties encountered during war. That there are similarities in the types of problems before, during, and following World War II is apparent.

The effectiveness of counseling can be gauged in terms of the adequacy of the counselor, the readiness of the client to make use of such help, and the possibilities and limitations of counseling methods. This was illustrated in the case material. Many of the people who come for help have moved toward a solution before setting foot within the office. It is perhaps in these cases that counselors can make a significant contribution by consolidating the positive elements in the situation brought by the client. In other cases counseling seems to accomplish little or nothing and in yet others to fail completely. The functions of the counselor in the foregoing cases included his being an educator, a confessor, a kindly parental surrogate, a sounding board for the emotions of his client, and a stimulator of understanding of emotional processes. How the counselor was used depended on the individual situation.

Situations brought to a counseling agency and the ways in which persons meet them afford continual and often dramatic evidence of the complexity of human values, growth, and life, of the uniqueness of each individual, and, for the most part, of the resilience and strength of human beings.

10

The Process of Counseling

DURING THE YEARS in which case material for this study was collected, increasing interest was directed by many professional and lay groups toward what is involved when two people work together to solve the personal problems of one. Semantics have both aided and detracted from efforts to understand and clarify the dynamics of this process. Words such as casework, counseling, treatment, therapy, and psychotherapy have been and are being used. These terms have been defined and redefined in a kind of interprofessional badminton to reflect the thinking of persons with different background, training, and points of view. The interrelationships between casework, counseling, psychology, psychiatry, and psychoanalysis, and the relationships of these practices with other allied professions have also been discussed and dissected (Aptekar, 1949). In the main, this has been done with constructive purpose—to clarify the working concepts and techniques, and to enlarge the perspective of professional groups whose function it is to assist in promoting better adjustment in human behavior (Fiedler, 1950), (Kasius, ed., 1950), (Karpf, 1937), (Rockmore, 1949), (Gomberg and Levinson, 1951).

This chapter will not attempt to survey this area historically. It will present procedure and practice at a functioning marriage counseling service in detail, as this is applied in case situations brought for service (See Chapters 8 and 9). It will comment also on important contributions to treatment methods basic to thinking in this field, and relate this material to current techniques and philosophy in marriage counseling.

When Marriage Council of Philadelphia was first organized in 1932 the term "counseling" was suggested by members of the Committee of Sponsors in an attempt to differentiate the proposed work with young persons "about to be or recently married" from the work of family agencies which, at that period, received requests for help predominantly from families after difficulties were well advanced. There was hope that the term counseling might have a positive appeal without the connotation of economic dependency and distress then ascribed by many members of the community to those who applied for assistance to social agencies.

It was not until later (Foster, 1937), (Groves, 1940), (Mudd, 1938), (Sauer, 1939), (Ware, 1940) and particularly during the war years that the term counseling grew in popularity in the United States (Burgess, 1943), (Goldstein, 1945), (Gomberg, 1948), (McElroy, 1947), (Rasey, 1943), (Rogers, 1942), (Schmidl, 1949), (Taft, 1946). As the term became more widely used, there arose the need for definition. Marriage Council's interpretative folder describes the work: "Counseling before and after marriage consists of confidential interviews which provide an opportunity to talk over questions or problems with a well-trained and understanding person. Primarily, people gain perspective on whatever situations they are facing and counseling aims to help people deal with these situations in the manner best fitting their particular needs."

The philosophy of this agency defines the happy family as "one which manages to solve its problems, not one which has no problems" (Levy and Munroe, 1938). It attempts to offer the individual a positive and dynamic approach to his problems which may result in a better understanding of self, greater assurance, and an enhanced capacity to live adequately. It is interpreted through the attitudes of the staff counselors.

In considering a philosophy and method of counseling there

178

are two main points: (1) What do the persons who come for help want and need?; and (2) How can they best be helped to attain what they want and need within the limits of the social order? First, the counselor should recognize that all human beings need to be wanted (loved), to be appreciated, to experience some variety, to have the chance to achieve, and to have some security. Secondly, the counselor should understand that all people are, at times, lonely and anxious, the difference being only in degree. It is therefore of great importance that those seeking help know that counselors are interested in them and concerned about their distress. This does more than anything else to ease the loneliness, to enable the client to feel free to express his anxiety, fear, or other feelings in manner or word and so to use help. Thirdly, the counselor should have general optimism about the worth-whileness of counseling, even though he is aware that he cannot expect to be helpful in every case.

It takes time for people to change, to grow, to make adjustments. Therefore, the counselor should offer patience rather than haste, sympathy not indulgence, tolerance not criticism, and should support an individual's efforts to adjust, even though success is not immediate. Above all, the professional counselor should show a warm, human responsiveness that denotes keen understanding of human differences. The goal of counseling is to help people over the rough spots, and to make this a strengthening process so that they can better help themselves and each other and pull their own weight in the community (Mudd, 1945).

This general philosophy and approach has been influenced by the experience and findings of leaders in the fields of psychiatry, psychology, and casework (Alexander and French, 1946), (Allen, 1942), (Appel, 1944), (Deutsch, 1945), (English and Pierson, 1945), (Garret, 1942), (Gomberg, 1946), (Hamilton, 1940), (Hollis, 1949), (Horney, 1939), (Menninger, K., 1942), (Menninger, W., 1948), (Plant, 1937), (Robinson, 1942), (Rogers, 1942, 1951), (Taft, 1946). It has also grown through actual experimentation by staff members in the many aspects of marriage counseling.

General and specific methods and procedures in use currently, within the general philosophical framework just summarized, indicate processes which our experience leads us to believe assist in change in the client's attitudes, behavior, or situation. These procedures were formulated gradually by the staff as a group during many case conferences (see *Acknowledgments*). Some were the result of meetings with the Medical Supervisory Committee. They are constantly reviewed in current staff case discussions, and are reformulated when need arises.

Each counselor brings elements of his personality to his work that make his approach different, in some degree, from any other counselor. There is no rigid use of general or specific procedures approved by the agency, but they are recognized and available when the counselor wants them. Experimentation with methods and techniques is discussed by the counselor in supervision and is encouraged to the extent that it seems to aid the total process of counseling.

ASPECTS OF COUNSELING CONSIDERED ESPECIALLY IMPORTANT

The following aspects of counseling hold special interest for our staff: procedures for client application, intake policy, first interviews, special techniques for premarital interviews, working with partners in marriage, joint interviews, the place of information giving and supplementary reading, time limits for total client-worker contact, the effects on clients of the personal attributes of counselors, use of fee as an integral part of counseling, medical referral of clients, counseling with disturbed clients, in-service supervised training, the effects of obtaining research material in counseling, and follow-up procedure.

Procedures for Client Application

Procedures for client application usually follow this sequence:

1. The client requests appointment by letter, phone, or in person. The receptionist offers an appointment time and explains that an interview takes approximately an hour. She states that the agency is nonprofit and charges a fee which will be worked out with the counselor on the basis of the client's financial situation. Her expla-

nation that a folder describing the work of the Council and listing its Board of Directors, sponsors, and staff will be sent or given to the client in the office before the first interview eliminates the necessity of becoming involved over the telephone.

2. The client's first appointment is scheduled one-half hour before the time he will see the counselor. After he settles in the waiting room, he is given a schedule by the receptionist to check before seeing the counselor, with the explanation that this is routine procedure. This "Background Schedule" contains information similar to that required for most social agency records and can usually be checked in about ten minutes. There is a second schedule which is an aid in interviewing if checked before the interview. For an engaged client it is "Schedule E" which covers attitudes and experiences during engagement and toward marriage. A married client is given schedule "Adjustment A," which covers various aspects of the marital adjustment. If the client is pressed for time, questions or objects to this procedure, or is obviously disturbed, the counselor may see him immediately and suggest the schedules be checked after the interview.[1]

3. Sometimes information about the client's situation is available through the source of referral but often, especially in the case of self-referral, little is known before the client talks with the counselor. Almost always it is known whether one or both partners are planning to come for a particular interview. Whatever is known is written on an application slip by the receptionist and, together with any correspondence about the case, is given to the counselor before the appointment. After schedules are checked, the counselor and clients decide together whether the first interview will begin separately or jointly with both partners if a couple is present.

B. Intake Policy

Until 1951, clients have been assigned to the staff counselor who has the first mutually convenient free time, and they continue with the same counselor unless there are unusual complications. Open hours are indicated to the receptionist weekly

---

[1] A paper entitled "Some Effects on Casework of Obtaining Research Material" giving detailed discussion of the use of schedules as an integral part of casework has been published by *Social Casework* (Mudd, Froscher, Preston, Peltz, January, 1950). Reprints are available at Marriage Council of Philadelphia. The schedules have been copyrighted by permission of the United States Public Health Service and are also available at cost.

by each counselor marking the main appointment book. New clients may fall in the premarital group desiring one or two interviews only, often within time limits of wedding dates. They therefore cannot be handled adequately by the usual intake procedures of family agencies in which the intake worker has a first interview and then assigns the client to another worker for treatment (Maeder, 1942), (Berkowitz, 1943). This was an additional reason why selection of staff counselors has been limited to workers who have had a minimum of three years' related experience in addition to their graduate degree, and why supervision of a new worker for approximately a year seems essential. It has been also one of the reasons why it has not been suitable for the agency to accept students in field-work placement from an accredited school of social work.

The initiation of an in-service training program at the agency for graduate physicians, under the Veterans Administration in 1947, and the recent expansion of this program, under grant from the Grant Foundation, to other workers with graduate degrees in related fields have made it necessary to modify this policy. Clients about whom the agency has no information now are assigned to experienced staff counselors in order that they may have the counselors most suited to their needs, and that counselors in training may start their work with the less difficult cases.

Case records are kept by all counselors on face sheets used routinely in the agency and on additional sheets of narrative chronological recording dictated following the interviews. Each client is referred to as X or Y and given a number in the office file. A cross file for names is available only to counselors and especially selected stenographers for use, if the client so wishes, in follow-up or other contacts with the agency.[2] As has already been mentioned, the fact that written records are kept is shared with any client who inquires, with the explanation that these help the counselor in working with the client. The client is assured that his situation will be treated confidentially. The

---

[2] A very occasional client in particular circumstances preferred to remain anonymous. Such requests are honored if the client still so desires after the disadvantages are discussed by the counselor with the client.

agency has always considered carrying out this assurance essential to ethical performance.

The First Interview

The term "first interview" may be used to denote the establishing of rapport and may actually take more than one session.[3] In a first interview the counselor considers carefully the following factors, any one of which may come up again in subsequent interviews (examples of the application of these principles may be found in the first interviews recorded in Chapter 8, Cases I, II, III and IV):

1. What the client has put into coming to Marriage Council and what it means to him to be here.

2. Interpretation to the client of agency function—including discussion of how he can use the agency for his purposes.

3. What the client feels the problem to be and the most distressing parts of the problem area, including something of the partner's situation.

4. Acceptance by the counselor of where the client is in feeling tone and general disturbance.

5. Sufficient material for the counselor to determine if Marriage Council is equipped to deal with the problem.

6. Some plan for the counseling contact—at least tentative—acceptable to the client and within agency function. The counseling may be completed within this one interview, it may continue on a trial basis until more definite arrangements seem appropriate, or a plan may be set up for a number of interviews, six to eight on the average.

The Premarital Interview

Premarital clients are usually younger, more open-minded and flexible with patterns of relationship to the opposite sex, less well established than postmarital clients. They are often still in some stage of weaning from the parental home and therefore the emotional relationship to the parent is of great

---

[3] This criterion does not necessarily apply to the general premarital interview where the focus is on preparation for marriage and not on a problem. These contacts are often for one interview only.

importance. Counseling may be predominantly educational with this group or it may be concerned with emotional disturbances (Mudd, Freeman, and Rose, 1941). The initial premarital interview is potentially the most difficult and subtle of any first interview in agency experience. For this reason, such applications are not assigned to a new staff member or counselor in in-service training until he has worked several months in the agency with postmarital clients. In a first premarital interview the counselor considers carefully the following:

1. A premarital client may fall in one of the three major classifications of agency intake: (1) *general* preparation for marriage (see Chapter 9, Case II); (2) a *specific* situation or problem (Chapter 8, Case I and Chapter 9, Case X); (3) involved disturbance and/or problem (Chapter 8, Case III, and Chapter 9, Case IX).

2. Often nothing more is known about premarital clients in advance of counseling than that they wish to discuss their engagement or approaching marriage (Chapter 9, Case II).

3. There is nearly always the time limit of an engagement announcement or a wedding date within which solutions are sought or decisions must be reached (Chapter 9, Case III). Often the application is made shortly before the predetermined date.

4. Because of the age of most premarital clients, and often the economic and legal dependence of one or both partners (usually the girl), parents may actually be in the picture more closely than in most postmarital situations (Chapter 9, Case X) and may also request an agency interview. Contact with parents, however, is rare. It may involve counseling with several different persons, all under conflicting pressures and concerned about the same situation.

5. The counselor must be adequately informed himself and be able to handle comfortably the giving of information on sexual and/or practical matters if it is desired (Chapter 9, Case XI). This includes familiarity with bibliography suitable for the particular couple if occasion arises.

6. An engaged couple are apt to come together for premarital counseling and, often, in the general "normal" preparation for marriage—problem free situation—expect to come only once. The counselor usually sees each partner individually and the couple together (Chapter 8, Case I).

7. In those unusual situations where either or both partners have severe doubts about the proposed engagement or marriage, seem unable to reach a decision, or are upset out of proportion to the

184

situation (Chapter 9, Case III), the counselor may consider the possibility of psychiatric referral. Limitations of time often necessitate a quick decision on the part of the counselor, who must weigh the advantages of stirring up sufficient anxiety to warrant acceptance of such a referral at a time when definite plans for a wedding may have already been made. Under such conditions, this arousing of anxiety hangs in delicate balance between the possibility of the client's becoming acutely ill if the proper help is not forthcoming or going into marriage with so many unresolved problems that the expectation of a constructive and lasting relationship is doubtful.

8. In a dysgenic marriage, such as where one partner is *hereditarily* epileptic, deformed, or the like, the counselor has to evaluate the total situation and the agency's responsibility in it. Consultation with a physician and/or a psychiatrist should be suggested in an evaluation of possible effects of marriage on each partner and children. For example, a statement such as the following might be made to the client: "In our experience, marriages undertaken when there are known conditions of physical pathology, or severely disturbed feelings or attitudes resulting from the pathology, almost always incur difficulty for the couple involved and for their possible children, etc." The alternative of raising no issue means the acceptance of responsibility for saying nothing, which superimposes the counselor's doubts or feelings on clients who themselves are not aware of serious question as to whether the marriage should take place.

9. Although it has already been indicated that anxiety is a condition which the counselor must constantly take into consideration, it cannot be stressed too much in thinking of the premarital interview. One gynecologist, who devotes some time to marriage counseling, has said that he believes anxiety is present in 100 per cent of the premarital patients who come to him.[4] There is always a question as to whether it is the kind of anxiety the individual can handle and use constructively, or whether it is a major problem, requiring psychiatric treatment.

10. When a counselor observes that fear of the approaching marriage is present, he must question its basis. If it is based on ignorance or misinformation, it may be a relatively simple matter to allay such fear—when, for example, the only need is for more ade-

---

[4] We are indebted to some of the lecturers in the in-service training program at Philadelphia Marriage Council for some of the views expressed in the following paragraphs, but particularly to Lovett Dewees, M.D., and William Fittipoldi, M.D.

quate sexual knowledge. However, if there are emotional problems involved, the client may be unable to accept the new information. Perhaps several interviews will be required to help establish new attitudes before the new information can be accepted. In some cases psychiatric referral may seem desirable.[5]

11. Feelings of guilt are very common in the premarital group—guilt over masturbation, over traumatic childhood experiences not associated with masturbation, over premarital sex play, premarital intercourse, or homosexual activity. Some one or a combination of these activities is likely to have been a part of the experience of almost every individual, and guilt feelings may be present.

12. The counselor who is sensitive to the anxiety, fears, and guilt that the client may be experiencing and alert to the problems and situations that may be causing trouble will be better able to help the client bring these out in the open. The counselor's attitude will be more important than any information or suggestions he may have to offer. Acceptance of all kinds of behavior without moral judgment,[6] the indication of concern, warmth, understanding, empathy—these are the essential ingredients of a good counseling relationship, and they are all reflected in the counselor's speech and manner. To offer this responsiveness without becoming emotionally involved, the counselor must achieve a fine balance between sympathy and objectivity.

13. The counselor must be prepared not only to offer education to those who lack information but to correct misinformation in the field of sexual knowledge. Occasionally a more sophisticated client may have been confused by his reading and may need help in interpreting what he has read. Discussions, books, pamphlets, physiological charts and models are all useful, and the nature of the questions as well as the kind of individual one is working with will dictate which are to be used in each situation. It is always wise to point out that a mutually satisfying sexual adjustment is highly individual. There are no rules governing frequency of intercourse, positions, timing, and all the elements that go into developing a satisfying relationship. Whatever provides satisfaction for both partners and leaves them comfortable and healthy is best for them, but it may take time for them to adjust to each other. To avoid the disillusionment that can develop so easily when a couple has ex-

---

[5] Psychiatric referral occurs in approximately 9 to 11 per cent of total client intake.

[6] Where a client wishes to obtain moral judgment in connection with a situation, referral to a priest, minister, or rabbi is suggested.

pected immediate perfection in the sexual relationship, many counselors like to inject a note of warning here to encourage patience.

14. Some premarital clients bring questions about homemaking to a marriage counseling service. Discussion and, sometimes, reading are helpful here. When specific legal questions arise, the client is referred to a lawyer. If medical questions are raised, the client is of course referred to a doctor. If the client has not already made plans for a premarital medical examination, the counselor usually discusses this with the client, and suggests a visit to the family doctor. If the client has no family doctor and wishes suggestions, a referral is made through the local County Medical Society or the agency Medical Supervisory Committee.

15. When the question of child-spacing arises, the counselor must of course be aware of the attitude and regulations of religious groups and must respect the client's religious background. If medical referral is requested in this connection, it should be made whenever possible and desirable to a physician or agency of the same religious affiliation as that of the client. Certainly no effort should be made to superimpose the counselor's viewpoint in this respect, but the counselor should be ready to help the client when the latter has determined what he wants to do.

16. Problems of continued dependence on parents and of possessiveness on part of the parents are, naturally, among the most common in this group. The counselor's efforts to aid in the client's growth toward independence, without loss of affection for the parents, are frequently hampered by the brevity of the period allowed for counseling before the wedding date. However, sometimes a process begun during counseling before marriage may continue after the counseling has ceased, and a client is always welcome to return for counseling with or without the marriage partner if and when the need is felt.

Counseling with Partners in Marriage

Working towards shared responsibility between partners is one of the goals of marriage counseling (Schmidl, 1949); therefore, we are most interested in trying to get both to do something about the situation. However, undue or premature pressure along this line is inadvisable. Sometimes partners come at the same time for their initial interview. This is an important dynamic to work with. Keeping from overidentification with one to the detriment of the other requires all the skill of the experienced counselor. The counselor should consider carefully the following:

1. In the first or within the first few interviews the place of partnership in marriage and the advantages of working with two people should be mentioned. This helps the client to evaluate the degree of responsibility each partner is taking for the marriage. It helps to approach the problem less in terms of the individual, but more in terms of what has gone astray in the relation (Chapter 8, Cases II and III, Chapter 9, Case III).

2. Early in the contact, the counselor should inquire about the possibility of the partner coming for counseling or at least checking schedules similar to those checked by the client. Schedules may sometimes serve as a springboard for the partner who comes into counseling later.

3. If the client is sure his partner will not come for counseling or if he does not want to tell his partner he himself is coming for counseling, the significance of such a situation for the marriage should be discussed.

4. Counseling should be focused on the person who wants to do something about his situation and on the aspect of the situation on which he wants to work (Chapter 8, Case III). If both partners have an equal desire to do something about their problem, the counselor should work with each accordingly (Chapter 9, Cases III and IV). Constructive results sometimes come in a few interviews when both partners are equally alerted to improvement in each other and anxious to modify their own behavior and preserve the marriage.

5. When husband and wife both come for counseling it seems better usually to have the same counselor work with both clients, irrespective of whether they are seen jointly or separately (Chapter 8, Cases I, II, III, IV). Although usually the skillful counselor can work equally well with clients of both sexes, the advantages in rare instances of a client working with a counselor of the same or of a different sex should be borne in mind. If the conflict between the two partners is of such severity that seeing one counselor only intensifies the elements of conflict and competition, then two counselors may be necessary.

6. Our policy accepts the concept that a counselor should never advise an individual or couple to marry, separate, or divorce (Chapter 9, Cases VI and IV). Such advice transfers the responsibility from the persons who are involved and inhibits development of maturity and independence. In addition, it has possible legal

implications which do not fall within the function of marriage counseling and might later involve the counselor in litigation. The client could be told that our experience at Marriage Council has demonstrated that people with feelings and attitudes similar to those he and his partner have expressed toward each other and toward marriage seldom make a go of marriage unless they can change their attitudes. ∠

Joint Interviewing

The joint interview with both partners occasionally is considered of possible therapeutic value, although it requires considerable skill, tact, and stamina on the part of the counselor. Under such conditions a man and woman may, for the first time, see each other with objectivity, because of the protecting presence of the counselor. Often each accepts feelings and needs in the other or in himself which had not been appreciated before. Such an interview has always been available as part of routine agency structure.

Possible hazards, however, should be borne in mind. A joint interview may serve as a means of avoiding a problem. If the counselor does not have equally good rapport with each partner, one partner may feel rejected or pressured in these circumstances. Such an interview may degenerate into a free-for-all if the partners are not able to move or give but want only an opportunity to tell each other off. Final decision as to the use of this procedure is in the hands of the counselor and supervisor. In considering a joint interview, the following points are important:

1. When clients come together for the first appointment or wish to be seen together at some time in the contact, a joint interview should be considered and arranged if and when it seems desirable to clients and counselor (Chapter 8, Case I, first interview of second opening).

2. If the entire time of the first interview is spent with both clients together, they should not be seen again jointly unless each has been seen at least once alone in the interim.

3. A joint interview should not be held when one partner has previously had an individual interview and the second partner has not yet been seen by the counselor. In such a case, the second partner can easily feel that the counselor has identified with the one

already seen and resent not having the opportunity of giving his own account privately to the counselor before he is, as it were, put on the spot.

4. If the client and his partner come alone and do not ask for a joint interview, the counselor should consider the possibility of a joint interview at some time during the total contact for part or all of a counseling hour. Whether this should be actually mentioned to the client, or when, depends upon the discretion of the counselor (Chapter 8, Case IV).

5. There should not be pressure from the counselor for a joint interview if clients are not interested (Chapter 8, Case III).

6. If there is a joint interview, it need not cover the full hour; both individual and joint interviews can be used in the course of a single appointment (Chapter 8, Case II, first interview).

7. A joint interview may be particularly helpful in stressing the co-operative aspect in counseling which can be carried over into the marriage (Chapter 9, Case II).

8. It is important that the counselor not allow himself to identify or be identified with either partner individually in the case of such an interview (Chapter 9, Case III).

9. It is necessary to interrupt if a vindictive argument ensues between the partners.

10. The joint interview furnishes the opportunity for fantasy and reality to meet and for the clients to make a distinction between them (Chapter 8, Case IV, Chapter 9, Case II).

11. The joint interview may assist in relieving the anxiety some clients have over feeling they are very different from their partners (Chapter 9, Case XIII). In such situations, it may be helpful for the counselor to support the client in accepting his difference as an individual from his partner.

Information Giving and Supplementary Reading Material

The counselor should be equipped to furnish information relevant to marriage to those clients who seek for this type of assistance and who, in the counselor's judgment, are ready and able to utilize it. Information may be requested in connection with community resources, with a description or explanation of some event which the client or his partner is anticipating with apprehension, such as a medical or psychiatric examination, or treatment, or hospitalization, or pregnancy (Stern, 1942), (Gould, 1950), (Zabriskie, 1925). It may be in the

190

realm of general or specific sexual performance.[7] Particularly in premarital interviews various types of questions are frequently brought up which have to do with relationships in the sexual sphere (Chapter 9, Case II).

In all areas of information giving, the counselor should be confident of the reliability of his statements. If he does not know the answer, he should state this fact clearly and if it is important, offer to find out before the next interview. Clients will respect an admission of ignorance, and an occasional instance of not having all the answers will present the counselor as a fellow human being rather than the ultimate authority, which no one person should be for any other. In areas in which the counselor is not trained, such as law, no specific information should be given and referral to reliable sources of legal aid should be made.

The counselor should consider the suggestion of reading material to supplement the information he has given or to substitute for giving information (Mackay, 1946). To do this he should be familiar with at least part of the agency's well-rounded lending library (Timmons and Caraway, 1947). He should recommend only books with which he himself is familiar, and always make clear that he would welcome discussion of the client's reactions to this material[8] (Mudd and Whitehill, 1938), (Twyeffort, 1942), (Menninger, K., and Devereux, 1950).

In either the verbal giving of information or the suggestion

---

[7] *A Sex Knowledge Inventory for Marriage Counseling* by Dr. Gelolo McHugh and an advisory committee of well-known authorities in their field is published by Family Life Publications. Although to date the author has not used the material clinically, it seems reasonable to believe, and others report, that it would be helpful in certain counseling cases.

[8] In Marriage Council of Philadelphia about half of the clients utilize the lending library under the supervision of their counselor. Although there are well over one thousand books and fifty pamphlets which allow wise choice to suit the particular client and his problem, it is found, nevertheless, that counselors tend to suggest certain books for their clients on the basis of satisfactory results. Books by the following authors fell in the category of the ten most used books from 1948 to 1950: Butterfield, E. Duvall, English and Pearson, Fishbein and Burgess, Foster, E. Groves, Levy and Monroe, Saul, Stone and Stone, Strecker and Appel.

of collateral reading material, particularly in sexual matters, the counselor should not only be aware of the client's motivation in indicating desire for such information, but should be able to take responsibility for assessing the degree of insecurity, anxiety, or emotional disturbance represented by the request and the subsequent reaction to the material. He should know that the client who repeatedly requests literature on specific subjects such as personality deviation, sexual information, and so forth is almost inevitably emotionally blocked and cannot be helped in this way.[9] On the other hand, he realizes, absurd as it may seem to those inexperienced in this field, that many individuals in all age groups are pitifully ignorant of the most elementary factors pertaining to sex, personality, and emotional difficulties. Discussion of facts, the using of adequate vocabulary with a counselor who is informed and comfortable during the process, often has amazing cathartic effects and therapeutic benefits to the client who has never before had the opportunity of going over such material with anyone whom he trusted and respected. In this connection, "Schedule 1B," which has to do with detailed sexual material, is found to be extremely useful and helpful. It is used only during an interview and at the discretion of the counselor (See Chapter 8, Case II). The client is given a copy to examine and talks over his answers while the counselor checks a duplicate copy. Discussion covering one point in the Schedule may occupy most of one interview, and it takes from one to two interviews to complete the Schedule.

Time Limits for Client Contacts

Time is one of the basic dynamics in counseling. In this agency, as in most casework agencies, time limits are important in defining and clarifying the client's relation to seeking and using the kind of assistance which the agency offers. Except in rare emergencies, interviews are scheduled at definite times and for approximately an hour. This procedure is explained to the client, who knows that the period arranged for in his counselor's time will be saved for him. The skilled counse-

---

[9] It should be noted here again that persistent sexual difficulties are considered as expressions of total personality involvement and as symptoms of neurosis.

lor utilizes this structure and its limits carefully as a conscious tool in his relationship with the client. He is able to learn a great deal about his client through his use of his hour. He learns something of how he makes use of or considers other people, how much he tries to control or dominate, how hard it is for him to accept limits other than his own, how difficult it is emotionally for him to come for help. The client's pattern may reflect his behavior with his marriage partner. If this is so, it enables the counselor to utilize the pattern in one way. On the other hand, it may be very different from his usual pattern and so serve as the basis for a new use of himself in an environment in which he is sufficiently secure to give him the courage to experiment in other settings.

When appointments are not kept according to plan, this may mean that anxiety or resistance has been stirred up at the first or some subsequent interview to such a degree that the client is unable to return for further counseling without help. Attitude and current behavior of the partner may be closely involved. A friendly note expressing interest and understanding and offering the possibility of another interview may be important in bridging this block. On the other hand, there are situations in which there may be more therapeutic value in not contacting the client (Chapter 9, Case XVI). From understanding of his client's personality and individual situation the counselor can base his decision regarding the wisest choice.

A planned ending should be utilized consciously by the counselor in all possible cases regardless of the duration of the contact. Where there is a one-interview, premarital contact or where the client fails to return, this is naturally impossible. The situation of each partner must be considered separately as well as the total marriage situation (Chapter 8, Cases II, III and IV). The ending of counseling, if worked out carefully by the counselor, can be an important factor in enabling the client to carry on alone freely and comfortably without undue feelings of guilt or rejection.

Counselor Attributes and Their Effect on Clients

The impression which a counselor makes on clients is of great importance. This reaction is more apt to be in the realm of unspoken feelings than in verbal exchange. Certain attributes such as the background training and experience, sex of the counselor, appearance, manner, and speech are obvious and may affect the client. Whether the counselor is married, is a parent, and to what race, nationality, and religion he belongs are less obvious, but again may influence the client's reaction to counseling. The client may ask the counselor directly, or indirectly hint at his desire to know some of these personal factors, and it is important that the counselor handle his answers in such a way that they aid rather than block or detract from his relationship with the client. It is generally agreed that attitudes spoken and unspoken are basic in their impression on the client.

Certain clients may work better with a man counselor because of personality characteristics, situational experiences, or particular emotional needs; others may do better with a woman counselor. However, it is conceded in general that the skilled counselor can usually handle these preferences, identifications, or differences as part of therapy. Very occasionally the reaction of either a client or a counselor to each other or the problem involved stirs up so much emotional overtone that it seems best to transfer the client to another counselor.

Any or all of these attributes may be important in aiding or detracting from the counselor's ability to provide a warm, understanding, supporting relationship for the client. If one believes that some transference takes place during counseling, then it is vital for the counselor to be cognizant of these factors and make constructive use of them if the client is going to effect positive change.

Use of Fee as an Integral Part of Counseling

The policy of quoting a fee has always been considered an essential part of the structure of Marriage Council. The fact that there is a fee and that this is flexible on the basis of income is stated in agency interpretive literature and in response to telephone inquiries. Clients are informed of a minimum fee and told that the exact amount for them per interview will be worked out individually with the counselor. The counselor, in turn, has the agency fee scale at hand. This begins with a small income, below which fees are waived, and quotes a minimum and maximum for increasing, graduated, yearly incomes. The counselor discusses this schedule when he shows it to the client and together they work out a fee per interview acceptable to the client and suitable to the agency. The amount decided on is noted on a printed slip prepared for the purpose and given the client, who in turn shows it to the receptionist-secretary when paying the bill at the end of each interview. Cumulative payments or billings are discouraged as expensive to the agency and interfering with the therapeutic aspects of meeting the responsibility for each interview at the time.

Within this process (as in the use of time limits) is the beginning of a give-and-take relationship in connection with which the client can test out patterns of old and new behavior. He can show his need to control, to possess, to give little, to vacillate, and to undervalue himself or the marriage partner. Our experience also leads us to believe that interesting insights into a client's sexual behavior and attitudes are often obtained through study of his attitudes towards paying for counseling (Mudd and von Minckwitz, 1951). The payment of a fee, even if small, is believed to enable the client to use the service more freely, with more self-respect and with less guilt. These facts make the ending of the counseling contact, in particular, easier and more constructive for the client (Chapters 8 and 9, all cases).

Medical Referral of Clients

A medical check-up should be suggested by the counselor in any case where physical abnormality or distress is obvious or a possibility. If the client has a personal physician, he should be urged to arrange for a consultation. If he does not know of a doctor, he should be referred to the information service of his County Medical Society (Chapter 8, Case I, Chapter 9, Cases II and III).

Counseling with Psychiatric Implications

It is always necessary to evaluate how disturbed or ill the client is, and whether counseling or psychiatric service should be considered by the counselor and referral suggested to the client, if the latter seems preferable. Disturbance cannot be measured alone by the presence or lack of overt distress symptoms at any one interview, but rather by the continuing of such symptoms unabated or their increase over a series of interviews. Serious disturbance is certainly indicated by a client whose statements or behavior are conspiciously unrelated to reality or who gives evidence of acute neurological symptoms or ill health. In 1947 "directives" were prepared by the Medical Supervisory Committee to guide staff with regard to relationships with psychiatrists as follows:

1. Some clients have had psychiatric help either before coming to or before returning to Marriage Council for a renewed contact. Others return after being referred to a psychiatrist. When previous psychiatric help seems to relate to the client's current situation, the counselor, after obtaining the client's permission, should check with the psychiatrist as to the suitability of Marriage Council working with the applicant. If the psychiatrist states that nervous or mental disease exists and requires treatment, or there is a strong possibility of such disease developing, then the counselor should explain to the client that his situation does not fall within the agency's function, and he should then be referred back to a psychiatrist as constructively as possible.

2. Psychiatric referral should be made by the counselor when a client is obviously so emotionally disturbed at the first interview that psychiatric diagnosis seems indicated; when the client after several interviews seems to be making no further progress and is becoming more disturbed and upset by his problem (Chapter 9, Case III); when a psychiatrist's opinion is wanted by the client or some member of the client's family in connection with a specific situation, i.e., a considered marriage, planning for a child, a marital break-up or reunion, and so on (Chapter 9, Case XIII).

Follow-Up of Client Cases

Follow-up policy at Marriage Council has remained much the same through the years. Among the married clients there has been to date no routine procedure. The decision as to whether to get in touch with an individual, some weeks or months after counseling has terminated, is left to the discretion of the counselor and is related primarily to the welfare of the client rather than to the interest of the counselor or the agency in knowing what happened.

In the group of clients who come for counseling before marriage, procedure is quite different. Here a follow-up to be sent three to six months after marriage is discussed with the clients during their interview. Until 1945 it was explained as interest on the part of the counselor and agency in knowing how things were going after marriage. After the research schedules were developed and put into use it was explained that a schedule similar to the one they had checked on engagement adjustment, but geared to marriage, would be sent both partners to fill out and return to the counselor. This suggestion is usually welcomed by the clients, and unless there is objection the schedules are sent according to plan with a friendly letter. A further suggestion is made in the letter to the effect that it has been found helpful to go over material on sexual adjustment also, and because of the nature of the material this is done only in an interview in the office. The clients are offered such an interview without charge with the same counselor they saw previously, on the basis that this cooperation on their part is helpful to the agency research program. In turn, they are free to raise any questions they wish.

Response has been good on the whole to this systematic and routine postmarital follow-up although, quite naturally, fewer clients make the office visit than check the schedules. Unfortunately, many contacts are made impossible by the clients having moved to a distance after marriage.

A systematic follow-up of groups of cases is being considered in relation to the current evaluation of effectiveness of service. There are as yet many obvious and unsolved difficulties and complexities to such a program in addition to the moot question as to whether, if these could be overcome, results obtained would really answer the question of whether counseling helped.

STAFF TRAINING AND RESEARCH

In-Service Supervised Training

In 1947 in-service training in marriage counseling was initiated at Marriage Council of Philadelphia for physicians, at the request of the Veterans Administration program in neuropsychiatry. After the expansion of this program in 1950, under grant from the Grant Foundation, to include trainees with other professional backgrounds and experience, we have been aware increasingly of the effects of this activity on the process of counseling. The administration of this program carries triple responsibility; namely, to the client, to the trainee, and to the agency as a community service. We indicate here only the responsibility to the client, which is accounted for mainly through the medium of continual close individual supervision of the trainee's work by experienced staff counselors. In terms of everyday office routine, there is a great deal for the trainee to learn in addition to the principles and techniques of counseling which he gradually absorbs only over a period of time. The length of this time period must of necessity vary with the individual trainee's ability to grasp and utilize new material, his awareness of self as it pertains to his use of the counseling situation, and the degree of his insight into the meaning of the tremendous gamut of problems presented in interpersonal relationships. At the present time, there are arrangements for a minimum of six months to a year, which has already been extended in several individual instances.[10]

Clients do not know the status of their particular counselor. This is similar to other casework agencies where students from a school of social work are serving a field placement but are not differentiated from the rest of the staff so far as clients are concerned. This of necessity raises the question of intake selection. To date, cases with known community implications and referrals from professional sources where the problem is known to be complex are not assigned to trainees. Premarital appointments also, as already mentioned, are not usually given to trainees until they have been counseling for approximately four months.

Case Conferences

The regular biweekly staff case conference has a very important place in the training program as well as in the routine

---

[10] Information concerning requirements for admittance to this program, content, length of training, etc., can be obtained by writing Marriage Council of Philadelphia, Philadelphia 2, Pa.

work of the agency. The trainee attends this hour and a half conference regularly with the full agency staff. During the first months cases are presented by members of the counseling staff and the trainee participates in the discussion as he feels inclined or is called on by the chairman of the conference. Later in his training he is given the opportunity at different times to present one or more of his own cases.

Such an opportunity is full of challenge for the trainee. In presenting his own case, he brings to the case conference something of himself in which he has an important stake and basic feeling of worth. He has been over this case with his supervisor and probably much feeling has gone into its selection. He has heard others present cases and is familiar with the type of direct comments of surprise, commendation, disapproval, or disagreement which may follow from the group. He is used to the process and this give-and-take, but it is a new and different experience when his own case, and he as counselor, is subjected to this same frank scrutiny. If the group reaction is critical, the trainee, quite naturally, may react strongly, according to his pattern in traumatic situations. He may become defensive, hostile, threatened, fearful, or depressed, or he may be able to assimilate this experience as part of the total learning experience without undue reaction.

It is important for the staff chairman to be aware of what is going on and, without overly protecting the trainee, make him feel the security of the agency and his supervisor behind him in sharing the responsibility for whatever happened in his case. This experience, the group comments, and the trainees' reaction to them should be discussed further in the privacy of the next supervisory hour. When skillfully handled this procedure furnishes the trainee with possibilities of seeing his own reactions under stress and gaining real insight into his ways of relating to others. It offers invaluable guides to the degree of professional maturity to which the trainee has attained. Its importance can hardly be overemphasized.

Effects of Research on Counseling

A large-scale research project is under way with the aid of a grant from the United States Public Health Service. It aims to study marital adjustment and to evaluate the effectiveness of marriage counseling. As one step in reaching these objectives, the schedules described on page 181 were developed.

In a study of the effects of using the schedules on the case work program it was found that, for the most part, clients have accepted the schedules without question or comment. Where very occasionally an objection is raised, it is often associated with other negative reactions to counseling. Schedules are also used in follow-up after marriage of those clients seen premaritally and there appears to be a high degree of co-operation from this client group. On examination of their cases, counselors have felt that the schedules in general contribute to more economic and effective use of the interview time. They help both client and counselor to see the focus of the problem, gain perspective, raise questions for discussion, and affect clients' attitudes constructively.

Other effects of the research program are evident as staff counselors and trainees participate in the detailed analysis of case records to determine the type and variety of problems brought for counseling, the clients' part and the counselor's part in the counseling process, and the judgments as to the results of these contacts [11] (Preston, Mudd, Peltz, Froscher). This procedure illustrates to each case reader the great individual variation in case recordings, and in many instances the lack of systematically recorded information, particularly in connection with the counselor's activity. This experience, in turn, stimulates counselors to be more critical, not only of their own dictation but also of their own counseling procedures.

In addition, the impress of research is felt as it necessitates the interchange and co-operative efforts of trained personnel from different professional disciplines. This takes place both in the research team itself, which includes a psychologist with specialization in dynamic statistics, an analytically trained psychiatrist, a social worker from the family field, and the agency director, and in the varying procedure required of the eighteen or more case readers (Froscher, 1951). The reper-

---

[11] Project under way 1947 to 1951 by grant from the United States Public Health Service.

200

cussions of these interdisciplinary exposures prevent undue rigidity, develop respect for the effectiveness of different approaches (Fiedler, 1950), broaden perspective, and stimulate dynamic thinking.

TREATMENT METHODS

Treatment methods and procedures described thus far (with a few variations having to do mainly with premarital work) are essentially those used by most family caseworkers (Hertel, 1949), (Martens, 1944), (Waelder, 1947). Evidence for this statement can be found by referring to Chapter 4, which quotes from the Family Service Association of America, to Appendix B, which includes reports from three of its member agencies, and to the articles edited by Kasius (1950). In the eighteen years of Marriage Council's experience, general criteria, techniques, and procedures which have proved their usefulness in counseling practice were tested daily, reviewed in staff conferences, and revised or discarded whenever new theories or experience seemed to suggest improvement.

In considering the role of the counselor, the agency research team, assisted by staff members, after months of studying agency records reached agreement about the ways in which they believed counselors at Marriage Council were active. Although records differ in the extent to which they report systematically the counselor's activity, the following were felt to be used, in varying degrees, by counselors in their day-by-day work: discussion of agency function and structuring client's relation to the agency; exploration of client's feelings and behavior; exploration of situation or problem; providing a sympathetic listener, reassurance, and approval; offering of information and education; interpretation; offering suggestions, advice, and proposal of activity; discussion of referral. Through evaluation and the appropriate use of these activities, the counselor hopes to give psychological support and clarification, and ultimately, in some instances, to aid in the development of increased insight.

Obviously the use in specific cases or individual interviews of any of these processes depends on factors in each client's personality and in his situation. The skilled counselor, quite naturally, is sensitive to the prime importance of the individualization of all techniques and processes in relation to the varying needs and reactivity of every client. And these technical processes are only parts of the *total relationship* between the client and the counselor, the essence of which is reflected in the effectiveness of the results of counseling.

There seems nothing in this detailed description of the counselor's role in a marriage counseling service which, in the writer's opinion, is inimical to the classification of methods of treatment proposed independently by Florence Hollis (1949). This classification brings together recent casework thinking and the findings of psychiatry and analytic psychology. The reader may find it of interest to reconsider the recordings of cases in Chapter 8 in the light of these methods. Dr. Hollis states:

Psychological support covers such steps as: encouraging the client to talk freely and express his feelings about his situation; expressing sympathetic understanding of the client's feelings and acceptability of his behavior; indication of the caseworker's interest in the client, his desire to help; expression of the worker's confidence that a way can be found to improve the situation, confidence in the client's ability to solve his difficulty, to make his own decisions; indication of the worker's respect for and approval of steps the client has taken or is planning where these attitudes are realistically warranted. All these are designed to relieve anxiety and feelings of guilt and to promote the client's confidence in his ability to handle his situation adequately. Also included in psychological support is the direct encouragement of attitudes that will enable the client to function more realistically as well as more comfortably. . . .

When psychological support is the predominant treatment method, it rests upon a warm, good-parent type of relationship between client and worker. . . .

The dominant note in clarification (sometimes called counseling) is understanding—understanding by the client of himself, his environment, and/or people with whom he is associated.

Insight development involves carrying understanding to a deeper level than that described in clarification. Sometimes conflicting feelings and strong emotions lead the individual to distort reality so seriously or react to it so unappropriately that understanding is impossible without the deeper perception we are referring to as insight.

To achieve insight, current and past emotions must be relived in a therapeutic atmosphere in order that some of the affect may be discharged and in order that irrationalities may be brought so clearly to the surface that they can be recognized, at first in the safety of the treatment relationship and later in real life.

Insight development is always accompanied by some degree of clarification and of psychological support.

Some readers may wonder how this development of insight differs from that achieved in psychoanalysis. The chief distinction is one of depth—depth of the transference, of the worker's comments, and of the material reviewed by the client.

Different techniques are used to elicit material on these different levels. Face-to-face interviewing, a time lapse of at least several days and usually a week between interviews, limiting explanations to conscious and near-conscious material, refraining from interpretations of highly symbolic material, absence of the insistence on free association, or of comments on dream material except where the meaning is obvious from the manifest rather than the latent content, all are designed to keep the treatment from entering the realm of the deep unconscious.

Dr. Robert Gomberg (1947), Executive Director of Jewish Family Service in New York City, contributes his concepts of the four basic essentials for adequate marriage counseling. To achieve these the counselor should have "fundamental psychological and psychiatric understanding of personality growth; a full understanding of the psychodynamics of family life, a psychology of treatment, and family-close individual supervision." We believe that acceptance of these requirements for personnel in Marriage Counseling practice is implicit in the criteria and methods already described.

DIFFERENTIATION BETWEEN MARRIAGE COUNSELING AND PSYCHIATRIC TREATMENT

Authorities in both casework and psychiatry have contributed to defining the similarities and differences, the areas of overlapping and of supplementation in these professions. There is widespread agreement to the effect that therapy takes place in each approach. Having familiarized ourselves to some degree with methods and procedures in casework as they apply to marriage counseling, we can consider how various psychiatrists, active in the development of this field, have described counseling.

Dr. Frederick H. Allen, a child psychiatrist for twenty-five years, the first chairman of the Board of Directors and later of the Medical Supervisory Committee of Marriage Council of Philadelphia states:

Marriage counseling can help a couple work through to a new quality in family living on the basis of getting together on mutual concerns and finding out what they really want to do.

The nature of the agency service needs to be defined in the first interview in terms of marriage, stressing that both partners are involved and explaining how the agency can come in as an outside force to help them get together on their problem. If the focus is kept on the service and how it can be used by those who seek it, the counselor is less liable to become involved in details or in other areas of concern and lose sight of what he is there to do as a helping person. The focus on function and use of service is one of the essential differences of counseling and psychotherapy. The exploring of what is available for the client brings out anxieties, questions, doubts, and negative reactions, and in the end, a clarity of purpose which the client elects to pursue.

The same counselor should work with both partners. By having two different counselors on a case, the focus, the dynamics, the interaction, the interweaving of the service toward a common goal, would be lost. It would be working with individuals instead of with marriage partners and complicate the problem for which help is sought.

Marriage counseling is a matter of *getting together on a decision*—which in terms of the marriage may mean either to stay together or to separate. The significance of a person coming to Marriage Council instead of going to a psychiatrist, or lawyer, etc., is very difficult to evaluate. It may, however, be very important as an indication of attitude and potentialities for getting together in a marriage.[12]

---

[12] Material presented by Dr. Frederick H. Allen, February 10, 1949, at a case conference for staff and in-service trainees of the Veterans Administration training program for neuropsychiatric residents at Marriage Council of Philadelphia. Quoted with permission.

Dr. Kenneth E. Appel, Professor of Clinical Psychiatry, Medical School, University of Pennsylvania, and psychiatric supervisor of the staff of Marriage Council since 1932 and chairman of the Board of Directors since 1948, writes in the introduction to an article for physicians on marriage counseling (1944):

Doctors' accustomed ways of therapy are so definite, concrete, aggressive, and authoritarian they are often awkward, ineffective, and anything but subtle. Their efforts in this field are frequently self-defeating, because their knowledge and skill are limited.

Fortunately there is an increasing group of workers with special knowledge and ability in dealing with the problems of interpersonal relationships, especially in marriage and the family. Practically, their work has helpfully supplemented that of physicians. There are, furthermore, many patients who are unable to discuss intimate and personal problems with many physicians, because of differences in temperament, but who can freely and profitably go over these matters with counselors whose knowledge, temperament, and training put such patients more at their ease. Many patients with marital problems who need expert help will not consult available psychiatrists because of the still all-too-persistent idea that psychiatrists treat only patients with mental disease.

Dr. O. Spurgeon English, Professor of Psychiatry, Temple University Medical School, and for five years a member of Marriage Council's Medical Supervisory Committee, commented in 1948: [13]

Marriage counseling stands in an ancillary relation to psychiatry; it is somewhat dependent upon it and yet contributes a great deal to psychiatric work. It also fills a very important mental hygiene function in the community. . . . It is in certain respects a special field and requires special preparation.

Although the emotional overtones in a marriage relation may be disturbed, they are not necessarily the same conflicts as those which produce a neurosis or cause people to be mentally upset in a psychotic way. Marriage counseling requires a high refinement of one's emotional measurement of the things which cause friction in everyday life. This takes special experience and skill. Psychiatrists may not necessarily want to include this specialization within their work

---

[13] Cf. footnote 12.

but they always can do so if they wish. They cannot practice psychiatry without meeting occasional marriage problems.

If a client turns out to be too neurotic, psychotic, or does not make the required progress, a consultation can be obtained and a decision made as to whether the case shall remain in a marriage council or be referred for psychiatric treatment. Where the relationship is close between the psychiatrist and a marriage council, I see no special problem of mishandling of the case if good will prevails on both sides.

Dr. S. Bernard Wortis, Professor of Psychiatry at New York University, and president of the American Association of Marriage Counselors in 1947, stated (1945):

Marriage counseling is fundamentally important work and should be carried out on a much wider scale. Most people coming to such clinics want general information, and only a minority require special psychiatric help. I emphasize this point because it is my belief that marriage counsel clinics are best organized outside of psychiatric institutions under close supervision of psychiatrically trained physicians. Too many people are afraid of the connotations of psychiatry and will not avail themselves of the help that is available in such hospital-linked clinics. The psychiatrist may be called in for the more difficult personality problems, just as the gynecologists will be called on to help with the structural problem, but most of the routine work can be carried out by the properly trained physician, the properly trained marriage counselor, and the liberal and enlightened clergyman.

Dr. Robert Laidlaw, chief of psychiatry at Roosevelt Hospital, New York, currently president of the American Association of Marriage Counselors, gave his point of view at the 1949 meeting of the American Psychiatric Association, later reported in the *American Journal of Psychiatry* (1950):

Marriage counseling is a form of short-term psychotherapy dealing with interpersonal relationships, in which problems relating to marriage are the central factor. The field is subdivided into premarital and postmarital counseling. It is an approach carried out essentially at a conscious level. The interview is conducted on a discussion basis in which the therapist actively participates. If, as therapy progresses, unconscious factors are discovered which necessitate long and involved psychotherapeutic techniques, the case ceases to be in the field of marriage counseling. Sometimes a relatively simple presenting problem will develop unforeseen complexities, while an apparently complex marital situation may yield to a simple short-term approach. In making the above distinction between marriage counseling and clinical psychiatry, therefore, the differentiation is based primarily upon the degree of complexity of the presenting problem and accordingly the types of therapeutic techniques necessary to meet it.

In a symposium of the Boston Psychoanalytic Society on Psychotherapy and Casework (February, 1949) Dr. Greta Bibring discusses her views on the relationship between these two approaches to assistance in individual adjustment and further enlightens the subject as follows:

Adjustive change through a specific experience, which probably happens only rarely in life, can be approximated in the therapeutic set-up, including casework therapy. . . . Such adjustive changes seem worth while, since many persons who could never be reached by the psychiatrist and many who do not need psychiatric treatment can be helped through this method. . . . I think therefore that casework should remain flexible and not take over one or the other of the existing *methods* of psychotherapy, but that it can and should assimilate within its own framework certain fundamental *principles* of psychotherapy and apply them according to its own goal and to the structure of the individual case.

And Dr. Jules Coleman (1949) in the same symposium gives his definite distinctions between the two fields:

Casework and psychotherapy look in different directions, and are interested in different aspects of the problem area in the total life situation of the person in distress. Many casework procedures are useful to the therapist, just as many therapeutic procedures become available to the caseworker. . . . Procedure and technique become adapted to separate value systems, separate philosophical presuppositions, and separate traditional professional attitudes, prejudices, and mythologies. Casework is the field of wider range and wider indication, since it is more closely related to social process and convention. Psychotherapy has a much narrower range of indication and its field of helpfulness is relatively limited. . . . It need not continue, as it still so often does, to duplicate and compete with casework practice. . . . The two fields can undoubtedly continue to enrich each other and find ways of mutual support and complementation, particularly as they seek out and respect their own uniqueness and distinctiveness.

The foregoing thoughtful material throws light on marriage counseling; for, although this field requires certain specialized knowledge and skill, it employs in the process of counseling many methods of social casework treatment as utilized at Marriage Council and other agencies. These methods are illustrated in the cases presented in Chapters 8 and 9.

Marriage counseling per se does not attempt to furnish medical and psychiatric examination or treatment, but such additional sources of assistance may be recommended when necessary. However, the purpose is to assist those partners, who so desire, to promote their ability to get along with each other in marriage. Therefore, the focus of all treatment is on the dynamics of the interpersonal relationship to a partner in connection with marriage. Such a focus reaffirms the belief that the philosophy and methods of casework and counseling are differentiated from and auxiliary to those of psychiatry.

People are feeling the need for help in interpersonal relations and evidencing this need by their requests for assistance from casework, counseling, and psychiatric service. This fact is reflected in current public interest in marriage counseling. In addition to the personal needs of individuals, marriage counseling, because it is practiced by members of professions representing many specialized fields, contains within its functioning many potentialities for interprofessional co-operation. Thus a mutual obligation as well as stimulus is encountered by these professional groups to pool their knowledge and experience in furthering the professional maturity of this field as well as the psychodynamics of human relations.

SUMMARY

In this chapter, the philosophy, methods, procedures, and goals of counseling in a functioning marriage council are formulated and certain aspects of the dynamics of counseling, deemed of particular importance, are explored. In this way, general criteria which have proved their usefulness and value through the years in the guidance of staff counselors and trainees are cited and discussed. Methods of treatment in this agency are compared and found to be basically similar to those of casework as formulated and defined by recognized authorities in the field.

Statements of psychiatrists related actively to marriage counseling define it and concur with other psychiatric authorities that casework and counseling utilize procedures separate from but auxiliary to the more profound procedures of psychotherapy under psychiatric or psychoanalytic auspices. The catalytic potentialities of the professional specialty of marriage counseling are suggested as factors in promoting constructive interprofessional co-operation.

Further pooling of knowledge among all professional groups involved in marriage counseling, together with team research on the psychodynamics of human relations, is indicated as essential in the continuing development of the field to professional maturity.

11

The Impact of Mobilization and
War on Clients of Marriage Council

A BOOK ON MARRIAGE counseling in these times would
be neither realistic nor complete if a discussion of the impact
of war was omitted.[1] Probably no one factor has a more over-
all disrupting effect on marriage and family relations than
world war. This is true even when the actual fighting is on
foreign soil, as it has been for the United States intermittently
since 1914. Men by the thousands are forced to leave their
families for military service or essential industry; wives and
children leave their homes to follow their men when possible.
Mothers whose income from their husbands' military pay is
inadequate to support their children are forced to find employment, and often to move their families in order to accomplish
this. Separation usually causes loneliness and frustration socially and sexually. Alternative companionship is sought or
may result quite unexpectedly from new contacts which could
hardly have occurred had the usual pattern of life not been
drastically disturbed. New roots are grown which become
quite naturally entangled with the old, and resulting behavior
taxes to the utmost the loyalties, love, and faith already invested in the marriage.

Where the past relationship has been limited and unsatis-

---

[1] Many writers have contributed information and insight into factors
precipitated by the war which produced or accentuated marriage and
family problems. Among them are: Abrams, ed., Bossard, Bowman, Burgess, Duvall, Glueck, Hill, Hollis, Hughes, Kitching, Kluckhohn, Mudd
and Gaskill, Rosenbaum, Strecker and Appel, Tregaskis, and Waller.

factory to one or both marriage partners before the disruption of war, the new experiences offer different and perhaps as yet unexperienced attractions. These in turn exert pressures which lessen the desire to continue former patterns. They also implement the urge to escape into a happier future. On the other hand, where the will to work things out is strong and the former relationship satisfying, the prognosis for finding a way through and out of the difficulties is good. Thus, the vagaries of war, although in the main destructive, may act as a catalyst for the stimulation of characteristics of sharing, communication, warmth, generosity, unselfishness, tolerance, flexibility, love, and sacrifice which are conducive to satisfying human relations. Both types of reactions are reflected in clients who come for marriage counseling during the impact of mobilization and war and have been illustrated in Chapter 9, Cases I–IX, and compared to situations in peace time.

These case descriptions are probably similar in type to situations experienced in many marriages throughout the country. In an effort to gain additional information and insights, over and above the difficulties of the individual, on some of the effects of war on marriage, the population of 1,033 clients studied in Chapter 6 was subjected to further systematic exploration. This consisted of a comparison of the sample in an era of peace, of war, and of postwar. Certain interpretations of the findings are offered.

The mid-point for the comparison between peace and war was originally set arbitrarily at December 7, 1941, the battle of Pearl Harbor, as this date was technically considered the actual beginning of war for the United States. With this mid-point in mind, 1,000 consecutive cases were selected, 500 of which had received counseling before Pearl Harbor and 500 after Pearl Harbor. These cases were studied as an entire population and also by yearly intake.[2] This examination showed that systematic changes in the Marriage Council sample began to be apparent during the year 1940 rather than in December, 1941. Referring to Chapter 2, "Current Events Affecting Mar-

---

[2] Complete charts of yearly intake, table for the year 1940, and all other statistical data referred to in this chapter are on file in Marriage Council's office.

riage Counseling in the United States, 1936–1949," one finds that in June, 1940, one and one-half years before Pearl Harbor, the first bill for compulsory registration of all men from eighteen to sixty-five years of age was introduced into Congress, had wide publicity, became a law in September the same year, and was followed by the first draft registration in October.

Because of these facts, it seemed important to ascertain more exactly the turning point at which the imminence of war was reflected in Marriage Council intake. Therefore, eight categories in client intake, with a total of eighteen subdivisions in which there were frequencies of over twenty during the year 1940, were tabulated by periods of three months. The analysis of this material, together with trends apparent in the charted data already referred to, indicated that July 1, 1940, the time that universal registration was publicized, is the date at which changes in trend occurred in Marriage Council client intake.

COMPARABLE PERIODS OF TIME ARE SELECTED BEFORE, DURING, AND AFTER THE IMPACT OF WAR

With a new mid-point established on the basis of information from the data, similar periods of time and a comparable number of cases were selected for the final comparison. This consisted of 469 cases seen in the four and one-half years between January 1, 1936, and July 1, 1940, a peacetime era, and 564 cases seen in the four and one-half years between July 1, 1940, and December 31, 1944, a war period. This selection made possible the comparison of frequencies and percentages in total client intake in all major categories studied during these nine years. In addition, data from cases seen between January 1, 1945, and December 31, 1949, a postwar era, also were presented, although these later data were not subjected to the same detailed statistical analysis. This material is summarized in Table 3 and serves as the basis for further discussion.

From Table 3 it is obvious that in the forty categories studied there are many in which the frequencies in the same category differ in the three periods studied. In those instances where percentage difference was over 4 per cent the same series of statistical tests, Chi-square, as described in Chapter 6, was applied to the period of peace and war. This was done in order to discern whether these differences were sufficiently large to be statistically dependable. From these data we may conclude with confidence that the differences associated with the two time intervals, January 1, 1936, to July 1, 1940, and July 1, 1940, to December 31, 1944, are unquestionably significant in the case of thirteen of the twenty-five tests. In the case of ten additional tests, the small difference may be regarded as due to variations in random sampling. In the remaining fifteen categories, with less than 4 per cent variation (among them five unknown classifications which were not tested), we have no reason to believe the groups were different.

DIFFERENCES IN TOTAL POPULATION RE-EXAMINED WITH MEN AND WOMEN CLIENTS CONSIDERED SEPARATELY

The tests already described dealt with only two variables at a time (for example, the relationship between *age* and *time*). In these tests there was no differentiation between sexes, that is, men and women were treated together as one group. It was believed that the differences discovered could be discussed much more intelligently if men and women clients were separated. This procedure would permit us to ask whether the war period reflected change in the composition of the samples of men and women in the same way. To illustrate this, Chart IV presents data on the sexes separately in the nineteen categories having frequencies of 140 or more.[3]

---

[3] In considering a differential response between men and women clients before and after July 1, 1940, certain limitations of the data must be borne in mind. The total frequency of men clients was only one-fourth that of women clients, totaling 245 in all. When this total is subdivided, before and after selective service, into seven categories with subdivisions in each category, it is inevitable that some of the frequencies on which percentage comparisons are based are very small. This is true even though there is a frequency of 140 or more in each category when the sexes are considered together. In such instances, the results can be suggestive only and may occasionally be misleading or not capable of substantiation if frequencies of a more suitable size were available for study. One can only call attention to these limitations and comment that there would also be definite limitations in any conclusions drawn from the data if no statistical tests had been applied.

Examination of this chart shows that it is possible to ask whether in the case of both males and females an increase is to be observed, after July 1, 1940, in the proportion of college students, of Protestant clients, and of married clients. In order to answer any question relative to the consistency with which the composition of male and female samples changed, a statistical procedure, in this case a tetrachoric r for the investigation of a triple interaction, was used.[4] In all, seventeen tests were made. Significant differences appeared in the case of six of the seventeen tests. In these instances it was signified that the sample of men clients and the sample of women clients as seen before and after selective service were differently constituted. There is probably a differential response between men and women in one category of reasons for coming to Marriage Council—sex difficulties. In the ten remaining categories tested a differential response between the sample of men and women clients did not exist.

The general relationships found in the examination of the data permit us to draw the following conclusions for which explanations will be advanced in terms of three general factors: the trends of the times, the development of Marriage Council, the impact of World War II.

1. The use of Marriage Council services by men was greater after the impact of war than before in the following categories: men between twenty-one and thirty-five years of age, men over forty-one, men with college education, men referred through private individuals, engaged men without specific problems, married men, and married men with sexual difficulties.

2. Men and women of higher educational level used Marriage Council in greater proportions during the period of the impact of war than did persons of a lower educational level,

---

[4] The tetrachoric correlation coefficient (tetrachoric r) shows the extent of correlation between two dichotomous variables. For a discussion of this statistic, see H. E. Garrett, *Statistics in Psychology and Education* (New York: Longmans, Green & Co., 1945), pp. 371 ff.; C. H. Goulden, *Methods of Statistical Analysis* (New York: John Wiley & Sons, Inc., 1939), pp. 38, 73. All tests made are on file in the office of Marriage Council of Philadelphia.

CHART IV

DIFFERENCES BETWEEN SEXES IN NINETEEN CATEGORIES
HAVING FREQUENCIES OF 140 OR MORE, SHOWING
PERCENTAGES BEFORE AND AFTER INTRODUCTION OF
SELECTIVE SERVICE BILL.

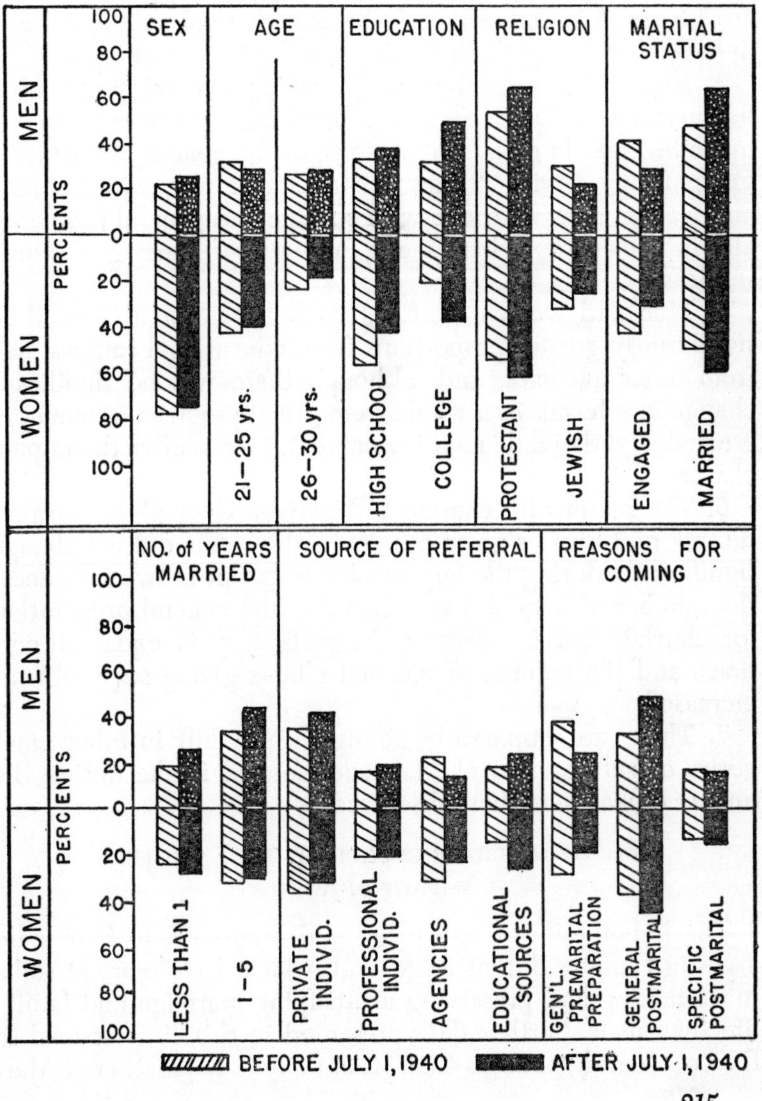

VZZZZZZ BEFORE JULY 1, 1940   ▬▬▬ AFTER JULY 1, 1940

and more persons were referred through educational sources.

3. There was an increase in Protestants, a decrease in Jews, and apparently no significant effect on the intake of Catholic clients using Marriage Council services during the impact of war. Nor was there any effect on the distribution of men and women within each religious classification. No explanations are advanced in connection with these particular data, nor any hypothesis relating these findings to the impact of war.

4. Engaged men and women seeking general preparation for marriage without recognized problems in their relationship made less use, in equal proportions, of the general preparation for marriage service during the impact of war, whereas men and women after marriage with specific and general problems, also in equal proportions, made more use of Marriage Council services.

5. Men and women were referred to Marriage Council in significantly greater proportions from educational sources, less from other agencies, and, although there was no significant change in referrals as a whole from private sources, women decreased slightly while men increased 1.3 times after the impact of war.

6. The reasons for coming to Marriage Council, or the presenting problems as given by men and women, did not change significantly during the impact of war except in two instances: the number of men and women using the general preparation for marriage service decreased significantly in equal proportions, and the number of married clients giving sex problems increased.

7. There was apparently no significant shift in other categories or subdivisions of Marriage Council intake during the impact of war than those discussed.

USE OF MARRIAGE COUNCIL BY MEN AND THE IMPACT OF WAR

The hypothesis was advanced and examined, in four main areas in Chapter 6, that in general women have more at stake in promoting and preserving a satisfying marriage and family life than men. Further data presented in this chapter lead to the collateral hypothesis that insofar as the population of Marriage Council of Philadelphia is concerned, this apparent difference between men and women in relation to marriage is lessened during the impact of war. Certain facts will be explored in connection with this hypothesis from the three general factors mentioned—the trends of the times, the development of Marriage Counsel, the impact of World War II.

From general considerations it seemed reasonable to expect that the total number of men using Marriage Council services would decrease between July 1, 1940, and December 31, 1944, and the number of women increase (Moore, 1947). The majority of men of the age groups using Marriage Council were serving in military units during this period. However, although the number of clients of both sexes increased, the proportion of men to women did not change in the total population in spite of significant differences in certain categories. In this connection it should be borne in mind that military life made many men more mobile and brought some in contact with chaplains, Red Cross, U.S.O. personnel (Mudd and Gaskill, 1945), and educational courses (Mudd and Freeman, 1945), and so on, which sometimes exposed them to new ideas in connection with preparation for and adjustment in marriage and also afforded the opportunity for referral to counseling facilities.

Within the agency, during the war period, there was no change in counseling facilities or intake policy for acceptance of clients. There was, however, a large decline in the amount of lectures, discussions, and group counseling requested and accepted. Table 10 indicates that the total number of men and women in contact with members of Marriage Council staff through group contacts between January 1, 1940, and December 31, 1943, was less than during the three years examined before the war. And among those contacted, men decreased whereas the proportion of women to men attending groups increased by 22 per cent. These facts lend support to the contention that changes occurring in agency development would lead to a decrease in the proportion of men clients after the impact of war. Total group attendance of both men and women increased in the three-year period after World War II. The proportion of men increased over the war level but was not as high as the prewar level, whereas the proportion of women decreased from the war level but was still higher than the pre-war level.

The general trends of the times outside of war influences seem to offer no data pertinent to the point under discussion,

TABLE 10

GROUP COUNSELING

LECTURES AND MEAN ATTENDANCE IN THREE-YEAR PERIODS

MARRIAGE COUNCIL OF PHILADELPHIA

	Before War 1/1/37–12/31/39			During War 1/1/41–12/31/43			Following War 1/1/45–12/31/47		
	Frequency	%	% of 9 yrs.	Frequency	%	% of 9 yrs.	Frequency	%	% of 9 yrs.
Lectures in Schools....	4			3			24		
Lectures in Colleges....	59			39			67		
Total Lectures in Schools and Colleges	63			42			91		
Men Attending......	755	23		505	19		1366	24	
Women Attending...	2325	77		2075	81		4254	76	
Total Persons Attending Schools and Colleges..	3080		26	2580		24	5620		49
Lectures in Community.	165			58			125		
Men Attending......	1815	33		555	16		1585	21	
Women Attending...	3790	67		2875	84		6237	79	
Total Persons Attending	5605		33	3430		20	7822		47
Total Lectures to All Groups...........	228			100			216		
Men Attending......	2570	29		1060	18		2951	22	
Women Attending...	6115	71		4950	82		10420	78	
Total Attendance....	8685		31	6010		21	13371		48

unless perhaps a gradually greater acceptance of counseling due to its popularization in the periodicals. It is practically impossible to determine how much such writing and discussion was speeded up by the war. It seems reasonable, therefore, to conclude that *the impact of war was influential in the fact that men clients did not decrease* at Marriage Council of Philadelphia between July 1, 1940, and December 31, 1944.

Age, Sex, and the Impact of War

The increase in the proportion of men between twenty-one and twenty-five might be expected during this period as a logical corollary of the facts just discussed. In Chapter 6, Table 6, it is stated that the median age in 1940 for men in the United States to marry was twenty-five to twenty-nine years. The impact of war and perhaps especially the draft precipitated many young people into quick marriage (Burgess, 1942). It would be expected, therefore, that more men proportionately of a somewhat younger age level would use Marriage Council during this period than formerly.

Just why more men proportionately over 41 years of age should use Marriage Council at this time can merely be surmised. Perhaps in this age division one would expect to find a large majority of men who might be exempt from active duty because of age, health, and job essentialness. This exemption in some instances undoubtedly produced relief, in others a sense of guilt, restlessness, and frustration. Other men of this age voluntarily enlisted in military units and were allowed to serve. Cases seen at Marriage Council illustrate these points although it was not possible to give examples.

Many motivations for voluntary enlistment of men of this age were evident. Some enlistments from stable family groups were motivated and carried out with constructive initiative, planning, and sharing of responsibility by both husband and wife (Chapter 9, Case V). Others were sought as a means of escape from irksome and unsatisfactory responsibilities, from a dulling middle-age ennui to an uneventful, mediocre, day-by-day existence, and from marital relationships in which disappointment, bitterness, and hostility—true enslavement in marriage—absorbed the majority of free time and energy without the possibility of acceptable social or legal release. Under these latter circumstances, either the decision to go into military service or the return home on leave or discharge could be expected to precipitate emotional or environmental crises for which help at Marriage Council might be sought (Chapter 9, Case VIII).

Education: Use of Marriage Council by Men and Women and the Impact of War

The change in educational status in the Marriage Council sample before and after July 1, 1940, is apparent in a percentage decrease, greater for men than women, in clients of grammar school level, and in clients with some or all of high school education. This is accounted for entirely by women clients, as the men in the high school group increased slightly. These decreases seemed to be offset in large measure by an increase of clients of both sexes with some or all of college education in approximately equal amounts.

As it was believed that developments in the agency might bear upon the educational status of its clients, attendance of men and women of various levels of education at group meetings, conducted by the agency staff, was explored further in Table 10. Figures in this table give no evidence which would lead to the expectation of an increase in intake during the impact of war among Marriage Council clients with college education. On the contrary, they might well lead to the expectation of a decrease in the college group based on the decrease in first-hand contact of students in college at this period with Marriage Council staff members. The actual decrease in clients of less than college education, on the other hand, comes at a period when the contacts with community groups, in which the majority of persons attending have high school education, is definitely lowered.

Consideration of this matter is next focused on trends of the times, which might be reflected in changes in educational procedure in the community from which Marriage Council clients were drawn. The literature records increased interest and activity between 1936 and 1949 in education for marriage and family life in schools and colleges (see Chapter 3). The assumption seems in order that the increased activity in this field within colleges and universities was a result both of the trends of normal times and the increased impetus given these trends by the demands of war (Reimer, 1947).

In line with the evidence presented, we can conclude with reasonable assurance that influences resulting from the war were in part responsible for the increase in clients in the college group, as well as for the increase of referrals from educational sources. It is of interest that these trends continued after demobilization (Chart I and Table 3).

Facts are not yet available to enable us to form a conclusion as to how much war or other influences accelerated an increase in discussions or courses in family life education in the public or private junior high or high schools. It is known that such education as carried on by the National U.S.O. for their junior hostess groups during the war reached predominantly women who had had high school or less education. As the drop in clients of part or complete high school education was due entirely to a decrease in the women clients in that group, it might be surmised that women of this level of education jumped more precipitously into marriage during the war era and did less to prepare themselves or try to work out conflicts (if they had them) after marriage than the more educated members of their sex. On the other hand, they may not have known as much about the availability of Marriage Council services and were not influenced by the importance of thoughtful preparation for marriage or by the possibility of their using marriage counseling facilities either before or after the wedding.

The facts relating to the significant shift in the educational level of clients at Marriage Council during this period seem to bear out the hypothesis that persons of college education are more apt than persons with less education to make use of services which attempt to prepare for the job ahead—in this instance marriage and family life—and to try to continue the job undertaken constructively by utilizing, when indicated, reputable available assistance (*Education and the Cultural Process*, 1943).

Referral: Use of Marriage Council by Men and Women and the Impact of War

The increase of 10 per cent of Marriage Council clients through educational sources has been discussed in the preceding paragraphs. The decrease of 9 per cent from agencies seems to be due largely to a decrease in 1943 and 1944 of nearly 50 per cent in referrals from one agency—the Central Maternal Health Center of Philadelphia. This change resulted from the fact that in 1943, when the first research funds were received by Marriage Council, the donor required that Marriage Council establish headquarters independent from the

Maternal Health Clinic, which had proffered office space at low cost to Marriage Council for nearly nine years. The move was made in October, 1943, and eliminated the easy means of communication between members of the staffs of the two organizations, as well as the easy access formerly enjoyed by patients of the Maternal Health Center in the use of Marriage Council's facilities.

It seems natural then that referrals from this source should have dropped. They have decreased even more in recent years as the Philadelphia Maternal Health Center, following the policies of the national organization in its field, has experimented in the establishment of some marriage counseling facilities for its patients under its own auspices. This decrease in referrals from agencies seems then to be related to a special factor in agency development and the trends of the times rather than to be influenced by the impact of war.

Mention should also be made here of the fact that a significantly greater proportion of men than women came to Marriage Council referred through private sources during the war period than before World War II. One of the largest subdivisions under referral from private sources was "former client." Apparently, even though the men had less chance to learn directly about Marriage Council, they were more interested or open-minded to the remarks or suggestions of their partners and other friends or acquaintances who had been clients than they were before war influences.

Marital Status, Reason for Coming to Marriage Council, and Impact of War

On the basis of clinical experience at Marriage Council the hypothesis seemed logical that the proportion of engaged clients seeking general premarital counseling would decrease during such exigencies of war as time limitations, actual or contemplated separation, specific fears of personal harm, and generalized anxieties. On the same grounds, the hypothesis seemed reasonable that the married clients and the number of married clients giving sexual difficulties as their reason for coming for counseling would increase.

When this change is considered in relation to the types of

problems presented by both groups of clients during these two periods, it is discovered that the significant *decrease* which existed in the engaged clients who used Marriage Council of Philadelphia was not for help in working out a problem, but for the *general preparation-for-marriage interview* (described in Chapter 8, Case I, and Chapter 9, Case II), when this category is compared with all other reasons for use of the agency. The *increase* in the subclassification of married clients with sexual problems seems to account largely for the increase in the category of general marital problems.

Many an engaged couple who had made plans for a reasonable period of engagement and preparation before their marriage were forced to abandon all arrangements by sudden overseas orders for men, cancelled leaves (Marquand, 1945), changes in military assignments, and so on. Under such circumstances many thoughtful couples rushed into a sudden wedding ceremony at home or at a military camp and were prevented thus, through lack of time or by distance, from using the premarital service which they had planned to use a month or so before the expected wedding date. However, as this group of clients continued to decrease in the postwar period (see Chart II), the question can logically be raised as to whether the increase in courses on marriage, already discussed, together with the easier availability of satisfactory literature on this subject, may not have taken the place of individual interviews for those couples who felt no specific problems. Thus, although the marriage rate was highly accelerated in 1941–42 (see Table 4 and Chart I), we see two possible reasons why the use of premarital service offered by Marriage Council of Philadelphia decreased rather than increased.

Individuals married under war circumstances often took the first opportunity to come to Marriage Council together or, if this was not possible, to come separately (Chapter 9, Case IV). This probably accounted in part for the slight increase among younger married clients. On the other hand, it might also be mentioned that many of the marriages responsible for the increase in the marriage rate during this period were entered into, according to the statements of recognized authorities, thoughtlessly, selfishly, and with little or no care for the future (Bossard, 1941), (Abrams, 1943). Material presented by clients and discussed in Chapter 10, Cases VII and IX, illuminates this point. It would hardly be expected that individuals so motivated would avail themselves before marriage of the services of a marriage council. Rather they might be expected to apply for service when the married state did not bring to one or both partners the satisfactions either had counted on. Although the aforementioned approach to marriage undoubtedly did exist and may throw light on the decrease in the use of the premarital service, no material in this study allows us to add information on the percentage of marriages undertaken because of such motives during war.

As already mentioned, the major part of the increase in the general problems of married clients was accounted for by those who gave sexual difficulties as their reason for use of the service (Chapter 9, Cases IV and VII). Sexual performance satisfying to partners from backgrounds of high school and college education, similar to the majority of clients of Marriage Council, is thought by well-known authorities to be correlated positively with lack of pressure and fatigue, relaxation, patience, leisure time, and a general spirit of comfort and security (Dickinson, 1931), (Duvall and Hill, 1945), (Ellis, H., 1935), (Folsom, 1943), (Hirsch, 1948), (Mudd, 1941), (Stokes, 1948), (Stone, 1939). Practically all of these criteria were affected adversely by the most prevalent exigencies of war (Marquand, 1945). It therefore seems reasonable to expect an increase in sexual difficulties among the married as the basis for use of a marriage counseling service during the impact of war.

Examination of the data when divided into separate groups of men and women (Chart III) throws further light on the above discussion in that there was no significant difference found before and after July 1, 1940, in the way men and women reacted in the engaged group coming for general or total reasons for premarital counseling as compared with all other reasons. In other words, the proportions of men and women tended to increase or decrease in the same way. However, although the frequencies were so small as to make results questionable, there was a (probably) significant difference found between married men and women with sexual problems as their presenting reason for coming to Marriage Council as compared with other postmarital reasons given by clients.

Thus we see that data resulting from the analysis of total intake with men and women together and, subsequently, with men and women separated, lead to the substantiation of this hypothesis, insofar as the material presented illuminates the matter: during a period of war it is to be expected that fewer engaged and more married persons would use the services of a marriage council, and that among the married group there would be an increase in sexual problems.

It is perhaps of even greater interest to learn, on the basis of the data presented, that there was no reason to believe that the impact of war, trends of the times, or the development of the agency influenced the proportions of clients or the proportions of men to women within other subdivisions than the ones discussed. It should be noted, however, that the frequencies in the majority of subdivisions of reasons for coming, in which no change was apparent, were so small that the significance of the figures could well be questioned.

In concluding this discussion of the impact of war on clients using a marriage counseling service, attention should be focused on the fact that before the repercussions of World War II have been assimilated, a new war is impressed upon the world. Already teachers, counselors, physicians, and others who come in contact with young people within draft ages are aware, cogently, of the beginning repetition of the natural anxieties, pressures, dislocations, and behavior patterns so familiar in former wars.

In addition to the conditions undergone in 1940–45, the five-year period since the cessation of hostilities in 1945 has been much shorter than the twenty-two years between World Wars I and II. This fact is extremely significant for all professional persons involved in marriage counseling. It means that many of the same young people who survived the stresses of World War II will be involved through present military activities in bearing over again strains and suffering similar to those which they themselves have already experienced. For some this may mean greater strength and perspective in facing current difficulties because the past was survived. For others it may mean increased tension and supersensitivity as feelings, attitudes, and patterns of behavior, incurred through deeply traumatic experience, are reactivated.

The endurance level of the client (the camel's back that may be broken by the straw), while always of importance in marriage counseling, becomes under the conditions at least of the next decade, 1950–60, of extraordinary meaning for those counselors who work with young people. The prognosis for the years immediately ahead necessitates understanding on the part of the adequate marriage counselor of the repercussions of war on men and women of all ages and on marriage and family adjustment, and, in particular, of the fact that these repercussions will be part of the thinking, feelings, and experience of a large majority of the individuals whom they will be called upon to counsel.

SUMMARY

This chapter has emphasized the importance of a realistic point of view concerning the impact of war on marriage adjustment. To further this end, certain characteristics of a total population of clients, and of men and women clients separately, who came to a functioning service for counseling were subjected to comparison through statistical means in a period of peace and a period of war. The selection by experimental means of a mid-point for the study of the impact of war on the 1,033 consecutive clients seen in these periods is described. Material on a period following demobilization was presented also, although this was not subjected to the same detailed statistical examination.

The following hypotheses were advanced: (1) In the importance felt by women and men in the preservation and development of satisfying marriage and family life, the impact of war lessened the differential between women clients on the one hand, and men clients on the other of twenty-one to thirty-five years of age and over forty-one, as well as those with high school and undergraduate college education. It was responsible, at least in part, for the increased effort made by college men and women clients for seeking help in marriage adjustment, and also for lessened effort in seeking such help on the part of women clients of high school or less education and men and women clients of grammar school education. (2) The impact of war, along with trends in the times, influenced the number of men and women clients referred to Marriage Council from educational institutions, and the number of men clients referred from private sources. Both of these factors also influenced the decrease in the number of engaged men and women clients who used the services of Marriage Council for general preparation-for-marriage (without specific problems), and for the increase in men and women clients after marriage with problems of sexual adjustment. It apparently had no significant effect upon the number of men or women clients between twenty-six and thirty years of age, the number of single clients, the number of years clients were married, and the other reasons given by clients for coming to Marriage Council. Explanations substantiating these hypotheses were submitted on the basis of the trends of the times, changes in the agency, and the impact of war.

Attention was called to the obvious limitations in the data due to the small frequencies in subdivisions of men clients. It was recognized also that discussion of the data without the application of statistical tests would be definitely limited.

Finally, the prognosis of unsettled and anxiety-producing times, due to war and its aftermath, is made for at least the decade 1950–60. Marriage counselors are urged to consider the importance of being aware of and understanding the significance of such conditions on men and women in marriage and family adjustment, and in particular the double strains projected upon young people who have already participated, only five years ago, in World War II.

12

Conclusion: Marriage Counseling and the Future

MARRIAGE IN SOME FORM is an institution of all social systems and so of major interest to society in general within both national and international boundaries. The foundations upon which this institution is built and the material and design from which it functions are developing, forever changing, living, human beings. Men and women with all their likeness and difference, their frailties and strength, their mutual and conflicting desires, needs, feelings, and reactions, seek each other, attract and repel, live together, and reproduce their kind. For the large majority a major part of life and energy is invested in this institution.

The processes promoting the elementary search for completeness and unity, as they are in part exemplified in marriage, are impelled by forces many of which as yet elude the analyses of modern science. Customs, rituals, and group mores of wide variety have grown up in different civilizations and localities to foster and continue this search. Nature's method of adaptation and survival of the fittest is in evidence, for unless ectogenesis becomes a practical reality, the continuation of the human race depends on the processes involved.

Within the nucleus of the relationship of man and woman to each other can be enacted the gamut of human feeling and emotion: warmth, friendliness, self-sacrifice, exaltation, love, ecstasy; anxiety, fear, despair, revulsion, antagonism, and hate. Human striving, ambition and success, frustration and failure, compromise and survival, are dependent in large measure on

228

this relationship. The elements and attributes conducive to group survival are herein engendered, for as the man and woman are molded, so in part will be their children.

Marriage counseling deals daily with men and women through whose children a new growth of world society must be achieved. It deals with the family as a "connecting link in the chain of life" (Bossard, 1949). Its record bears witness of the dynamic quality of personality characteristics when men and women in partnership feel toward each other, their young, and their fellow beings a warmth and sharing, openmindedness, tolerance and love as expressed in the true breadth of Christ's teachings. This same record emphasizes the devastating effect on human relationships, well-being, and creative effort of anger, hostility, and hate. The complexity of human value systems as well as behavior are clear, as are the uniqueness of personal individuality and interrelatedness. Through all this, for the counselors who do the work, belief is crystallized in the inner strength and resilience of men and women.

"The struggle" (of man with his instincts) states Saul (1947) "represents the essential adventure of the human spirit . . . Out of this struggle come sublimations and projections in art, science and thought." Dr. Chisholm (1949), director-general of the World Health Organization, challenges: "Dare any of us say that he or she can do nothing about the desperate need of the world for better human relations? Whoever is reasonably informed in any aspect of human emotional-mental-social development, whoever can do something to clarify thinking even a little and very locally . . . by that knowledge, training, insight or ability, is made responsible to do what he can in all places."

Marriage counseling as an art is old, as a science newly born. If it can, even in a small way, enable men and women to use their inner strength to lessen prejudice, soften hate, and increase tolerance, understanding, and love it will have accepted responsibility for contributing toward the possibility of permanent human relations. Now, and in the next decades, it has the opportunity through its vital experimental processes, its interprofessional curiosity, co-operation and good will, its openmindedness and ingenuity to make substantial progress.

Bibliography

Abrams, R. H. "Residential Propinquity as a Factor in Marriage Selection—50 year trend in Philadelphia," *American Sociological Review*, 1943, 8, pp. 288-94.

———, ed. "American Family in World War II," *The Annals of the American Academy of Political and Social Science*, September, 1943.

Adams, C., and Packard, V. *How to Pick a Mate*. New York: E. P. Dutton & Co., 1946.

Aldrich, C. Anderson, and Mary M. *Babies Are Human Beings*. New York: The Macmillan Co., 1938.

Alexander, Franz, and French, Thomas M. *Psychoanalytic Therapy*. New York: Ronald Press, 1946, p. 164.

Alexander, Paul W. *Report by American Bar Association Committee*. National Conference on Family Life, Washington, D.C., May, 1948.

Allen, Frederick H. *Psychotherapy with Children*. New York: W. W. Norton & Co., 1942.

American Bar Association Committee Report, National Conference on Family Life, 1948.

Anderson, W. A. *Marriages and Families of University Graduates*. Ithaca, N. Y.: Cornell University Press, 1950.

Angell, Robert C. *The Family Encounters the Depression*. New York: Chas. Scribner's Sons, 1936.

Appel, Kenneth E. Introduction to "Marriage Counseling," *The Cyclopedia of Medicine, Surgery and Specialties*. Philadelphia: F. A. Davis Co., 1944, pp. 450-60.

———. "Psychiatric Therapy," chap. 34, *Personality and the Behavior Disorders*, J. McVicker Hunt, ed. New York: Ronald Press Co., 1944.

————. "The Role of Women in Personality Growth." Lecture for the National Committee for Mental Hygiene of Canada and McGill University, Montreal, February, 1946.

————. "Science, Psychiatry and Survival," Centennial Volume, American Association for the Advancement of Science, Washington, D.C., 1950.

Aptekar, Herbert H. "Case Work, Counseling and Psychotherapy—Their Likeness and Difference," *Jewish Social Service Quarterly,* December, 1950.

Ayrinhac, Very Rev. H. A. *Marriage Legislation in the New Code of Canon Law.* New York: Benziger Brothers, Inc., 1949. (Revised and enlarged by Rev. P. J. Lydon)

Baber, Ray E. "A Study of 325 Mixed Marriages," *American Sociological Review,* II, October, 1937, pp. 705-16.

————. *Marriage and the Family.* New York: McGraw-Hill Book Co., 1939.

Barnett, James H. *Divorce and the American Divorce Novel 1858–1937,* thesis. Philadelphia: University of Pennsylvania Press, 1939.

Beach, Frank A. "A Review of Physiological and Psychological Studies of Sexual Behavior in Mammals," *Physiological Review,* Vol. 27, No. 2, April, 1947.

————, and Ford, C. S. *Patterns of Sexual Behavior.* New York: Harper & Bros., 1951.

Beard, Mary. *Woman as Force in History.* New York: The Macmillan Co., 1946.

Becker, H., and Hill, R., eds. *Marriage and the Family.* Boston: D. C. Heath & Co., 1949. (Revised edition)

Benedict, Ruth. *Patterns of Culture.* Boston: Houghton Mifflin Co., 1934.

Benz, Margaret A. *Family Counseling Service in a University Community.* New York: Columbia University Press, 1940.

Bergler, Edmund. *Divorce Won't Help.* New York: Harper & Bros., 1948.

————. *Unhappy Marriage and Divorce.* New York: International Universities Press, 1946.

Berkowitz, J. "An Approach to the Treatment of Marital Discord," *Journal of Social Casework,* Vol. 29, No. 9, November, 1948, pp. 355-61.

————. "Techniques of Intake Interviewing in Marital Problems," *The Family,* Vol. XXIV, October, 1943, pp. 209-14.

Bernard, L. L. "The Teaching of Sociology in the United States," *American Journal of Sociology,* Vol. XV, 1908, pp. 164-213.

Bibby, Cyril. *Sex Education.* New York: Emerson Books, Inc., 1946.

Bibring, Grete, "Psychiatric Principles in Casework," *Journal of Social Casework,* Vol. XXX, No. 6, June, 1949, pp. 230-35.

Boie, Maurine, "The Case Worker's Need for Orientation to the Culture of the Client," *Proceedings: The National Conference of Social Work.* Chicago: University of Chicago Press, 1937, p. 112.

Bossard, James H. S. "The Age Factor in Marriage," a Philadelphia Study, *American Journal of Sociology,* Vol. 38, January, 1933, pp. 536-47.

————."Family Problems in War Time" (Psychiatry), *Journal of the Biology and Pathology of Interpersonal Relations,* Vol. 7, No. 1, February, 1944.

————. *Sociology of Child Development.* New York: Harper & Bros., 1948.

————, ed. "Toward Family Stability," *The Annals,* Vol. 272, November, 1950.

————, "War and the Family," *American Sociological Review,* Vol. 6, June, 1941, pp. 330-44.

————, "What Are We Educating for in Marriage," *Journal of Social Hygiene,* June, 1949.

————, and Boll, Eleanor S. *Ritual in Family Living.* Philadelphia: University of Pennsylvania Press, 1950.

Bowman, Henry. *Marriage Education in the Colleges.* New York: Social Hygiene Association, 1948–49.

————. *Marriage for Moderns.* New York: McGraw-Hill Book Co., 1942.

————. "The Teacher as Counselor in Marriage Education," *Marriage and Family Living,* Vol. IX, No. 1, February, 1947, pp. 1-7.

Bradway, John S. "Some Domestic Relations Laws that Counsellors in Marital Difficulties Need to Know," *Social Forces,* 17.1, October, 1938, p. 83.

Bridgman, Ralph P. "Guidance of Marriage and Family Life," *The Annals of the American Academy of Political and Social Science*, March, 1932, pp. 144-64.

Brown, Muriel W., Groves, Gladys H., and Rustad, Ruth M. "How to Conduct an Institute," *Marriage and Family Living*, Vol. VII, No. 3, Summer, 1945, pp. 49-51.

Bryson, L., Finkelstein, L., and MacIvor, N. M., eds. *Learning and World Peace*. New York: Harper & Bros., 1948.

Buck, Pearl S. *Of Men and Women*. New York: John Day Co., 1941.

Burgess, E. W. "The Effect of War on the American Family," *American Journal of Sociology*, 38, 1942, pp. 343-52.

————. "Marriage Counselling in a Changing Society," *Marriage and Family Living*, Winter, 1943, Vol. V, No. 1, pp. 8-10.

————, and Cottrell, Leonard S., Jr. *Predicting Success or Failure in Marriage*. New York: Prentice-Hall, 1939.

————, and Locke, H. *The Family*. New York: American Book Co., 1945.

————, and Wallin, Paul. "Predicting Adjustment in Marriage from Adjustment in Engagement," *American Journal of Sociology*, 49, 1944, pp. 324-30.

Burgess, J. Stewart. "The College and the Preparation for Marriage and Family Relationships," *Marriage and Family Living*, Spring and Summer Issue, 1939, pp. 39-42.

Busser, Ralph C., Jr. "Is Divorce Incurable?" *The Shingle*, Vol. 12, No. 1, January, 1949, pp. 10-13.

Butterfield, O. M. *Marriage and Sexual Harmony*. New York: Emerson Books, Inc., 1950. (Revised)

Carden, Marie. "The Organization of Family Consultation Centers," *Marriage and Family Living*, Vol. IV, No. 3, Summer, 1942, pp. 61-62.

Cavan, Ruth S., and Ranck, Katherine H. *The Family and the Depression*. Chicago: University of Chicago Press, 1938.

Chisholm, George Brock. "Social Responsibility," *Science*, Vol. 109, January, 1949, p. 27.

Christensen, Harold. *Marriage Analysis*. New York: Ronald Press, 1950.

Ciocco, A. "On the Mortality of Husbands and Wives," *Pro-*

ceedings of the National Academy of Sciences, 26, Washington, D.C., 1940, pp. 610-15.

Coleman, Jules V. "Distinguishing Between Psychotherapy and Casework," *Journal of Social Casework,* Vol. XXX, No. 6, June, 1949, pp. 244-51.

Commission on Marriage and the Home, Federal Council of the Churches of Christ in America. *Building the Christian Family,* 1948.

Corner, G. W. *Attaining Manhood.* New York: Harper & Bros., 1938.

———. *Attaining Womanhood.* New York: Harper & Bros., 1939.

Cottrell, Leonard S., Jr. "The Adjustment of the Individual to His Age and Sex Roles," *American Sociological Review,* Vol. 7, No. 5, October, 1942, pp. 617-21.

———. "Present Status and Future Orientation of Research on the Family," *American Sociological Review,* Vol. 13, April, 1948, pp. 123-36.

———. "Research on the Family," *Social Science Research Monograph.* (In preparation, 1951)

Cox, Rachel D. *Counselors and Their Work.* Harrisburg: Archives Publishing Company of Pennsylvania, 1945.

Crampton, C. W. *Live Long and Like It,* Public Affairs Pamphlet No. 139. New York: Public Affairs Committee, Inc., 1948, pp. 1-32.

Cuber, John F. *Marriage Counseling Practice.* New York: Appleton-Century Crofts, Inc., 1948.

Curran, Charles A. *Personality Factors in Counseling.* New York: Grune & Stratton, 1946.

Davis, Katherine B. *Factors in the Sex Life of 2200 Women.* New York: Harper & Bros., 1929.

Davis, Kingsley. "Statistical Perspective on Marriage and Divorce," *The Annals,* Vol. 270, November, 1950, pp. 9-21.

De Schweinitz, Karl. *Growing Up.* New York: The Macmillan Co., 1935. (Revised)

Deutsch, Helene, *Psychology of Women,* Vols. I and II. New York: Grune and Stratton, 1945.

Dewees, Lovett. "Contraception in Private Practice—A

Twelve Year Experience," *Journal of American Medical Association,* Vol. 110, April, 1938, pp. 1169-72.

Diagnosis and Treatment of Marital Problems, Family Service Association of America, New York. Copyright, 1947–49.

Dickinson, Robert L. *Human Sex Anatomy.* Baltimore: Williams and Wilkins, 1941.

————, and Bean, Lura. *A Thousand Marriages.* Baltimore: Williams and Wilkins, 1931.

Dicks, Russell. *Comfort Ye My People.* New York: The Macmillan Co., 1947.

————. "Pastoral Work" Section, *The Pastor,* Monthly Volumes, 1949–50–51, Nashville, Tenn.

Drinker, Sophie H. *Music and Women.* New York: Coward-McCann, Inc., 1948.

Drown, Frank S., ed. "The Municipal Court of Philadelphia, Annual Reports 1936–49." Philadelphia: Municipal Court.

Duvall, Evelyn Millis. *Building Your Marriage,* Public Affairs Pamphlet No. 113. New York: Public Affairs Committee, Inc., 1946.

————. *Family Living.* New York: The Macmillan Co., 1950.

————. "Loneliness and the Serviceman's Wife," *Marriage and Family Living,* Vol. VII, No. 4, Autumn, 1945, pp. 77-81.

————, and Hill, Reuben. *When You Marry.* New York: Association Press, 1948.

Duvall, Sylvanus M. "The Minister as Marriage Counselor," *Marriage and Family Living,* Vol. IX, No. 3, Summer, 1947, pp. 63-65.

————. *Before You Marry.* New York: Association Press, 1949.

"Education and the Cultural Process," Symposium. *American Journal of Sociology,* Vol. XLVIII, No. 6, May, 1943, pp. 629-32.

Elliott, H. S., and Bone, Harry. *Sex Life of Youth.* New York: Association Press, 1929.

Ellis, Albert, "A Study of Trends in Psychoanalytic Publications," *American Imago,* Vol. 5, No. 4, December, 1948.

Ellis, Havelock. *Psychology of Sex.* New York: Emerson Books, Inc., 1935.

Elmer, M. C. *Sociology of the Family.* New York: Ginn and Co., 1945.

English, O. Spurgeon, and Pearson, Gerald H. *Emotional Problems of Living.* New York: W. W. Norton Co., 1945.

Farris, Edmond J. *Human Fertility and Problems of the Male.* White Plains, N.Y.: The Author's Press, Inc., 1950.

Fiedler, Fred, E. "A Comparison of Therapeutic Relationships in Psychoanalytic, Nondirective, and Adlerian Therapy," *Journal of Consulting Psychology,* Vol. 14, No. 6, December, 1950.

Fishbein, M., and Burgess, E., eds. *Successful Marriage.* New York: Doubleday & Co., Inc., 1947.

Fisher, Mary S. "The Development of Marriage and Family Counseling in the United States," *Parent Education,* Vol. 3, April–May, 1936, pp. 3-9.

Folsom, Joseph K. *The Family and Democratic Society.* New York: John Wiley & Sons, 1943.

Fosdick, Harry Emerson. *On Being a Real Person.* New York: Harper & Bros., 1943.

Foster, Robert G. *Marriage and Family Relationships.* New York: The Macmillan Co., 1950. (Revised)

————. "Servicing the Family through Counseling Agencies," *American Sociological Review,* Vol. 2, No. 5, October, 1937, pp. 764-70.

————, and Wilson, Pauline Park. *Women After College.* New York: Columbia University Press, 1942.

Frank, Lawrence K. *Society as the Patient.* New York: Basic Books, Inc., 1948.

Garrett, Annette. *Interviewing—Its Principles and Methods.* New York: Family Welfare Association of America, 1942.

Gaskill, Evelyn, and Mudd, Emily H. "A Decade of Group Counseling," *Social Casework,* Vol. XXXI, No. 5, May, 1950, pp. 194-201.

Gaylord, Gladys. "A Marriage Counseling Center," chap. XIV, *You and Marriage,* ed., Helen M. Jordan. New York: John Wiley & Sons, 1942, pp. 256-76.

Gesell, Arnold, and others. *Vision: Its Development in Infant and Child.* New York: Paul B. Hoeber, Inc., 1949.

Glueck, Eleanor T. "Wartime Delinquency," *Journal of Criminal Law and Criminology,* Vol. 33, 1942, pp. 119-35.

Glueck, Sheldon, and Eleanor. *Unraveling Juvenile Delinquency.* New York: Commonwealth Fund, 1950.

Goldstein, Sidney E. *Marriage and Family Counseling.* New York: McGraw-Hill Book Co., 1945.

Gomberg, M. Robert. "Counseling as a Service of the Family Agency," in *Family Case Work and Counseling, A Functional Approach,* Jessie Taft, ed. Philadelphia: University of Pennsylvania Press, 1948, pp. 191-219.

————, Stevenson, G., Mudd, E., Searle, R., and others. "Whose Job Is Marriage Counseling," *Better Times,* New York City Welfare News Weekly, Vol. 28, No. 26, March 21, 1947, pp. 6-8.

Gould, Lawrence. *Common Sense Psychoanalysis.* New York: Garden City Press, 1950.

Gregg, Allan. "Lessons to Learn," *Bulletin of the Menninger Clinic,* Vol. 12, No. 1, January, 1948.

Groves, Ernest R. *Case Book of Marriage Problems.* New York: Henry Holt & Co., 1941.

————. *Christianity and the Family.* New York: The Macmillan Co., 1942.

————. *Conserving Marriage and the Family.* New York: The Macmillan Co., 1944.

————. "Consultation Service in Connection with Instruction in Preparation for Marriage at the University of North Carolina," *Parent Education,* II, 1936.

————. "A Decade of Marriage Counseling," *The Annals of the American Academy of Political and Social Science,* Vol. 212, November, 1940.

————. "The First Credit Course in Preparation for Family Living," *Marriage and Family Living,* Vol. III, 1941, p. 67-69; *Social Forces,* XIX, 1941, pp. 236-43.

Gruenberg, Benjamin C. *How Can We Teach About Sex,* Public Affairs Pamphlet No. 122. New York: Public Affairs Committee, Inc., 1946.

Guest, Charles Boyd. "The Position of Women as Considered by Representative American Authors Since 1800," *Summaries of Doctoral Dissertations of the University of Wisconsin,* Vol. 8, 1943, pp. 197-99. (Dissertations unpublished)

Hagedorn, Hermann. *The Bomb That Fell on America.* New York: Association Press, 1950. (New revised edition)

Hamilton, G. V. *A Research in Marriage.* New York: A. and C. Boni, Inc., 1929.

Hamilton, Gordon. *Theory and Practice of Social Case Work.* New York: Columbia University Press, 1940.

Harding, M. Esther. *The Way of All Women.* New York: Longmans, Green & Co., 1933.

Hart, Hornell, and Ella. *Personality and the Family.* New York: D. C. Heath & Co., 1941. (Revised edition)

Hartman, Carl G. *Sex Education of the Woman at Menopause.* Chicago: American Medical Association, 1948. (Revised)

Hertel, Frank J. "Family Social Work," *Social Work Year Book.* New York: Russell Sage Foundation, 1949, pp. 190-96.

Hill, Reuben. "Returning Father and His Family," reprinted from *Marriage and Family Living,* Vol. VII, No. 2, Spring, 1945, pp. 31-34.

———. *Families Under Stress.* New York: Harper & Bros., 1949.

Hiltner, Seward. *Pastoral Counseling.* Nashville, Tenn.: Abingdon-Cokesbury Press, 1949.

Himes, Norman E. *Practical Birth Control Methods.* New York: Modern Age Books, 1938.

———. *Your Marriage: A Guide to Happiness.* New York: Rinehart & Co., 1940.

Hirsch, Edwin W. *The Power to Love.* New York: Citadel Press, 1948.

Hollis, Florence. "Effect of the War on Marriage Relationships," *Papers in Honor of Everett Kimball.* Northampton: Smith College Studies in Social Work, September, 1943, p. 57.

———. *Women in Marital Conflict.* New York: Family Service Association of America, 1949.

Horney, Karen. *New Ways in Psychoanalysis.* New York: W. W. Norton & Co., 1939.

Hughes, Gwendolyn S. *Mothers in Industry.* Impact of the War on Family Life. New York: Family Welfare Association of America, 1942.

Hunt, J. McVicker. "Measuring Movement in Casework," *Jour-*

nal of Social Casework, Vol. 29, No. 9, November, 1948, pp. 343-51.

————, ed. *Personality and the Behavior Disorders,* Vols. 1 and 2. New York: Ronald Press Co., 1944.

Hunt, T. C. "Occupational Status and Marriage Selection," *American Sociological Review,* No. 5, August, 1940, pp. 495-504.

Hutton, L. *The Single Woman and Her Problems.* Baltimore: Williams & Wilkins, 1937.

Johnson, Gerald W. "American Writing, American Life," *New York Times Book Review,* May 1, 1949.

Karpf, Fay. "Dynamic Relationships Therapy," *Social Work Technique,* March–August, 1937.

Kasius, Cora. *A Comparison of Diagnostic and Functional Casework Concepts.* New York: Family Service Association of America, 1950.

————, ed. *Principles and Techniques in Social Case Work.* New York: Family Service Association of America, 1950.

Kelly, E. Lowell. "Marital Compatibility as Related to Personality Traits of Husbands and Wives as Rated by Self and Spouse," *Journal of Social Psychology,* No. 13, February, 1941, pp. 193-98.

Kinsey, A. C., Pomeroy, W. B., and Martin, C. E. *Sexual Behavior in the Human Male.* Philadelphia: W. B. Saunders Co., 1948.

Kirkpatrick, C. "Factors in Marital Adjustment," *American Journal of Sociology,* 1937, pp. 270-83.

Kitching, Howard. *Sex Problems of the Returned Veteran.* New York: Emerson Books, Inc., 1946.

Kluckhohn, Florence, "Women in America," Bevier Lecture Series, University of Illinois, Urbana, Ill., 1950.

Komarovsky, Mirra. *The Unemployed Man and His Family.* New York: Dryden Press, 1940.

Koos, Earl L. *Families in Trouble.* New York: Kings Crown Press, 1946.

————. *The Middle Class Family and Its Problems.* New York: Columbia University Press, 1948.

Kopp, Marie. "Marriage Counseling in European Countries;

Its Present Status and Trends," *Journal of Heredity,* April, 1938, pp. 153-60.

Koster, Donald M. *The Theme of Divorce in American Drama 1871–1939,* 2518 S. Cleveland Avenue, Philadelphia, 1942.

Laidlaw, Robert W. "The Psychiatrist as Marriage Counselor," *American Journal of Psychiatry,* Vol. 106, No. 10, April, 1950.

Lamson, Herbert D. "Next Steps in College Education for Marriage," *Marriage and Family Living,* Vol. XI, No. 2, Spring, 1949, pp. 46-47.

Landis, Carney, *et al. Sex in Development.* New York: Harper & Bros., 1940.

Landis, Judson T., and Mary G. *The Marriage Handbook.* New York: Prentice-Hall, 1948.

Landis, Paul H. *Your Marriage and Family Living.* New York: McGraw-Hill Book Co., 1946.

Leclercq, Jacques. *Marriage and the Family.* New York: Frederick Pustet Co., 1949.

Levine, Maurice. *Psychotherapy in Medical Practice.* New York: The Macmillan Co., 1943.

Levy, John, and Monroe, Ruth. *The Happy Family.* New York: Alfred A. Knopf, 1938.

Lichtenberger, J. P. *Divorce, a Social Interpretation.* New York: McGraw-Hill Book Co., 1931.

Liebman, Joshua Loth. *Peace of Mind.* New York: Simon & Schuster, 1946.

Locke, Harvey, J. "Predicting Marital Adjustment by Comparing a Divorced and a Happily Married Group," *American Sociological Review,* Vol. XII, No. 2, April, 1947.

———, and Klausner, W. J. "Marital Adjustment of Divorced Persons in Subsequent Marriages," *Sociology and Social Research,* Vol. 33, No. 2, November–December, 1948.

Lundberg, Ferdinand, and Farnham, Marynia. *Modern Woman: The Lost Sex.* New York: Harper & Bros., 1947.

Mace, David. *Marriage Counseling,* Marriage Guidance Council, 78 Duke St., London W 1, England.

Mackay, Richard V. *Law of Marriage and Divorce Simplified.* New York: Oceana Publications, 1946.

Maeder, LeRoy M. "Generic Aspects of the Intake Interview," *The Family,* Vol. 23, March, 1942, p. 14.

Marquand, John P. *Repent in Haste.* Boston: Little, Brown and Co., 1945.

"Marriage and Family Education in the Schools," Symposium. *Marriage and Family Living,* Vol. XI, No. 2, Spring, 1949, pp. 40-45.

Martens, Elsie. "Case Work Treatment of Emotional Maladjustment in Marriage," *The Family,* Vol. 25, No. 8, December, 1944, pp. 297-304.

Mautz, W. H., and Durand, J. D. "Population and War Labor Supply," *Journal of American Statistical Association,* March, 1943, p. 37.

McBride, Katherine E. "What Is Women's Education?" *The Annals of the American Academy of Political and Social Science,* Vol. 251, May, 1947, pp. 143-53.

McElroy, Catherine. "Marriage Counseling," *Journal of Social Casework,* 28, 1947, pp. 211-27.

McHugh, Galolo. *Sex Knowledge Inventory and Marriage Counselors Manual.* Durham, N. C.: Family Life Publications, 1950.

Mead, Margaret. "What is Happening to the American Family?" *Journal of Social Casework,* Vol. 28, No. 9, November, 1947, p. 323.

————. *Male and Female.* New York: William Morrow & Co., 1949.

Menninger, Karl, with collaboration of George Devereux. *A Guide to Psychiatric Books.* New York: Grune and Stratton, 1950.

Menninger, Karl. *Love Against Hate.* New York: Harcourt, Brace & Co., 1942.

Menninger, William C. "Facts and Statistics of Significance for Psychiatry," *Bulletin of the Menninger Clinic* (Topeka), Vol. 12, No. 1, January, 1948.

————. *Psychiatry: Evolution and Present Status.* Ithaca, N.Y.: Cornell University Press, 1948.

Merton, R. K. "Intermarriage and the Social Structure—Fact and Theory," *Psychiatry,* 4, August, 1941, pp. 361-74.

"The Modern American Family," *The Annals of the American Academy of Political and Social Science,* Vol. 160, March, 1932.

Monahan, Thomas P. *The Pattern of Age at Marriage in the United States.* Philadelphia: Stephenson Bros., 1951.

Moore, Bernice M. *Women After the War.* U.S.O. Division, National Board, Y.W.C.A., New York, 1947.

Morgan, Mildred I. "Course Content of Theory Courses in Marriage Counseling," *Marriage and Family Living,* Vol. XII, No. 3, Summer, 1950, pp. 95-99.

Mowrer, Ernest R. "Recent Trends in Family Research," *American Sociological Review,* Vol. 6, No. 4, August, 1941, pp. 499-511.

Mowrer, Harriet R. *Personality Adjustment and Domestic Discord.* New York: American Book Co., 1935.

Mudd, Emily H. "Analysis of 100 Consecutive Cases in Marriage Council of Philadelphia," *Mental Hygiene,* Vol. 2, No. 2, April, 1939, pp. 198-217.

————. "Counseling, a Philosophy and Method," *The Cyclopedia of Medicine, Surgery and Specialties.* Philadelphia: F. A. Davis Co., 1945.

————. "How Women Adjust to Marriage," Part 5, Chapter 6, in *Successful Marriage,* Fishbein, M., and Burgess, E., eds. New York: Doubleday and Co., 1947.

————. "Marriage Counseling," *The Cyclopedia of Medicine, Surgery and Specialties,* Vol. 11. Philadelphia: F. A. Davis Co., 1951.

————. "Marriage Counseling as Afforded by Recently Developed Marriage and Family Counseling Clinics," *The Family,* Vol. XVIII, No. 9, January, 1938, p. 310.

————. "Sex Education for the Married Couple," *Hygeia,* Vol. 19, August, 1941.

————, and Freeman, Charlotte Hume. *Some Effects of the War on Women,* Official U.S.O. Bulletin No. 29. New York: Woman's Press, 1945.

————, Freeman, Charlotte Hume, and Rose, Elizabeth Kirk. "Premarital Counseling in the Philadelphia Marriage Council," *Mental Hygiene,* Vol. XXV, No. 1, January, 1941, pp. 98-119.

————, Froscher, H. B., Preston, M. G., and Peltz, W. L. "Some Effects on Casework of Obtaining Research Material," *Social Casework,* Vol. 31, No. 1, January, 1950.

————, and Gaskill, Evelyn. *When Your Man Comes Home,* U.S.O. Division, National Board, Y.W.C.A. New York: Woman's Press, 1945.

————, and Preston, M. G. "The Contemporary Status of Marriage Counseling," *The Annals,* Vol. 272, November, 1950.

————, and Whitehill, Jean L. "Use and Misuse of Books in Counseling," *Parent Education,* Vol. IV, No. 3, February, 1938.

National Marriage Guidance Council, *Syllabus for the Training of Marriage Counselors* (London, W.C. 1, 1949).

National Resources Committee. *Problems of a Changing Population.* Washington: Government Printing Office, 1938, p. 143.

Nelson, Janet F. *Marriages Are Not Made in Heaven.* New York: Woman's Press, 1947. (Revised)

Nimkoff, Meyer. *Marriage and the Family.* Boston: Houghton Mifflin Co., 1947.

Odegard, O. "Marriage and Mental Disease—A Study in Social Psychopathology," *Journal of Mental Science,* 92, 1946, pp. 35-59.

Ogburn, William F., ed. *American Society in War Time.* Chicago: University of Chicago Press, 1943.

Osborne, Ernest W. *Family Scrapbook.* New York: Association Press, 1951.

Parsons, Talcott. "Age and Sex in the Social Structure of the United States," *American Sociological Review,* October, 1942, pp. 604-17.

Patients in Mental Institutions, 1944, U.S. Department of Commerce, Bureau of the Census. Washington, D.C.: Government Printing Office, 1947.

Pavlov, Ivan Petrovich. *Lectures on Conditioned Reflexes,* Vol. 1, tr. by W. Horsley Gantt. New York: International Publishers, 1928, p. 41.

Plant, James S. *Personality and the Cultural Pattern.* New York: The Commonwealth Fund, 1937.

————. "Present Problems of Marriage Counseling," *Mental Hygiene,* Vol. XXIII, No. 3, July, 1939, pp. 355-62.

Popenoe, Paul. "The First Ten Years of the American Institute of Family Relations," *Mental Hygiene*, XXI, 1937, pp. 218-23.

————. *Modern Marriage*. Los Angeles: American Institute of Family Relations, 1945. (Revised)

Porter, E. H., Jr. *An Introduction to Therapeutic Counseling*. Boston: Houghton Mifflin Co., 1950.

Powdermaker, Florence, and Grimes, L. I. *Children in the Family*. New York: Farrar & Rinehart, 1940.

Preston, M., Mudd, E., Peltz, W., and Froscher, H. "An Experimental Study of a Method for Abstracting the Content of Social Case Records," *Journal of Abnormal and Social Psychology*, Vol. 45, No. 4, October, 1950, pp. 628-46.

Pritchett, H. L. "Marriage Teacher-Counselor Relationships," *Marriage and Family Living*, Vol. XI, No. 2, Spring, 1949, pp. 47-50.

Public Assistance Reviews. Pennsylvania Department of Public Assistance, 1936–49.

Rasey, Mabel. "Marriage Counseling in a Family Agency," *The Family*, Vol. 24, No. 2, April, 1943, pp. 65-71.

Rauch, David. "The Caseworker in Family Life Education," *Journal of Social Casework*, Vol. 29, No. 9, November, 1948, pp. 362-65.

Reimer, Svend. "Married Veterans Are Good Students," *Marriage and Family Living*, Vol. IX, No. 1, 1947, pp. 11-12.

Reynolds, Frank W., and Price, David E. "Federal Support of Medical Research through the Public Health Service," *American Scientist*, Vol. 37, No. 4, 1949.

Robert, David E. *Psychotherapy and a Christian View of Man*. New York: Chas. Scribner's Sons, 1950.

Robinson, Virginia, ed. *Training for Skill in Social Case Work*. Philadelphia: University of Pennsylvania Press, 1942.

Rockmore, Myron J. "Social Case Work as Therapy," *Journal of Psychiatric Social Work*, Vol. XVIII, No. 4, Spring, 1949.

Rockwood, Lemo D., and Ford, M. E. N. *Youth, Marriage and Parenthood*. New York: John Wiley & Sons, Inc.; London: Chapman & Hill, Ltd., 1945.

Rogers, Carl R. *Counseling and Psychotherapy*. Boston: Houghton Mifflin Co., 1942.

——. *Client Centered Therapy*. Boston: Houghton Mifflin Co., 1951.

Rose, Elizabeth Kirk. "Clinical Aspects of the New Premarital Medical Examination Law," *Weekly Roster and Medical Digest*, Vol. XXXV, No. 41, June 1, 1940, p. 1233.

Rosenbaum, Milton. "Emotional Aspects of Wartime Separations," *The Family*, Vol. 24, No. 9, January, 1944, pp. 337-41.

Ryan, W. Carson. "Family Life Education in the Schools," *Marriage and Family Living*, Vol. XI, No. 2, Spring, 1949, pp. 40-41.

Sauer, Mary L. "Marital Counsel in a Catholic Case Work Agency," *Pennsylvania Social Work*, Vol. 6, No. 1, July, 1939, pp. 26-28.

Saul, Leon J. *Emotional Maturity*. New York: J. B. Lippincott Co., 1947.

——. "The Individual's Adjustment to Society," *The Psychoanalytic Quarterly*, Vol. XVIII, No. 2, April, 1949.

Scheidlinger, Saul. "Group Therapy—Its Place in Psychotherapy," *Journal of Social Casework*, Vol. 29, No. 8, October, 1948, pp. 299-304.

Schindler, Carl J. *The Pastor as a Personal Counselor*. Philadelphia: Muhlenberg Press, 1942.

Schmidl, Fritz. "On Contact with the Second Partner in Marriage Counseling," *Journal of Social Casework*, January, 1949, p. 30.

Slater, Elliott. "A Note on Jewish-Christian Intermarriage," *Eugenics Review*, 39, April, 1947, pp. 17-21.

Sorokin, P. A. *Social Philosophies of an Age of Crisis*. Boston: Beacon Press, 1950.

Spock, Benjamin. *Pocket Book of Baby and Child Care*. New York: Pocket Books, Inc., 1946.

Staples, Edmund D. "Role of the Church in Education for Marriage and Family Life," *Marriage and Family Living*, Vol. XI, No. 2, Spring, 1949.

Statistical Bulletin, Metropolitan Life Insurance Co., Vol. 28, No. 4, April, 1947; Vol. 28, No. 10, October, 1947; Vol. 29, No. 7, July, 1948; Vol. 29, No. 9, September, 1948.

Steiner, L. R. *Where Do People Take Their Troubles*. Boston: Houghton Mifflin Co., 1945.

Stern, Edith M. *Mental Illness, A Guide for the Family.* New York: The Commonwealth Fund, 1942.

Stokes, Walter. "Family Counseling," *Medical Annals* of the District of Columbia (March, 1951).

———. "Legal Status of the Marriage Counselor," *Marriage and Family Living,* Vol. XIII, No. 1, Summer, 1951.

———. *Modern Pattern for Marriage.* New York: Rinehart & Co., 1948.

———. "New Frontiers in Parenthood Planning Clinics," *Clinics,* Vol. V, No. 3, 1946, pp. 698-707.

———. "Psychiatric Insights in Marriage Counseling," *Marriage and Family Living,* Vol. XI, No. 2, May, 1949, pp. 68-70.

Stone, Abraham. "Marriage Education and Marriage Counseling in the United States," *Marriage and Family Living,* Vol. XI, No. 2, Spring, 1949, pp. 38-39.

Stone, Hannah, and Stone, Abraham. *Marriage Manual: A Practical Guidebook to Sex and Marriage.* New York: Simon & Schuster, 1939. (Revised edition)

Stone, A., and Levine, L. "Group Therapy in Sexual Maladjustment," *American Journal of Psychiatry,* Vol. 107, No. 3, September, 1950.

Stouffer, S. A., and Lazarsfeld, Paul F. *Research Memorandum on the Family in the Depression,* Bulletin 29. New York: Social Science Research Council, 1937.

Strain, Frances B. *Being Born.* New York: Appleton-Century-Crofts, Inc., 1936.

———. *New Patterns in Sex Teaching.* New York and London: Appleton-Century-Crofts, Inc., 1937.

Strauss, A. "The Influence of Parent Images Upon Marital Choice," *American Sociological Review,* 11, No. 6, 1946, pp. 554-59.

Strecker, Edward A. *Their Mothers' Sons.* New York: J. B. Lippincott Co., 1946.

———, and Appel, Kenneth E. *Discovering Ourselves.* New York: The Macmillan Co., 1943. (Revised edition)

———. *Psychiatry in Modern Warfare.* New York: The Macmillan Co., 1945.

Sullivan, Mark. "Our Times 1936–1946," *Life Magazine,* November 25, 1946, p. 125.

Super, Donald E. "Guidance and Counseling," *Social Work Year Book.* New York: Russell Sage Foundation, 1949, pp. 223-30.

Taft, Jessie, ed. "Counseling and Protective Service as Family Case Work," Pennsylvania School of Social Work, 1946.

Taylor, K. W. "Parent-Child Interaction," in *Marriage and the Family,* Becker and Hill, eds. Boston: D. C. Heath & Co., 1942.

Terman, L. M., et al. *Psychological Factors in Marital Happiness.* New York: McGraw-Hill Book Co., 1938.

Thomas, Dorothy. *Social Aspects of the Business Cycle.* New York: E. P. Dutton & Co., 1925.

Thorman, George. *Broken Homes,* Public Affairs Pamphlet No. 135. New York: Public Affairs Committee, Inc., 1947.

Timmons, B. T. "Preparation of Teachers and Leaders in Family Life Education," *Health Education Journal* (London), October, 1948, pp. 1-7.

———, and Caraway, Iris, "The Role of the Library in Family Life Education," *Marriage and Family Living,* Vol. IX, No. 1, February, 1947, pp. 13-15.

Tregaskis. Richard. *Guadalcanal Diary.* New York: Random House, 1943.

Truesdell, Leon E. *Patients in Mental Institutions, 1944,* U.S. Bureau of the Census. Washington, D.C.: Government Printing Office, 1947.

Twyeffort, Louis H. "Therapy in Psychoneurosis" (Bibliotherapy), *The Cyclopedia of Medicine, Surgery and Specialties,* Vol. XII. Philadelphia: F. A. Davis Co., 1942.

Waelder, Elsie M. "Casework with Marital Problems," *Journal of Social Casework,* May, 1947, p. 168.

Waller, Willard W. *The Family: A Dynamic Interpretation.* New York: Dial Press, 1938.

———. *War and the Family.* New York: The Dryden Press, 1940.

Ware, Anna B. "Family Counseling Through Family Case Work," *The Family,* Vol. 21, No. 2, November, 1940, pp. 231-34.

Watkins, Gordon S., ed. "The Motion Picture Industry," *The Annals of the American Academy of Political and Social Science,* Vol. 254, November, 1947.

Weeks, H. Ashley. "Differential Divorce Rates by Occupations," *Social Forces,* 21, March, 1943, pp. 334-37.

Wolf, Anna, ed. *The Parents' Manual.* New York: Simon & Schuster, 1941.

Women's Bureau, U.S. Department of Labor. *Why Women Work.* Washington, D.C.: Government Printing Office, 1946.

Wood, Leland F. *Making A Home.* Nashville, Tenn.: Abingdon-Cokesbury Press, 1938.

———. *Pastoral Counseling in Family Relationships* (Copyright 1948). Commission on Marriage and the Home, Federal Council of the Churches of Christ in America, May, 1949.

———. "The Training of Ministers for Marriage and Family Counseling," *Marriage and Family Living,* Vol. XII, No. 2, May, 1950, pp. 46-47.

Wortis, S. B. "Successful Sex Adjustment," *Journal of Contraception,* Vol. 4, No. 10, December, 1939.

Young, Kimball. *Personality and Problems of Adjustment.* New York: F. S. Crofts & Co., 1940.

Young, Louise M., ed. "Women's Opportunities and Responsibilities," *The Annals of the American Academy of Political and Social Science,* Vol. 251, May, 1947, pp. 1-224.

Zabriskie, Louise. *Mother and Baby Care in Pictures.* New York: J. B. Lippincott & Co., 1935.

Zimmerman, Carle C. *The Family of Tomorrow.* New York: Harper & Bros., 1949.

APPENDIX A

National and Local Organizations
and Their Addresses

RELATED NATIONAL ORGANIZATIONS

American Association of Marriage Counselors, Janet Fowler Nelson, Ph.D., Secretary, 270 Park Avenue, New York 17, New York. Has information about marriage counselors and marriage counseling services throughout the United States.

American Social Hygiene Association, Walter Clarke, M.D., Executive Director, 1790 Broadway, New York 19, New York. Member agencies in many states.

Family Service Association of America, Frank Hertel, Executive Director, 122 East 22nd Street, New York 10, New York. Has member agencies in cities over the country which offer casework services.

National Association for Mental Health, George Stevenson, M.D., Director, 1790 Broadway, New York 19, New York. Roster of mental hygiene and child guidance clinics available.

National Council on Family Relations, Evelyn M. Duvall, Ph.D., Executive Secretary, 1126 East 59th Street, Chicago 37, Illinois. National membership of professional persons from related fields in the United States, Canada, and several foreign countries.

Planned Parenthood Federation of America, Inc., D. F. Milam, M.D., Director, 501 Madison Avenue, New York 22, New York. Affiliated leagues in many states and cities.

RELATED RELIGIOUS ORGANIZATIONS

The three major religious faiths each have special organizations for the strengthening of marriage and family life. Their representatives are prepared to be of real assistance both in supplying literature and recommending other resources:

Catholic

Family Life Bureau
National Catholic Welfare Conference
1312 Massachusetts Avenue, N.W.
Washington, D.C.
Rev. Edgar Schmiedeler, Director

Jewish

Central Conference of American Rabbis
1124 Prince Avenue
Athens, Georgia
Rabbi Samuel Glasner, Director

Rabbinical Assembly of America
3080 Broadway
New York 27, New York
Rabbi Reuben M. Katz, Chairman of the Committee
on Marriage and the Family

Protestant

Commission on Marriage and the Home
National Council of the Churches of Christ in America
297 Fourth Avenue
New York 10, New York
Rev. Roswell Barnes, Associate General Secretary

FUNCTIONING SERVICES LISTED ALPHABETICALLY ACCORDING TO
STATES

Service	*Director, Executive Secretary, or Chairman*
California	
Family Relations Center 2504 Jackson Street San Francisco 15, California	Henry M. Grant
Family Service of Los Angeles Area 355 South Broadway Los Angeles 13, California	Mrs. Blythe W. Francis, R.S.W.

Service	*Director, Executive Secretary, or Chairman*
Marriage Counseling Service American Institute of Family Relations 5287 Sunset Boulevard Los Angeles 27, California	Paul Popenoe, Sc.D. Roswell H. Johnson, Ph.D.

District of Columbia
Counseling Service   Ray H. Everett, LL.B.
Social Hygiene Society of the
   District of Columbia
927 Fifteenth Street, N.W.
Washington 5, D.C.

Florida
The Marriage Counseling Service   Dean Johnson, Ph.D.
Florida State University
Tallahassee, Florida

Illinois
Counseling Center   Carl Rogers, Ph.D.
The University of Chicago
Chicago 37, Illinois

Marriage Counseling Service   Freda S. Kehm, M.S., Ph.D.
The Association for Family Living
28 East Jackson Boulevard
Chicago 4, Illinois

Kansas
Marriage   and   Pre - Marriage   Robert G. Foster, Ph.D.
   Counseling
The Menninger Foundation
Topeka, Kansas

Massachusetts
Counseling Service   Lester W. Dearborn
316 Huntington Avenue
Boston 15, Massachusetts

Service	Director, Executive Secretary, or Chairman
Michigan	
Counseling and Guidance Service of the Merrill-Palmer School 71 Ferry Avenue, East Detroit 2, Michigan	Mrs. Clara Lyndon, M.S.
Minnesota	
Family Life Division of the Department of General Studies University of Minnesota Minneapolis 14, Minnesota	Mrs. Dorothy T. Dyer, M.S.
Missouri	
Pre-Marital Counseling Service Stephens College Columbia, Missouri	Henry Bowman, Ph.D.
New York	
The Family Counseling Service · The Child Study Association of America 132 East 74th Street New York 21, New York	Mrs. Mildred B. Beck
Jewish Family Service 113 West 57th Street New York 19, New York	M. Robert Gomberg, M.S.W., Ph.D.
Jewish Institute of Marriage and the Family Synagogue House 30 West 68th Street New York 23, New York	Rabbi Sidney E. Goldstein, D.D.
Margaret Sanger Research Bureau 17 West 16th Street New York, New York	Abraham Stone, M.D.
Marriage Consultation Center of the Community Church 40 East 35th Street New York, New York	Abraham Stone, M.D.

254

Service	*Director, Executive Secretary, or Chairman*
Marriage Counseling Service Mothers' Health Center 44 Court Street Brooklyn, New York	Lena Levine, M.D.
Religio-Psychiatric Clinic at the Marble Collegiate Church 5th Avenue and 29th Street New York, New York	Rev. Norman Vincent Peale

North Carolina

Marriage and Family Council, Inc. Chapel Hill, North Carolina	Mrs. Gladys H. Groves

Ohio

Cincinnati Social Hygiene Society 312 West 9th Street Cincinnati 2, Ohio	Roy E. Dickerson, LL.M.
Consultation Service of the Maternal Health Association 2101 Adelbert Road Cleveland 6, Ohio	Mrs. Byron E. Jackson, M.S.
Family Service 312 West 9th Street Cincinnati 2, Ohio	Mrs. Anna Budd Ware, M.A.
First Community Church 1320 Cambridge Boulevard Columbus 12, Ohio	Rev. Roy A. Burkhart
Marriage Counseling Center Ohio State University Columbus 10, Ohio	Merton Oyler, Ph.D.
Marriage Counseling in a Family Court The Juvenile and Domestic Relations Court of Lucas County Toledo, Ohio	Ralph P. Bridgman, M.A.

Service	Director, Executive Secretary, or Chairman
Pennsylvania	
Family Service of Reading and Berks County 620 Franklin Street Reading, Pennsylvania	Mrs. Charlotte K. Hutchinson, M.S.
Marriage Council of Phila-delphia 1422 Chestnut Street Philadelphia 2, Pennsylvania	Emily H. Mudd, M.S.W., Ph.D.
Marriage Counseling Service School of Education Pennsylvania State College Burrows Building State College, Pennsylvania	Clifford R. Adams, Ph.D.
South Carolina	
Marriage Counseling Service Furman University Greenville, South Carolina	Aaron L. Rutledge, Ph.D.
Texas	
Marriage Counseling Services Southern Methodist University Dallas, Texas	Henry L. Pritchett, Ph.D.
Utah	
Bureau of Student Counsel University of Utah Salt Lake City 1, Utah	Rex A. Skidmore, Ph.D.
Marriage Counseling Service Utah State Agricultural College Logan, Utah	C. Jay Skidmore, Ph.D.
Virginia	
Pre-Marriage and Marriage Counseling Service 421 West Grace Street Richmond 20, Virginia	Mrs. Beatrice V. Marion, M.A.
Wisconsin	
St. Michael's Hosp. Family Clinic Milwaukee, Wisconsin	Sister Mary Regis, M.S.

APPENDIX B

Reports from Functioning Services as Furnished by Their Executives, October 1950–April 1951

Listed in the Sequence in Which They Are Mentioned in Footnotes of Chapter 4

Conditions in any functioning service may vary. Each report bears the date on which it was released by its executive. Changes occurring in the service following this date are not covered by this report.

THE FAMILY COUNSELING SERVICE

OF

THE CHILD STUDY ASSOCIATION OF AMERICA

132 East 74th Street, New York 21, N.Y.

(November 30, 1950)

History, Auspices, Support. The Family Counseling Service under the auspices of the Association was initiated in 1928 within the framework of a larger program of parent education. It is supported by the Association and is open to anyone who applies provided his problem falls within the agency's function. It is through this service that the Child Study Association has its most intensive contact with individual parents.

Staff. The director of the Child Study Association is Mrs. Mildred B. Beck. The Family Counseling Service has on its staff three counselors with extensive psychiatric training. There are in addition three psychiatrists who provide part-time consultative, supervisory, and diagnostic services.

Clients. The range of problems brought to the service is as follows: problems that center around or grow out of parent-child relationships, such as discipline, difficulties in feeding, toilet-

training, and sleeping; also fears, aggressiveness, school difficulties, social adjustments, etc. Most clients have had high
school education or above. The age range of the children
whose families come to our service is from birth through adolescence. The preponderance of cases falls within the pre-
school group. There is no statistical information with regard to
religious background.

Method and Philosophy. With the aid of psychiatrically trained
counselors, parents are helped to gain insight into their problems with their children. The primary focus is on the difficulties arising within parent-child relationships. The service is
concerned with the parents' adjustments to each other as well
as with their own personal difficulties, but primarily as these
problems affect the development of the children. Where the
problem is essentially that of personality difficulties of either
or both parents, referral is made to the appropriate community
resource. In this sense, the service is one of family rather than
marriage counseling as such.

Fee. Fees are individually determined according to the client's
ability to pay.

ACTIVITIES OTHER THAN INDIVIDUAL COUNSELING

Education. The Association has an extensive educational program.

Research. No activity.

In-Service Training. No activity.

MARRIAGE COUNSELING SERVICE
THE ASSOCIATION FOR FAMILY LIVING
28 East Jackson Boulevard, Chicago, Illinois
(November 15, 1950)

History, Auspices, Support. Originally called the Chicago Association for Child Study and Parent Education, the Association under its forty-one member board of directors carried on
a program of leadership to study groups for eleven years before its counseling service, inaugurated in 1936, was made

available to the membership and its group participants. Since 1943 this service has been available to the general public. It provides an opportunity to individuals to discuss the normal problems that are part of everyday family living and attempts to deal preventively with children's problems before they become too deeply rooted in the personality. Often cases coming for child guidance had problems rooted in the marital situation. Because groups included preparation for marriage as well as parent education, premarital counseling also came to be included as part of the counseling service.

Currently about one-fifth of the budget comes from the Community Fund provided a specified sum is raised in contributions by the agency. Fees for group work and counseling and memberships or contributions provide the balance of the funds.

Staff. The agency employs a full-time counseling supervisor and three part-time counselors. All have master's degrees in social work with psychiatric sequence and a minimum of five years previous experience in agencies of recognized standards. Psychiatric consultation has been available since 1945 to the director, Dr. Freda S. Kehm, and the counseling staff.

Method and Philosophy. In the counseling interview the client is offered opportunity to better clarify his problem by describing it to the counselor. He is encouraged to bring out his feelings, attitudes, and emotional needs. He may gain insight as to the dynamics of interpersonal relationships and the mechanisms of his own behavior. From time to time, the counselor helps him to make appropriate interpretations, particularly in terms of the causal relationship of past with present feelings and needs. The counselor is more or less directive depending upon the needs of the particular client. However, the usefulness of counseling is mainly dependent upon the client's ability to establish and use the relationship with the counselor. There are no joint interviews and each partner is seen by a separate counselor.

Clients. The age range of clients is between twenty and fifty, with the largest group being in the thirties. Thirty-four per cent are Jewish, 33 per cent Protestant, and 13 per cent Catholic. About one-tenth represent mixed religious marriages. More than one-third have some or more than college education. Vocationally, the clients tend to business and the professions, with sales work being the most frequent single occupation. Forty and seven-tenths per cent have a child guidance problem, 34 per cent a marital problem, 16 per cent a personal problem, and 6.3 per cent desire premarital counseling.

Fee. Since 1947 there has been a flat fee of $5 an hour. In past years this was less, and earlier the first interview was free to members and group participants. Fee is waived if client is unable to pay. During 1949, about one-fourth were served without fee.

Length of Contact. The majority of applicants are seen for one or two interviews. Others continue for supportive help for as long as six months. Each interview lasts an hour.

ACTIVITIES OTHER THAN INDIVIDAL COUNSELING

Education. Counseling is co-ordinated with the group work program of the agency. A program of parent and family life education is carried on by the group work staff. During the past year over 1,200 discussion groups were led by the staff— in which over 42,000 persons participated.

Research. A sample of 100 cases was studied last year. A similar study is now in progress with data from about 270 clients.

In-Service Training. None.

FAMILY SERVICE
312 West Ninth Street, Cincinnati, Ohio
(November 9, 1950)

History, Auspices, Support. Marriage counseling has always been accepted as an undifferentiated part of the direct casework service. However, in 1935, with the passage of the Social Security Act, Family Service has been in a better position to extend its counseling services to the economically independent group. An eighteen member board of directors determines policy, utilizing staff committees in the study and formulation of policies. The bulk of income derives from Community Chest, the balance from fees, donations, and income from monies willed the agency.

Staff. There are twenty-seven professional staff persons exclusive of homemaker and clerical staffs. This includes those who do mainly direct casework treatment, as well as administrative and supervisory personnel. All caseworkers, including the executive, Mrs. Anna Budd Ware, are graduates of accredited schools of social work. Several psychiatrists are available for consultation. Psychiatric seminars and other in-service training programs are participated in by staff continuously. The agency is a member of Family Service Association of America.

Clients. In 1949, 23 per cent of the 3,075 applicants requested help with marital problems. This represented an increase of 300 marital problems over the previous year. The largest number of married people were between the ages of twenty-five and forty and the majority had been married between two and ten years. The largest proportion of the husbands came from the skilled and semiskilled laboring groups. A few asked for casework help prior to their marriage.

Method and Philosophy. The casework method is used, and the following, based on the caseworker's understanding of the problem, are considered as possible procedures: (1) the maintenance of the status quo because of risk of undermining defenses, (2) offering supportive help which will enable the client to tolerate the situation, (3) attempting to help the client toward the achievement of insight into various factors as they affect his marriage. In every instance the caseworker appeals to that side of the client's personality which enables partners to be more giving to each other and to lessen their own feelings of resentment.

Fee. Fees are charged when there is ability to pay and the range is from $1 to $5 per interview, based on income and size of family. The service is the same irrespective of whether or not a fee is paid.

Length of Contact. Each interview lasts approximately forty-five to sixty minutes. Counseling ranges from short-time help with the focus being on environmental factors to continuing treatment of emotional relationships over a period of months.

ACTIVITIES OTHER THAN INDIVIDUAL COUNSELING

Family Life Education. This program involves educating parents to the normal and emotional development of children during specific age ranges, thereby helping parents evaluate their children's behavior as it relates to a particular period of development in which the child is. It helps parents to differentiate between behavior which is normal at a particular age and that which suggests that the child is having difficulty for which they should seek individual help.

Home Economist. To advise families on financial management problems.

Homemakers Service. Substitute mothers during temporary illness or absence of the mother in order to give the children security when remaining in their own homes.

Council of Churches. One member of the staff serves as an informational and referral resource for Protestant clergy and families they desire to refer.

Community Leadership. Family Service contributes to professional leadership—teaching, records, materials, study projects, joint school and recruitment projects. With other organizations it participates in promotion of social legislation and the improvement of community conditions affecting families.

Research. Research program temporarily discontinued due to limitation of funds. Efforts are being made to obtain monies from foundations. Only planned research at present is that undertaken by graduate students placed with the agency.

In-Service Training. Family Service is an accredited agency for field work training for students placed by graduate schools of social work. Agency has planned psychiatric consultation for staff, and monthly seminars under leadership of psychiatrists. Casework seminars are given by casework director to casework staff on a continuing basis.

FAMILY SERVICE OF LOS ANGELES AREA
355 South Broadway, Los Angeles, California
(November 6, 1950)

History, Auspices, Support. Family Service was organized in 1930 as a resource to assist people with the social and personal problems affecting family life. Until 1934 the chief concern was meeting basic economic needs of unemployed families. When public facilities took over this responsibility, the agency focused on a skilled counseling service. In 1945, the agency's interpretive material mentioned marriage counseling as a specific service for the first time. This service is nonprofit, supported by the Community Chest and managed by a thirty-three member Board of Directors. Mrs. Blythe Francis is the executive director.

Staff. The professional casework staff of twenty-two persons operate from six different district offices. They are all graduates of an accredited school of social work and the majority have five or more years of casework experience. All workers are supervised, and psychiatric consultation seminars and discussion groups are available to staff. A panel of psychoanalysts has been developed in co-operation with the psychiatric consultant.

Clients. To date, there has been no emphasis on premarital counseling. Approximately one-third of the families using Family Service present some marital conflict. Services are available only to persons in the Los Angeles area.

Method and Philosophy. During the initial period of exploration, from three to five interviews, the caseworkers attempt to understand the various manifestations of the problem and help the client clarify his concept of it. (1) It is determined whether help in the environmental area must be given before the marital problem can even be touched on. (2) Possibilities for bringing the other partner into counseling are explored through the client recognizing his problem as marital difficulty. He may then tell the partner of seeking counseling, or plan to bring the partner into participation with the agency. (3) If the partner does not participate, work can be with the client only. Following the exploratory period, a plan may be established with one or both partners to continue for a specified period of time. Joint interviews may be used at certain stages.

Fee. There is a sliding fee scale ranging from $1 to $3 per interview for those who are able to pay.

Length of Contact. Interviews are scheduled for forty-five minutes, usually at weekly intervals. The average length of contact is three months and ranges from those situations that require only one interview to those where contact lasts for six months or longer.

ACTIVITIES OTHER THAN INDIVIDUAL COUNSELING

Education. None.

Research. None.

In-Service Training. None.

JEWISH FAMILY SERVICE
113 West 57th Street
New York 19, New York
(December 28, 1950)

History, Auspices, Support. Jewish Family Service was created in 1874. Its history has been the usual history of family agencies. During its experience in helping families with concrete services it evolved a method of also helping with the usual psychological problems that are attendant upon people making an adjustment to marriage, children, work, and social relationships. It has its own board of directors, which assumes responsibility for the agency's function, its place in the community, and its relationship to the Federation of Jewish Philanthropies of New York, which assumes responsibility for the agency's financial support. A consultation service was established in 1935 as part of the agency's program. The agency has district offices set up at convenient transportation points in the boroughs of Brooklyn, Manhattan, and the Bronx. Office hours are 9:00 to 5:30, plus one evening a week for those clients who are employed.

Staff. The professional staff consists of three people with executive responsibility, eleven district supervisors, eleven associate district supervisors, and sixty caseworkers. Employment qualifications are graduation from an accredited school of social work and, if possible, some experience since graduation. The agency provides regular supervision, district and general staff educational meetings, seminars, and committee activity as part of the training program.

Clients. Clients represent all educational, economic, occupational, and social groups within the Jewish community.

Problems. The major number of problems for the unmarried group are personality difficulties, social adjustment, vocational adjustment, premarital counseling, and problems in relation to family living. The married group presents primarily problems in relation to the marriage itself, or parent-child problems.

Method and Philosophy. The agency's approach is based upon a psychological understanding of the client, his relationship to his problem, and the dynamics which will help the individual client toward a solution. Contact consists of helping a client determine the area of his problem and, in addition to himself, who is involved in its solution (husband and wife, parents and child, unmarried young adult and a parent). Interviews are to examine the client's current experience and help him find out the part he plays in his problem and what he can do to effect a solution. It is the client's experience in working on his problem with the counselor which enables him to effect a change.

Fee. The agency uses a sliding scale, related to family income; fees are 50¢ to $10 an interview.

Length of Contact. Clients are usually seen weekly. In many situations, two members of the family are seen concurrently. The average length of contact is six months.

ACTIVITIES OTHER THAN INDIVIDUAL COUNSELING

Education. Institutes of four to eight sessions for small groups who wish to work on a common problem and whose need is not for individual counseling.

Research. For the past two and a half years the agency has had a program concerned not only with the study of a specific aspect of the agency's work but also with developing a know-how for research in psychological processes.

MARRIAGE AND FAMILY COUNCIL, INCORPORATED
Chapel Hill, North Carolina
(February 13, 1951)

History, Auspices, Support. Marriage and Family Council, Incorporated grew through Professor Ernest R. Groves's increasing specialization in marriage and family life and from the marriage and family counseling he had been doing with college students and their families in the preceding quarter of a century. As his counseling load became more than he could handle even with the help of his wife, Dr. Groves suggested that Mrs. Gladys Groves and he, with a few professional associates, should incorporate to give a broader base to the marriage counseling done by each one. John S. Bradway, director of the Legal Aid Clinic, Duke University, applied to the state of North Carolina for incorporation of the Marriage and Family Council (a) to give advice and assistance in premarital and domestic problems, (b) to co-operate with other professional and lay groups in handling premarital and domestic problems, and (c) to do charitable and educational work in this field. Papers of incorporation were granted March 16, 1940.

This service functions independently, but its officers and advisory board are made up largely of professors in the departments of sociology, education, religion, gynecology, endocrinology, and law at the University of North Carolina, Duke

University, and North Carolina College at Durham. The organization has always been supported chiefly by contributions of time and money from its officers, who comprise the staff. It now has a few outside contributors.

Staff. The present officers consist, in addition to Mrs. Gladys Groves, of four members, all on the staffs of the University of North Carolina or North Carolina College. They have all had many years' experience in marriage counseling, plus a wide range of academic background and training. Each does his own secretarial work, or provides it.

Clients. The number of clients has never been large (since students are not included), averaging one new one weekly. Most cases come from this or nearby states, a few from greater distances. Most clients are married, a considerable number for many years.

Method and Philosophy. Each counselor uses his own methods and follows his own philosophy of counseling. In general, it has been the custom to use these two procedures: (a) to give the counselee unlimited time at each interview (due, in part, to the long distances traveled and the need for returning home soon); (b) to talk separately with husband and wife if both come, but also to see them together.

Fee. Most work of the Council has been free, with fees increasing gradually. In 1950, a policy of charging $5 in all but hardship cases has been followed.

Length of Interview. A few cases have run on for years, finally ending comfortably for the client, either with or without a major change in the outwardly troublesome circumstances. Most cases involve one interview only, either because the counselee got the help he wanted or a satisfactory referral, or because he could not be away from his distant home longer and must do further conferring by mail. Rarely have the Groveses suggested another interview to a client, since they felt that the initiative should come from the client. They have, however, encouraged the counselee's writing at any time.

ACTIVITIES OTHER THAN INDIVIDUAL COUNSELING

Education. In 1942 the Council started its circulating library service of books on marriage adjustment. Carried on largely by mail, this is available to lay and professional people in this and foreign countries. Publications of the staff are a part of their educational work connected with counseling, but are not listed as output of the Council. Best known of the Council's activities are the annual Groves Conferences on Marriage and the Family for marriage educators and counselors, at the University of North Carolina, Chapel Hill, and at North Carolina College, Durham, founded, respectively, in 1934 and 1941 by Ernest and Gladys Groves.

Research. Several Council staff members have done considerable work on their own researches, but nothing is yet ready to report as a product of the Council.

In-Service Training. None.

MARRIAGE COUNCIL OF PHILADELPHIA
1422 Chestnut Street, Philadelphia 2, Pennsylvania
(December 15, 1950)

History, Auspices, Support. This nonprofit community service was started in 1932 by a group of professional and lay persons in the community "to help young married couples and those contemplating marriage to a better understanding of what companionship in married life involves." It is supported by individual memberships, by grants for in-service training and research, and in lesser degree by fees for counseling and educational service.

Staff. The two full-time and three part-time counselors all have graduate degrees in social work, experience in previous case-work positions, and are married. A psychiatrist has always been a member of the staff on a call basis. Psychiatric consultation has been used constantly for individual cases and staff conferences. A psychologist especially trained in dynamic statistics and a psychoanalytically trained psychiatrist are research consultants. Emily Hartshorne Mudd, M.S.W., Ph.D., has been executive director since 1936.

Clients. There were 387 clients in 1949, 53 per cent of whom had some college or postgraduate education. They were predominately Protestant, with one-quarter Jewish, and 14 per cent Catholic. Thirty-eight per cent of the clients were under twenty-five and another quarter under thirty years of age. Twenty-three per cent were engaged, one-tenth single, and the remainder married. In 60 per cent of the cases the partners of clients also came for counseling.

Method and Philosophy. The council attempts to offer the client a positive and dynamic approach to his problem which may result in a better understanding of self, greater assurance, and an enhanced capacity to live adequately in his marriage. Counselors recognize that it takes time for people to change, to grow, and to make adjustments. Therefore, patience, warmth, and understanding, sympathy without indulgence, and tolerance are used to support the client in his effort to adjust. The goal of counseling is to help people over the spots that seem rough to them, and so enable them to grow, develop, and handle their own problems.

Fee. There is a sliding scale fee, based on income, from $2 per interview. This can be adjusted or waived if the client's financial situation warrants. About 84 per cent of Marriage Council clients paid fees averaging $3.20 per interview in 1949 as compared to 38 per cent who paid a much lower average in 1933. Clients' fees are felt to be of primary importance as a part of the agency's structure and of help in the process of counseling. Only in a few instances do they cover the cost of service.

Length of Contact. About half of the clients seen at Marriage Council have one counseling interview. Many of these are engaged individuals. Others with more involved situations are seen weekly, with ten to twenty or more interviews extending over a period of months.

ACTIVITIES OTHER THAN INDIVIDUAL COUNSELING

Educational. The group aspect of Marriage Council work is participated in by the counseling staff under the supervision of a staff member with special experience in teaching and personnel work. Each year this service brings three to five thousand persons in contact with the agency and is practically self-supporting. Preparation of publications for scientific journals and research are considered also to be major responsibilities of the agency staff.

Research. Since 1947 Marriage Council has been engaged in a research project supported by funds from the U.S. Public Health Service and directed towards a systematic evaluation of marriage counseling as a means for the promotion of good mental health. Prior to that time a foundation grant initiated research on the effects of premarital counseling.

In-Service Training. In 1947 the Veterans Administration contracted to use Marriage Council as one of the six Philadelphia clinics in the training program for their neuropsychiatric residents. The purpose was to furnish in-service supervised training in marriage counseling to the graduate physicians assigned. In addition, since the spring of 1950, the training program has been enlarged under grant from the Grant Foundation to include trainees from allied professional backgrounds who already have graduate degrees for a minimum supervised training period of six months to a year.

MARRIAGE COUNSELING SERVICE
THE AMERICAN INSTITUTE OF FAMILY RELATIONS
5287 Sunset Boulevard, Los Angeles, California
(November 9, 1950)

History, Auspices, Support. The Institute, opened in 1930, is incorporated as a nonprofit educational agency by a self-perpetuating group of about fifty people who are prominent in many different community activities. It receives support through its educational activities, sale of literature, and from client fees.

Staff. Paul Popenoe, honorary Sc.D., and Roswell H. Johnson, Ph.D., head the professional staff of more than thirty people who have had special training in marriage counseling. The counselors' backgrounds are varied and represent such fields as sociology, psychology, home economics, religious education, public health nursing, medical and psychiatric social work, and social biology. They have been selected because of their education, training, experience, and natural aptitudes. Graduation from college is a minimum requirement and many of the counselors hold graduate degrees. Once associated with the Institute, they are especially trained in techniques found most successful at the Institute and receive salary from it. Therefore, a continuous program of training in counseling methods is maintained as well as seminars in the use of personality tests. There are, in addition to staff, always a number of interns who are training to become counselors.

Clients. About 10 per cent of the total client group come for premarital help, 15 per cent are concerned with problems of heredity or personality without primary regard for marital difficulty, and the remainder seek help with marital conflicts. In the majority of situations, the husband also enters into counseling eventually.

Method and Philosophy. Methods are adapted to the problems in a given situation since the Institute adheres to no particular cult or body of doctrine, rather considering counseling a personal experience. Emphasis is placed on the counselors' resources, integrity, and ability to get satisfactory results. It has been found that strong adherents to either completely nondirective counseling or to the slow and ponderous Freudian psychoanalytic techniques find that a more eclectic and flexible approach in counseling improves their results. Wide use is made of personality tests.

Fee. There is a standard fee of $5 per interview hour or four interviews for $15. Free service is offered when a person is unable to pay but he is allowed in return to work by helping in the educational department, for example, addressing and stuffing envelopes.

Length of Contact. Interviews are an hour long and usually a series of four interviews, a week apart, is scheduled. Some clients need more time in which to work out their problems and in this situation may continue in the private practice time of their counselor. In such instances, the fees are then paid directly to the counselor.

ACTIVITIES OTHER THAN INDIVIDUAL COUNSELING

Education. This is the most important phase of the Institute's total activity. Continual classes and lectures are offered by staff members throughout Southern California. In addition, classes and seminars are conducted at the Institute. There is a circulating library, wide distribution of literature, and *Family Life* is published as a monthly bulletin. There are weekly radio and television programs. For parents and teachers there is a home study course in sex education.

Research. There is in progress a research project involving follow-up of people after they have become divorced. Marriage adjustment profiles have been done for thousands of clients and these will provide a basis for evaluating marital maladjustment. A study is also in progress which intends to correlate temperament traits with biological data, and also with other aspects of the individual history.

In-Service Training. None.

PRE-MARRIAGE AND MARRIAGE COUNSELING SERVICE
421 West Grace Street, Richmond 20, Virginia
(November 7, 1950)

History, Auspices, Support. This service was conceived as an extension of five existing agencies—Family Service Society, Memorial Guidance Clinic, Instructive Visiting Nurse Association, Richmond City Schools, and the Richmond Ministerial Union. They have assumed responsibility for its financial support and for general supervision of its policies and personnel. After more than a year of studying needs, co-operative community planning resulted in the establishment of this service in 1948 under the directorship of Mrs. Beatrice V. Marion. An executive committee composed of one representative from each of the five supporting agencies plus a layman and a physician administers the service.

272

About half the funds come from Community Chest, nearly a fourth from the Jewish and Protestant churches, and a like amount from the adult education funds of the local schools. Small income is derived also from sale of pamphlets and occasional fees for lectures in other communities or for counseling. The Council of Counseling Agencies, an advisory group made up of representatives from every community agency known to be doing counseling, serves as liaison between the Service and the community.

Staff. The director also serves as counselor. She has a master's degree in marriage education and counseling, has done college teaching, lecturing, and had a limited experience as caseworker in a family agency.

Clients. In a twelve-month period, 141 out of a total of 210 applicants were accepted for counseling. In about 20 per cent of the cases, both partners were seen and in these cases the initial applicant was as frequently the man as the woman. One client in five came for premarital counseling. Religious affiliation is overwhelmingly Protestant, 10 per cent Catholic, and 5 per cent Jewish or another faith.

Method and Philosophy. Counseling is client-centered in a somewhat broader sense than that associated with nondirective counseling. Casework includes such techniques as psychological support, clarification, and, to a limited degree, insight development. The primary goal is to help the individual achieve a better adjustment and secondarily to stabilize the marital situation.

Fee. No fees were charged to persons or organizations in the Richmond area during 1949–50. The policy of fee charging is being studied.

Length of Contact. Each interview lasts for sixty minutes or longer. The average length of contact is from one to four interviews.

ACTIVITIES OTHER THAN INDIVIDUAL COUNSELING

Education. The director's time is nearly equally divided between educational work with groups and individual counsel-

273

ing. A marriage relations course is taught at the Richmond Professional Institute of William and Mary College. A semi-weekly column is written for the local paper over a pen name. In a year, it was estimated that contact was made with 6,350 persons, representing the following groups, through lectures and group counseling: young people and young adults, parents in relation to their children's needs, professional groups regarding counseling techniques or family life educational materials and methods, general adult audiences in relation to marriage or marriage counseling service.

Research. None.

In-Service Training. None.

MARRIAGE COUNSELING IN A FAMILY COURT
THE JUVENILE AND DOMESTIC RELATIONS COURT OF
LUCAS COUNTY, TOLEDO, OHIO
(February 4, 1951)

History, Auspices, Support. The Court of Domestic Relations of Lucas County was established in November, 1924, when the voters of the County elected a judge who was designated Judge of the Court of Domestic Relations of the Common Pleas Court. Developing an idea that originated in 1914 in the Domestic Relations Court of Hamilton County, Cincinnati, Ohio, the primary purpose of this new court was "to rehabilitate disintegrated and broken families, and to guide and protect children in need of its special consideration and care."

In November, 1936, Paul W. Alexander was elected Judge of this Court. Previously active in community movements for the welfare of families and children, from his first day in office he strove to make court procedures more effective in conserving and strengthening marriages and in rehabilitating children who get into trouble.

In May, 1938, on the day when a permissive state statute became effective, Judge Alexander appointed one of the Court's woman probation officers to serve as marriage counselor. At first, under casework supervision, she worked only with marital partners in litigation who were referred by the Court. Later she included troubled partners who were considering whether or not to initiate litigation or how to work out better adjustments. Despite frequent changes in personnel, the service operated continuously throughout the years, and for one period of about a year there were two counselors.

These first twelve years of experimentation have made increasingly clear that adults with marriage troubles can be helped to understand their difficulties more realistically and to behave more rationally if, as with children, they can talk informally with professionally trained counselors before their cases are heard by the Court, or even after a preliminary hearing and before final disposition. It has been seen also that counseling services can facilitate administrative and legal procedures, and so work to decrease the over-all cost of Court operations.

As it now operates, this service is not a reconciliation department, of which there are many in the divorce courts. It is a casework and counseling service. In the words of Judge Alexander, it has the following functions: to help partners learn how to live together; to help partners who cannot or will not do this to compose their emotional and financial differences as peaceably as possible; with both groups to work out plans for the healthiest possible care and development of any children who may be involved; and to help those who have finally separated to prepare for single blessedness and/or future happier marriages. In addition, the Court expects its marriage counselors to work in the community for the development of marriage education and premarital counseling services. These ideas won acceptance increasingly, so that in the summer of 1950 it became possible to augment the staff by the addition of a second trained counselor and an apprentice counselor.

Staff. Three marriage counselors now comprise the staff, two women and one man, from widely differing backgrounds. One has a doctorate in social work and a law degree. Another has completed requirements except for publication for a doctorate in education, with a major in student personnel work and marriage counseling. The third counselor has a master's degree in home economics, and is now working towards a doctorate. All three have had extensive experience in their own major fields as well as additional work in marriage counseling.

These marriage counselors are members of a professional staff numbering thirty which mans the Juvenile Court, the Child Study Institute (a detention home operated as an in-patient child guidance clinic), and the divorce Court. Counselors' offices are in tiers which house Juvenile Court referees, intake workers, and probation counselors, and a secretarial staff of twenty which serves both juvenile and adult divisions of the Court. They work under casework supervision and integrate administratively with other Court functions. Through daily staff contacts and biweekly staff conferences, as well as with their own clients, they secure vivid first-hand knowledge about many different kinds of families and family troubles.

Clients. Clients are referred to marriage counselors (a) about 20 per cent by the Court in the course of litigation; (b) about 45 per cent by social and religious workers, physicians, relatives and friends, and attorneys, while litigation is under consideration or after it has been instituted, generally in the hope of forestalling or sidetracking it; and (c) about 35 per cent by themselves for help in understanding or adjusting their own marital difficulties. In every case there are potentially two counseling clients, and more if there are teen-age children or in-laws living in the family.

Method and Philosophy. All clients are assured of professional relationships with their counselors. In the case of a client in the first group, the counselor is generally asked to make a report to the Court on the interpersonal aspects of the failing marriage, including suggestions for Court action. With this the counselor has to make crystal clear his role and relationships. The judge considers himself and the Court bound by the American system of jurisprudence to render no decision or disposition of a case except upon competent evidence to which both sides must have access. The client is told that if his statements should be transmitted to the judge, they will not be used against him. In twelve years no client, litigant, or

276

lawyer has complained of this procedure. With this group, also, the counselor has to help the client reckon with court procedure and with the inescapable authority of the law, including past and possible future Court decisions and decrees.

With the second group, the counselor has the delicate responsibility of helping the client to examine and understand the pros and cons of the legal action that is being contemplated, especially its probable consequences on all who may be directly affected. With some, feelings run so deeply and compulsively that this is hardly possible. The drive to escape from the responsibilities of marriage or to punish a partner is overpowering and blinding. With other clients this understanding becomes possible through casework treatment in which the client gains a certain amount of insight into the emotional dynamics of his own personality. In these cases, especially, the counselor's objective is to foster acceptance of self and of the responsibilities of the marriage relationship, to the point where clients are able to make less emotionalized and more realistic decisions, and so to conduct relationships with partners on a more acceptable and satisfying level.

With the third group which comes for help in trying to keep their marriages intact, the counselor's purpose may be described as attempting to help clients reach such a point of self-acceptance and of freedom from inner and outer pressures that they are better able to mobilize their abilities for working out satisfactory adjustments with their partners.

On request, the Court's clinical psychologist and consulting psychiatrist are available for analysis and evaluation of counselors' diagnoses and treatment plans, and they are so used on about six cases a month. About four cases each month are referred to the Mental Hygiene Center, an independent community service staffed by a psychiatrist, psychologist, and social caseworker. On other cases, there is close co-operation with private and public casework agencies, with public relief organizations, and with socially and psychologically oriented pastors, physicians, and lawyers.

Figures collected recently during one year indicated that for every individual who sought marriage guidance from the private agencies of the community, there were about thirty who came to the Court and filed divorce actions.

Fee. No fees of any kind are charged.

Length of Interview. Intake interviews, with or without appointment, are available daily between 8:30 A.M. and 4:30 P.M. Monday through Friday, and between 8:30 A.M. and noon Saturdays. Marriage counselors take turns serving as intake workers. Being a public agency, every applicant is given at least one interview. Applicants include all kinds and conditions of persons, from business executives and professional people to clients of relief agencies. Women outnumber men in the proportion of three to two. Interviews last from half an hour to one hour and a half, depending on need and circumstances. There are at present eighty referrals and applications each month. Approximately three-fifths are seen only once and many of these are referred to other agencies. The other two-fifths are accepted as "major cases" and receive from two to a dozen or more interviews each, the average being six to seven per client. Clients generally are seen individually, occasionally jointly.

ACTIVITIES OTHER THAN INDIVIDUAL COUNSELING

Education. During the last four months of 1950, marriage counselors gave an average of four talks per month to community groups, such as parent-teacher associations, clubs, and church societies; and they gave lectures in professional training seminars and college courses at the rate of two per month. During the spring of 1951 one counselor conducted a marriage study seminar for engaged couples and a marriage adjustment seminar for young married couples (group counseling experiments meeting weekly for 6 to 8 weeks). These were sponsored by one of the community's group work agencies.

Research. A systematic study and evaluation of counseling procedures has been initiated. Beginning January 1, 1951, each major case is being analyzed by means of a schedule which tabulates pertinent facts, and which makes provision for estimating the manner in which counseling is used by the client and for measuring client movement. In constructing this instrument, concepts and categories developed by Marriage Council of Philadelphia (Emily H. Mudd, director), and by the Institute of Welfare Research of the New York Community Service Society (J. McV. Hunt, director), were borrowed freely. Its use is encouraging systematic and comparable methods of handling client relationships and recording interviews, and an attitude of inquiry and evaluation in daily operations.

In-Service Training. Consultation with the Court's clinical psychologist and consulting psychiatrist and the biweekly staff meetings on current cases and related professional problems constitute the only in-service training of staff members that is carried on at the present time.

MARRIAGE COUNSELING SERVICE
MOTHERS' HEALTH CENTER
44 Court Street, Brooklyn, N.Y.
(February 1, 1951)

History, Auspices, Support. The Marriage Counseling Service was inaugurated in 1947 under the auspices of the Mothers Health Center in Brooklyn. It is affiliated with the New York State League for Planned Parenthood and the Planned Parenthood Federation of America. After a year of experimental study, it was found that patients coming for contraceptive service often raised problems in relation to their lack of sexual response. The medical director, Dr. Lena Levine, and psychiatric social worker, working together, did a year of experimental study to determine whether, and in what way, marriage counseling service could help these patients. It was found that in many cases the problem was limited to the sexual area and could be helped by brief psychotherapy. It seemed expedient that this service be offered as a part of a family planning agency.

The Center is supported jointly by the Kings County Committee for Planned Parenthood and the Brooklyn Section, National Council of Jewish Women.

279

Staff. Counseling Service is handled by an experienced psychiatric social worker, in consultation with Dr. Levine, a psychoanalyst with extensive background in gynecology and marriage counseling.

Method and Philosophy. Diagnosis and treatment is offered concerning sexual difficulties related to the emotional adjustment of the individual and problems in the interpersonal relationships in marriage. Service is limited to brief psychotherapy, psychoanalytically oriented. Premarital counseling is offered individually or in groups. Premarital problems in the same area as marital problems are also treated.

Clients. In 1950, there were 97 clients who came for marriage counseling and 147 who wanted premarital counseling. Problems handled are those where the presenting problem is focused in sexual maladjustment. The majority of couples coming for help have been married less than five years.

Fee. Fees range from no charge to $6 per interview depending upon the client's income.

Length of Contact. Husbands and wives are usually interviewed separately, then together. Most cases average about three interviews. If long-time, intensive contact is required, the case is referred for psychiatric help.

ACTIVITIES OTHER THAN INDIVIDUAL COUNSELING

Education. Talks to groups of college students, nurses, medical students, clubs, veterans' groups, etc.

Research. Clinical research—a follow-up study of premarital and marriage counseling cases is now beginning.

In-Service Training. None at present.

THE MARGARET SANGER RESEARCH BUREAU
17 West 16th Street, New York City
(January 24, 1951)

History, Auspices, Support. Since the establishment of the Bureau in 1923, problems of marriage, particularly in the area of sex and reproduction, have been diagnosed and treated by the medical director and staff members of the Bureau. In 1943 a premarital program was instituted by Dr. Robert Laidlaw, and in 1945 a Premarital Consultation Service for couples was established. From 1945 to 1947 an experimental group in sexual maladjustment was carried on by the medical director, Dr. Abraham Stone, and Associate Director, Dr. Lena Levine. In 1946 an infertility psychotherapy service was established in which marital problems of the infertile couple are treated. The service functions under the auspices of the Margaret Sanger Research Bureau, which is supported by patient fees and voluntary contributions.

Staff. In addition to the medical director and associate director, the Bureau has two staff physicians, who have volunteered their services.

Clients. Patients are lower and middle class white persons, about 60 per cent Jewish, mostly of high school educational level, some of college level, native Americans, first or second generation.

Method and Philosophy. The treatment is preventive and curative. Preventive treatment consists of premarital consultation with the couple individually or in groups. Curative treatment is practiced with those who have premarital and postmarital problems. The techniques are: (1) support and reassurance; (2) information and advice; (3) intellectual insight. Short-term analytically oriented psychotherapy is used in a few selected cases.

Fee. A fee of $1 is charged.

Length of Interview. The premarital contact consists of one session from two to three hours. In the infertility service the treatment varies from two to fifteen hours.

ACTIVITIES OTHER THAN INDIVIDUAL COUNSELING

Education. (1) Orientation lectures on infertility, on sex and reproduction. (2) Orientation lectures on contraception. (3) Lectures to medical and nonmedical students, physicians, and nurses.

281

Research. (1) New project begun to determine sensitivity of vaginal mucosa and relationship to vaginal orgasm. (2) Group therapy. (3) Clinical research into methods of psychotherapy in infertile couples.

In-Service Training. Physicians are continually trained in premarital consultations as well as in group therapy.

CONSULTATION SERVICE OF THE MATERNAL HEALTH
ASSOCIATION
2101 Adelbert Road, Cleveland 6, Ohio
(November 27, 1950)

History, Auspices, Support. The Contraceptive Clinic of the Cleveland Maternal Health Association was established in 1928, and three years later, in 1931, the marriage counseling service was offered. It is supported mainly through contributions from interested persons in the community.

Staff. There are three counselors, including the director, Mrs. Hazel Jackson, all of whom are trained family caseworkers. Consultations are available to counselors with members of the medical or psychiatric staff when the need arises.

Clients. About 336 clients came for premarital guidance in 1949. In addition, 599 clients were carried jointly with other departments. Fifty per cent of clients are men. The age range is from sixteen to fifty-four. Educational levels range from high school to college graduates. All religious groups are served.

Method and Philosophy. In premarital counseling, the major functions are to provide sex education, to change unhealthy attitudes, to treat accessible personality problems responsive to limited contact, and, when indicated, to prepare for referral to other community resources. Counseling can be effective only through the use of established casework principles of understanding clients through observation and evaluation. In the postmarital group, the largest number of clients come with sexual problems. Treatment varies with the individual. One of the valuable aids in short-time treatment is the availability of early psychiatric consultation for the counselor or directly with the client. Follow-up procedure (which consists of letters and interviews) has supported the belief that the relief of anxiety and the insight that can be obtained have been sufficiently effective to enable many of these people to carry on the marriage relationship satisfactorily.

Fee. The fee is based on a sliding scale and ranges from 50¢ to $3 per interview. Agency policy permits waiving the fee in certain low-income situations.

Length of Contact. The length of each interview is usually one hour, although first interviews may require more time, especially when both partners are seen. The number of interviews per client ranges from one to five.

ACTIVITIES OTHER THAN INDIVIDUAL COUNSELING

Education. Lectures for graduate and undergraduate students regarding marriage counseling. Lectures and discussions for church and civic groups on education for family living.

Research. None.

In-Service Training. No formal training program. Many local and out-of-town professional workers come for knowledge and guidance.

FAMILY SERVICE OF READING AND BERKS COUNTY
620 Franklin Street, Reading, Pennsylvania
(November 28, 1950)

History, Auspices, Support. This service was initiated in February, 1948, with a gift of approximately $2,000 from the Planned Parenthood Federation. It functioned under a board of public-spirited citizens. In the summer of 1950 the work was incorporated with that of Family Service, and is now supported by Community Chest Funds.

Staff. A full-time trained caseworker carries on the counseling under the direction of Mrs. Charlotte K. Hutchinson, the executive of Family Service.

Clients. In 1949 approximately 75 clients were seen by the part-time counselor-director, Dr. Elmer Horst, a psychiatrist. Of these, 64 per cent were women, 19 per cent had less than ninth grade education, 47 per cent some or complete high school education. There were 52 per cent Protestant clients, 33 per cent Jewish, and 15 per cent Catholic. About 61 per cent were between eighteen and thirty-five years of age, the remainder older. Premarital counseling accounted for 20 per cent of the work. Since April, 1950, when Family Service took over the marriage counseling, there have been 54 applications from married couples. Only two were over thirty-five years of age. Forty-two per cent of the applications were made by men. Occupations of husbands: draftsmen, architects, attorneys, salesmen, skilled textile workers, truck drivers, and so on.

Method and Philosophy. Interviews of one hour are scheduled weekly for husband and for wife. As frequently as possible, when evaluation of the problem indicates, husband and wife have separate counselors. Joint interviews are used, depending on the problem and personalities of the individuals. When necessary, other community resources are used: medical, religious, legal, psychiatric, etc. The caseworkers review all cases with the agency's analytically trained psychiatrist consultant for guidance in counseling and correct diagnosis. The philosophy is based on Freudian psychology and the understanding of the dynamics of human behavior.

Fee. Marriage Council discontinued use of fees early in 1950 and is now preparing to study the possible establishment of a fee system some time in 1951.

Length of Contact. Until April, 1950, almost half the clients had only one interview and the remaining group had from two to five. Since April, interviews have varied from one to a total of sixty interviews for a couple. The average has been twenty-four interviews per case.

ACTIVITIES OTHER THAN INDIVIDUAL COUNSELING

Education. Marriage Council initiated a marriage counseling seminar for young people of the community—a series of six lectures and discussions. A selected group of high school teachers were instructed to conduct classes in preparation for marriage and family living and are carrying on the classes. Family Service continues these projects. All counselors speak frequently to civic and educational groups on the subject of marriage.

Research. None.

In-Service Training. None.

MARRIAGE AND PRE-MARRIAGE COUNSELING SERVICE
The Menninger Foundation
Topeka, Kansas
(February 26, 1951)

History, Auspices, Support. This service was organized during the summer and fall of 1950 and operates under the auspices of the Menninger Foundation, a nonprofit group concerned with psychiatric treatment, education, and research. At present, support for the counseling service comes both from the Menninger Foundation and from the Grant Foundation in New York City.

Staff. Robert G. Foster, Ph.D., marriage counselor, division of adult psychiatry, is the only member of the professional staff, although plans are being formulated for including a well-trained and experienced social caseworker. Psychiatric consultation, casework and psychological services, both at the Foundation and among professional people in the community, are utilized when needed.

Clients. The program is still too new to allow for evaluation of the client population; however, both premarital and post-marital counseling are offered.

Method and Philosophy. It is felt that various counseling methods must be adapted to the needs of the individual client. In this setting the counselor does not attempt to manipulate the environment but is concerned with the problem's reality factors as well as their relationship to the emotional feelings

285

and experience of the client. Counseling is primarily an educational approach and there is no attempt to basically reconstruct the individual's personality. No one school of thought dominates the approach to diagnosis and service given.

Fee. Fees are charged to clients in accordance with their economic circumstances, with a minimum fee of $10 an hour quoted. Although most people pay from $15 to $25 per interview, some are accepted for as little as $5.

Length of Interview and Contact. Fifty minutes are allowed for each interview. For the most part contacts are brief, ranging from one to twenty or thirty interviews.

ACTIVITIES OTHER THAN INDIVIDUAL COUNSELING

Education. Some educational work in connection with schools, churches, and other community agencies will probably get under way by the spring of 1951.

Research. None at present.

In-Service Training. This service is considering applications for training in counseling that will cover a minimum period of ten months to a year. Applicants must have a Ph.D. degree or its equivalent in social work, psychology, medicine, child development and family relations, or a closely related field.

ST. MICHAEL'S HOSPITAL FAMILY CLINIC
Milwaukee, Wisconsin
(December 26, 1950)

History, Auspices, Support. This clinic started officially in 1948 and functions within the Out-Patient Department of St. Michael's Hospital. It developed out of needs seen in the various out-patient services since their beginning in 1938. Social service and medical counseling had been done, but specialized help such as psychological, spiritual, and psychiatric services had to be requested from the various community agencies. Often individuals and families became discouraged and returned again and again with the same problems. Hence it was felt that a single service area was indicated to insure complete care and follow-up. Priests, doctors, social workers, nurses, psychiatrists, and psychologists now work together in a co-ordinated program to give such a service. There is no social service department in the hospital. All cases needing case-work and Family Clinic service are referred to the Out-Patient Department social service.

Staff. The director, Sister Mary Regis, is a certified public health nurse with a master's degree in nursing education. There are two social workers—one holds a master's degree in social work and the other is a registered nurse with public health nursing and social casework background. Four gradu-ate nurses, all with public health nursing backgrounds, assist with the general Out-Patient Department programs as the point of departure. The staff also includes a member of the Al-coholics Anonymous group whose work is invaluable in the program. The forty to fifty physicians who give their services to the general and special clinics are also indispensable to the Family Clinic program. This is especially true in the areas of maternity and gynecology, medicine, pediatrics, and so forth.

Clients. In addition to the hospital referrals, clients are re-ferred from any and all welfare agencies in Milwaukee County by the Courts, by Alcoholics Anonymous, by the Office of Catholic Education and the Public School Board, by parish priests and Parish Conferences, and by the Archdiocesan Chancery Office. Often referrals for spiritual counseling come from private physicians or psychiatrists.

The proportion of cases requiring postmarital counseling is 98 per cent, and 2 per cent for premarital counseling. Seventy-five per cent of the applications are from women. The age range of clients is from twenty to fifty, with the largest propor-tion falling in the group from thirty-five to forty-five years of age. A large number of children are being referred as well, and here the Clinic finds that it must work also with the parents.

Method and Philosophy. The Family Clinic is a total pattern of service—a Catholic pattern—all staffs serving in their specific capacities as members of the Mystical Body of Christ. The social mission of the Church as well as the social mission of the priests and physicians is activated through the Family Clinic service.

The social service work-up consists of a complete social history, release for medical and social information from other agencies, and a generalized evaluation of the problem at hand. Referral is made according to the immediate need, which is always considered first, whether it be medical, psychiatric, alcoholic, or any other. Intensive follow-through is delayed until the immediate problem has been alleviated. Where the problem is vague, a series of psychological tests are utilized in the clearing procedure and as a preparation for psychiatric care. The case is then referred according to findings. Clearing cases in the medical specialities is an important step in the Family Clinic program. For patients who can afford private medical care the co-operation of the family physician is secured. Family Clinic has aimed to build a good working relationship with the physicians—not only those of the hospital and Out-Patient Department staff, but with all the physicians in order to correlate family clinic work with the medical and psychiatric approaches to problem situations. Our records contain medical reports from physicians treating the cases that come to the Family Clinic for help. Sometimes the spiritual need is of foremost concern. The priest is called in and further clearing is done upon his recommendation. No set rule is followed. Co-operation between staff and the parish units and referring agencies is constantly maintained in the interest of the client. Much of the initiative for treatment is left to the client, who is told to call for further appointment if he wishes to follow through. Follow-up, including home visits when necessary, is deemed essential and is the responsibility of the social service department of the O.P.D.

Fee. There is no specific Family Clinic Fund as such. The Family Clinic is one of the services of the O.P.D. supported by the Hospital. Fees are charged on a sliding scale according to ability to pay. Patients not falling within the low income groups are asked to pay a registration fee according to their means—usually $3 on the first visit and on subsequent psychological service visits. No fee is charged for clergy counseling. Psychiatric service is given in the clinic to those who cannot afford private care. Others are referred to the psychiatrist's office.

Length of Interview. Depending upon the case, sometimes both husband and wife are seen separately and together at one visit. This would entail a period of several hours. The usual interview is one hour, although the client is given as much time as needed. Clients are seen from one month to several months, with revisits at intervals throughout the year as the client feels the need. Interviews, except in psychiatry and psychological testing, are not scheduled for a given time allotment. Some families are known to the department for seven or eight years.

ACTIVITIES OTHER THAN INDIVIDUAL COUNSELING

Education. The Cana and Pre-Cana Program conducted by Father J. J. Holleran in Milwaukee Archdiocese is a significant factor in the over-all Family Program. It accounts for the few requests for premarital counseling. Husbands and wives also are referred to the Cana Conference for supplementary help.

In the alcoholic program the aim is to intensify the spiritual phase through the St. Michael's League monthly program of Mass and Communion followed by a breakfast at which a member of the clergy speaks—not on alcoholism, but on some timely spiritual topic. The League is composed of Catholic alcoholics and their wives—who are active members of A.A. Through this activity we keep in close personal contact with the alcoholics and it gives them a feeling of belonging, along with the co-operation of A.A. Also a refresher course in religion is given twice weekly for those alcoholics who feel the need, and a day of recollection is offered once a year. Many family problems come to our attention through such programs.

Research. None.

In-Service Training. This consists of series of meetings of physicians and priests held periodically for refresher purpose;

series of lectures by the staff psychiatrist to priests on the psychiatric approach to family problems; series of lectures on moral problems to the clergy group. Staff educational activities are mostly through interstaff consultation, conferences, and case discussions.

JEWISH INSTITUTE OF MARRIAGE AND THE FAMILY
Synagogue House
30 West 68th Street, New York 23, N.Y.
(December 5, 1950)

History, Auspices, Support. The Institute was organized formally in 1936 with the co-operation of a committee composed of representatives from Orthodox, Conservative, and Reform groups in addition to representatives from Jewish social agencies. It grew directly out of pastoral and social service experience in the Free Synagogue and the courses in marriage and the family that the director, Rabbi Sidney E. Goldstein, D.D., has given since 1907 in the Synagogue, and since 1922 to rabbis in training in the Jewish Institute of Religion. Support is derived from contributions for services rendered to individuals, families, and social agencies.

Staff. In addition to Dr. Goldstein, who serves as director and consultant, there is a panel of experts from several professional spheres. Each client is first interviewed by the director and then referred to the panel member deemed most competent to deal with the major cause of distress.

Clients. Of the number of clients who used this service in 1949, about half were men and half were women. Many were college graduates, but most came from the high school level. The age range was from eighteen to over fifty. About 40 per cent came for premarital counseling and about 60 per cent for postmarital counseling.

Method and Philosophy. In the program of premarital conferences both partners are assigned readings on the various phases of marriage and family life, and the foundations of marriage and the family, which are fully discussed with them

290

in the course of the interviews. The Jewish concept of marriage is interpreted to every couple. In the program of post-marital consultation every effort is made to establish a correct diagnosis and to formulate a plan of treatment in accordance with accepted procedures and standards in casework and counseling. The Institute is especially concerned with assisting young people to build their marriage upon firm foundations, and endeavors to conserve family life and family values through a discussion of the structure, organization, and function of the family today. These programs of service take on added importance when it is remembered that to the Jewish people the family is not only a social institution, but a covenant with posterity.

Fee. No fees are accepted for Dr. Goldstein's services but each client arranges for a fee with the expert who is called into consultation, if the contact progresses to that point. Fees are then based upon the client's ability to pay.

Length of Contact. Each interview lasts from forty-five minutes to one hour, and the number of interviews depends upon developments in each case.

ACTIVITIES OTHER THAN INDIVIDUAL COUNSELING

Education. Many lectures and discussions on marriage and related subjects are conducted by the director and the panel of experts in answer to requests from the community and distant points.

Research. No information available.

In-Service Training. No information available.

FIRST COMMUNITY CHURCH
1320 Cambridge Boulevard, Columbus, Ohio
(November 9, 1950)

History, Auspices, Support. This program in marriage and family counseling, which began in 1935, is under the auspices of the church and has been supported through the church treasury. Counseling rooms are in the parish house.

Staff. In addition to the director, Rev. Roy A. Burkhart, who is the minister, the counseling staff consists of the parish pastor, a university graduate with extensive clinical training. The minister of men and women, who has a master's degree in education, also assists with counseling. The service is augmented by special church members who have unusual skill or were themselves helped through counseling. These people have understanding of child guidance and the relationships between marital partners. Two psychiatrists and several doctors collaborate with this program as it relates to premarital counseling and the less acute marital problems.

Clients. There is contact with at least 500 different families each year. This includes the 100 couples for whom the director performs the marriage service. Clients are predominantly Protestant and members of the parish. They range in age from eighteen to sixty and for the most part have at least a high school education.

Method and Philosophy. No information available.

Fee. There is no charge for counseling. If clients are not members of the church and are financially able, it is suggested that they might want to make a contribution to the church.

Length of Contact. Client interviews last approximately one hour, and the number per client varies from one to twenty.

ACTIVITIES OTHER THAN PERSONAL COUNSELING

Educational Group Work. Much work is done with young parents expecting their first child, and with older couples concerned with the various aspects of the parent-child relationship.

Research. There is a laboratory research project under way designed to evaluate "What is a good man?" and "How can a good society be developed?" The two psychiatrists who work with this program are active in intensive research projects. One, whose field is children, works with expectant mothers and those whose children are under five years of age. The other, a neuropsychiatrist, concentrates on marital relations and problems of children from six through twelve years of age.

In-Service Training of Marriage Counselors. One seminary student is accepted each year for training in counseling.

The Marriage Consultation Center of the · Community Church
40 East 35th Street, New York 16, N.Y.
(November 8, 1950)

History, Auspices, Support. This service was originally established at the Labor Temple of New York in 1930 by Drs. Hannah and Abraham Stone. In 1932 the center moved to the Community Church of New York under whose auspices it has been functioning continuously ever since as an independent unit with its own staff, under the direction of Dr. Abraham Stone. The Church provides the quarters, telephone and janitorial services, and all staff members contribute their services without remuneration, so that practically no expense is involved in conducting the consultation service.

Staff. The present staff consists of the medical director, two psychiatrists, three gynecologists (with special interest in marriage counseling), a psychiatric social worker, and a nurse and educator who has been under training in marriage counseling at the Center for the past three years.

Clients. Slightly over half the clients are Jewish, about 25 per cent Protestant, and 13 per cent Catholic. Half have high school education and about 42 per cent some college training. Premaritals, which account for about 20 per cent of the service, are seen either individually or occasionally in groups. Postmaritals are always seen individually. From time to time, series of group discussions are held for individuals presenting common postmarital problems. The most recent example was a series of discussions with men troubled with sexual incapacity.

Method and Philosophy. During the interviews, information is provided about the physical, emotional, and social aspects of the marital relation which would help the couple to a better

293

understanding of their own marital situation. An attempt is made to make an early diagnosis of the focal area of maladjustments to determine whether it lies primarily in the personality of the individuals involved, in their interpersonal relationship, or in environmental factors. Counseling is directed also at developing insight into the motivations of behavior of the client and his partner. The aim is to have individuals achieve their own solutions. Directive counseling and guidance are resorted to when necessary.

Fee. A fee of $1 is charged for each consultation and goes to the church treasury. Patients referred by social agencies are seen without fee.

Length of Interview and Contact. The average interview lasts from thirty to sixty minutes. The average number of contacts is about four, although many patients are seen only once, and some as many as a dozen or more times. Patients requiring long-term therapy or psychiatric care are referred to other agencies. However, short-term analytically oriented psychotherapy is used in selected cases by the staff psychiatrist.

ACTIVITIES OTHER THAN INDIVIDUAL COUNSELING

Education. Premarital group discussions are held for individuals without specific problems, lectures for married couples and parent-teacher groups within the church. Lectures are also given by staff members outside the church—in colleges, settlement houses, welfare organizations, and so on.

Research. Studies are under way as follows: the value of the Minnesota Multiphasic Test in premarital and postmarital counseling; short-term group psychoanalytically oriented psychotherapy of personality problems in marriage and potency disturbances in the male.

In-Service Training. A psychiatric social worker and public health nurse, both psychoanalyzed, and taking postgraduate courses for marriage counseling, have been trained for a period of two years and are now members of the staff. A psychiatrist now in analysis and analytic didactic training is being trained.

RELIGIO-PSYCHIATRIC CLINIC
OF THE MARBLE COLLEGIATE CHURCH
Fifth Avenue and 29th Street, New York 1, N. Y.
(April 5, 1951)

History, Auspices, Support. The founding of the Religio-Psychiatric Clinic was the work of Dr. Norman Vincent Peale, the pastor of the church, as an answer to "what to do" about the complex personal problems confronting human beings in our civilization. Dr. Smiley Blanton, who had for many years been interested in the close relationship between psychiatry and religion, was asked to help Dr. Peale meet this need. Founded in 1937, it was one of the first clinics sponsored by a church to deal with human problems through the combining of religion and psychiatry.

The purpose of the clinic is to bring value and meaning to life. It is the function of psychiatry to unearth and reveal the blockings in the unconscious mind that keep a person from leading a normal, healthy, emotional life. But the clinic is based upon the concept that religion and psychiatry can, as therapies, accomplish more together than either can accomplish separately. Religion and psychiatry alike teach that a person can remake his life once he has altered the character of his disturbed unconscious drives. Spiritual regeneration is a basic concept in the theory of human behavior. Man *can* and *does* change.

The clinic hopes to provide help for people suffering from anxiety, excessive fear, depression, and irritability, and for people who have difficulty getting along with others. It has put a special emphasis on helping in marital and family difficulties.

Staff. The staff is composed of Norman Vincent Peale, D.D., and Smiley Blanton, M.D. The associate staff includes two pastors, six physicians, six psychologists, and a secretary. The psychiatrists are doctors of medicine who are specialists in the treatment of mental and emotional disturbances. With certain other specialized training, they may also be psychoanalysts. The psychologists are college graduates, usually with a postgraduate degree of Ph.D., who have specialized in psychology: some in giving vocational, intelligence, and emotional tests, and some in counseling and guidance. The psychologist is especially valuable in the evaluation of habit reactions, and of the structure of the personality. The pastor's contribution is both analytical and therapeutic. He studies and evaluates the person's relationship to moral and spiritual values, and, through his knowledge of the avenues of spiritual experience, helps him to adjust himself to the Divine Source of strength and security.

Method and Philosophy. As the clinic was eventually organized, the staff was composed of ministers, psychiatrists, and clinical and consulting psychologists. The patient is first seen by either a minister or a psychiatrist, and is then assigned to the counselor best suited to his needs. In the routine of the clinic a person may be seen once a week or, occasionally, twice a week, but if he requires more frequent treatment over an extensive period he is referred to a competent and sympathetic psychiatrist outside the clinic who can care for him on a private basis. Clinic patients with similar needs are organized into groups for therapy, for the gaining of additional insight, and for companionship. The troubled person must be made acquainted with the forces that exist in the depths of the unconscious mind and with the conflicts hidden there that disturb his adjustment to his everyday life. The minister and the psychiatrist work together to restore the patient's emotional health by removing the causes of these conflicts, by building up his faith in God and in his own inner powers, and by encouraging him in a more mature philosophy of life.

In some cases patients are referred to psychiatrists or ministers nearer to their own home. Since part of the objective of the clinic is the training of ministers and psychiatrists in this particular type of counseling, it is the hope of the staff to have, eventually, a more extensive list for referral.

Clients. Help is offered to all who come to the clinic, regardless of religious affiliation, place of residence, race, or financial status. But because of the large number of people seeking help, it is necessary for the clinic to select cases in the following order: (1) members of the Marble Collegiate Church; (2) attendants at services in Marble Collegiate Church; (3) patients referred by ministers of other churches; (4) people from the surrounding area; (5) people from distant places who write the clinic seeking help. If no time is available when an interview is requested, the person's name is placed on a waiting list.

The age range of the large majority of patients seen is between nineteen and fifty-five. Most are of high school and college education and are from the major Protestant denominations, but there are also some from non-Christian religions and non-Protestant groups. The vocational status is varied. Approximately 70 per cent come for counseling after marriage and 30 per cent before marriage.

Fee. The staff of the clinic contributes its services and no charges are made to the patients.

Length of Contact. The number of interviews for the majority of applicants seen ranges from one to forty. Each interview lasts thirty to fifty minutes.

ACTIVITIES OTHER THAN INDIVIDUAL COUNSELING

Education. (1) In 1951 a course on "Human Behavior" for ministers, physicians, and social workers, consisting of fifteen lectures. Staff includes ministers, psychiatrists, clinical psychologists. (2) Clinic patients with similar needs are organized into groups. Three groups now in session.

Research. None.

In-Service Training. Two ordained ministers, both with several years of pastoral and clinical experience, are having special training.

CINCINNATI SOCIAL HYGIENE SOCIETY
312 W. 9th Street, Cincinnati 2, Ohio
(January 24, 1951)

History, Auspices, Support. The Cincinnati Social Hygiene Society, organized in 1917, is a Council of the Cincinnati Public Health Federation and an affiliate of the American Social Hygiene Association. It is a wholly autonomous organization with its own budget, board of directors, and staff, financed by the Community Chest of Cincinnati and Hamilton County, and housed in the Chest building. In its pioneer days the first task was the closing of the red-light district in Cincinnati. Over the years it has developed a unique, many-sided, community-wide program in which special emphasis is placed upon education for successful marriage and family life. This emphasis is carried out through group work and individual counseling. The society has no record of when it first undertook marriage counseling. Such services have evolved with the general development of the program.

Staff. The staff consists of an executive secretary, Roy E. Dickerson, LL.B., LL.M., who directs the entire program, supervises all the interviews, and conducts the majority of them himself; and three assistants (one a part-time volunteer) and a secretary-receptionist. The director studied extensively in mental hygiene and principles of psychiatry. He teaches classes, on the graduate level, at Teachers College, University of Cincinnati, in Social Hygiene Aspects of Human Relations and Education for Family Life. He directs institutes on Education for Family Life and Counseling in other colleges and universities, and is the author of numerous books, articles, and pamphets. The three other staff members are college graduates who have had graduate courses in related fields; one is a public health nurse, another a former college dean of women.

Method and Philosophy. About 225 interviews are sought annually, mostly for help with marital discord. Clients present the usual range of premarital and marital difficulties and are dealt with according to recognized principles of counseling on the assumption that the Society's function is to help the individual solve his own problems. When indicated, these persons are referred to physicians, psychologists, psychiatrists, clinics, and other sources of help. Frequent conferences regarding individual cases are held with a psychiatrist who is a board member. Contraceptive advice is not given.

Clients. Breakdown of age, education, number of premaritals, number of men and women, etc., is not available.

Fee. No fees are charged to residents of Hamilton County.

Length of Contact. Interviews vary in length but usually take an hour, and average three or four per individual.

ACTIVITIES OTHER THAN INDIVIDUAL COUNSELING

Education. Most of the time and resources of the Society are devoted to services which include the following: a varied program for Negroes under a Negro staff member; preparing curriculum outlines for the integration of family life education at all grades in the Cincinnati public schools; directing teacher training seminars for the Board of Education; conducting parent education classes in P.T.A. and other groups; counseling with boys and girls referred from the juvenile court; providing classes for girls in the Detention Home; maintaining, for research and circulation, a library of more than a thousand books and pamphlets and several hundred digests of magazine articles; publishing with the Cincinnati Public Library an annotated guide to readings in sex education; supplying the Health Department with 9,000 copies annually of a leaflet distributed to resident women who have recently become mothers, encouraging them to begin sex education of their children early; setting up a rehabilitation service for girls released from state and local corrective institutions; directing institutes for clergymen; conducting hearings before the City Council leading to the employment of policewomen; and conducting blood testing programs.

Research. None in a formal sense.

In-Service Training. All staff members are provided time and tuition for an occasional college training course or private psychiatric seminar.

COUNSELING SERVICE
316 Huntington Avenue, Boston, Massachusetts
(October 26, 1950)

History, Auspices, Support. The director of the Service, Mr. Lester Dearborn, established it in 1925 as a counseling service for personal and marital problems. In 1926 it was sponsored and financed by the Boston Y.M.C.A., and this continued until 1934 when the Y.M.C.A. entered into a co-operative arrangement with the Massachusetts Society for Social Hygiene. At the present time, support comes from the Society for Social Hygiene through the Community Fund. Office space is provided in the Y.M.C.A. and the facilities of that organization are accessory to the counseling service, the relationship being reciprocal. A board of consultants representing other professions, such as medicine, law, etc., is available. They meet regularly with the director for case discussion and critical appraisal of counseling procedure.

Staff. Mr. Dearborn is the only paid professional counselor. He is a college graduate, a teacher and author, and has had specialized training and long experience in sex education and research methods. In addition, he is a psychological consultant on the staffs of Franklin Technical Institute and the Boston Y.M.C.A., and in private practice.

Clients. Of the 224 new clients counseled in 1948, 67 per cent had education beyond high school, 74 per cent were under thirty-five years of age, 20 per cent came for premarital counsel.

Method and Philosophy. The work of this service is in three main areas: information, education, and guidance and adjustment. In counseling couples, premarital or married, they are seen first separately and then in a joint interview. In addition to thorough exploration of early relationships and attitudes, a sexual inventory is taken. This includes the individual's sexual feeling and behavior from date of earliest recall. Whatever information the client needs is given by the counselor in the interview, and this is supplemented by recommended reading. Terman's "Ten Points in the Prediction of Marital Happiness" are used with those contemplating marriage. Proper attitudes are continually stressed as being of great importance. In cases of guidance and adjustment the procedure is, first, exploration on the part of the counselor, then the client's catharsis, and finally reassurance and re-education from the counselor. Problems of a deep-seated nature are referred to psychiatric resources.

Fee. There is no set fee. Clients are urged to make a contribution to the service but no pressure is brought to bear.

Length of Contact. The average length of an interview is one and a half hours. Slightly over half the clients had one interview, one-fifth had two, one-tenth had three, and the remaining 16 per cent had up to ten interviews.

ACTIVITIES OTHER THAN INDIVIDUAL COUNSELING

Education. The director gives a ten-lecture course in modern marriage three times a year at the Boston Y.M.C.A. The course is limited to twenty-five members, a mixed group consisting largely of young married couples and those about to be married. He also gives a ten-lecture course in The Psychology of Personality, likewise to a mixed group, but not limited in number. Short unit courses of four or five lectures on such subjects as The Sex Factor in Human Relations, Problems of Marriage Adjustment, The Sex Life of Your Child, and The Psychology of Personality are given to many groups throughout the state. Individual lectures on the same subjects are given at local schools, colleges, churches, and P.T.A. groups.

Research. The director has carried on research on subjects such as masturbation as related to adult behavior, the significance of erotic fantasies in sexual stimulation and response, the sado-masochistic factor in marriage adjustment, the effect of corporal punishment on personality development, and causes of orgastic impotence.

In-Service Training. No arrangements have yet been made.

FAMILY RELATIONS CENTER
2504 Jackson Street, San Francisco 15, California
(October 14, 1950)

History, Auspices, Support. The Center, a nonprofit organization, is an outgrowth of an experimental sex education program which the Community Chest made available to local agencies in 1926 and 1927. It began in 1928 as a private organization governed by a board of directors and an advisory council. The name was changed from "Social Hygiene Education Association" to "Sex Education Society," and the present name was taken in 1934. In the early years, courses in sex education were conducted in various welfare organizations, parent-teacher associations, and club groups. These were eventually extended to two of the local colleges. As family life and sex education have become incorporated into the programs of many other organizations, the Center has increasingly confined its activities to personal counseling. The Center's sponsors include business, professional, and educational leaders in the community. Approximately 80 per cent of support is derived from fees, with the remainder from contributions and memberships.

Staff. The counselor is Mr. Henry M. Grant, a university graduate who has had extensive experience in developing sex education programs.

Clients. About 5 per cent of the clients come for premarital counseling, 5 per cent for general adolescent counseling, 15 per cent have miscellaneous problems such as sexual deviation and general maladjustment, and the remainder are marital problems. Sixty-three per cent of the clients are women.

Method and Philosophy. A workable blend of directive and nondirective counseling is used. Direct value judgments are carefully avoided. Clients are seen individually, except that very occasionally a married couple is seen jointly and sometimes an engaged couple is given a final interview together.

Fee. There is a fee of $10 per interview for those able to pay. Nearly half are seen free or for a nominal charge.

Length of Contact. Except for the initial interview, which is frequently two hours, the average interview lasts an hour. The average number of interviews per client is five.

ACTIVITIES OTHER THAN INDIVIDUAL COUNSELING

Education. No activities.

Research. None.

In-Service Training. None.

COUNSELING SERVICE
SOCIAL HYGIENE SOCIETY OF THE DISTRICT OF COLUMBIA
927 Fifteenth Street, N.W., Washington 5, D.C.
(November 2, 1950)

History, Auspices, Support. When this service was initiated in 1933 by the District of Columbia Social Hygiene Society, the director, Ray H. Everett, LL.B., was almost immediately asked to assist in many marital problems. The service was sustained through the efforts of the board, whose president was a well-known psychiatrist and whose membership included representatives of the major specialties useful in marriage counseling. The Society has always been supported by Community Chest funds.

Staff. The director, well known as a teacher, lecturer, writer, does about three-quarters of the counseling. The remainder is handled by an educational assistant who is a registered nurse and has taken special courses in psychology. Everyone on the staff is married.

Clients. In 1949 there were 714 clients, of whom 85 per cent were white. Almost half were Protestant, 29 per cent Catholic, and 12 per cent Jewish. Almost 60 per cent were referred from government agencies. In 1949 the numbers who sought counseling prior to marriage increased to approximately 20 per cent of the total counseling load.

Method and Philosophy. It is felt that premarital guidance can accomplish far more than postmarital mending. More than 150 persons were counseled in groups during 1949, but more intimate and personal problems frequently require individual conferences. Approximately 65 per cent of professional time goes into counseling and sex education. The usual procedure is a conference first with the client, then with the mate, then with both. In many instances, however, the mate most in need of counseling refuses to seek or accept it. Books are found useful. There is a lending library in the office but many clients are referred to the public library.

Where long-range casework and follow-up are indicated, the case is referred to a caseworking agency. Those who want specific contraceptive help are referred to Planned Parenthood Clinic unless they are of the Catholic faith.

Fee. There is no fee. However, with the continuing failure of the Chest to attain its campaign goals, the board has given much thought to the possibility of instituting fees. Since so many of the clients are in low income groups, many of the board members would prefer to continue the policy of free service.

Length of Contact. A first interview lasts from fifty to ninety minutes. About 50 per cent of clients have only one interview, and the remainder have from two to five sessions at varying time intervals.

ACTIVITIES OTHER THAN INDIVIDUAL COUNSELING

Education. Seminars for ministers; lectures and seminars for students—especially those in postgraduate groups majoring in education, sociology, or health and physical education; lectures and classes for church groups of so-called "marriageable young people."

Research. In major causes of marital disruption; why the preponderance of June weddings?; does marriage counseling make for lower divorce rates?; is Washington a good marrying city for girls?; and other questions.

In-Service Training. Nothing of a routine curricular nature.

COUNSELING CENTER
The University of Chicago, Chicago 37, Illinois
(December 4, 1950)

History, Auspices, Support. The Counseling Center was established in October, 1945, as one of the functions of the University of Chicago. Such a center had been proposed by a university committee, and Dr. Carl R. Rogers was brought to the University in part to establish it. From the first the purpose of the Center has been threefold: (1) to provide counseling service for individuals with personal maladjustments—both students of the University and a limited number of nonstudents; (2) to conduct an intensive training program in psychotherapy for advanced graduate students in clinical psychology and related fields; (3) to undertake research investigations in psychotherapy, and personality dynamics as related to psychotherapy.

The Counseling Center has been organized under the Office of the Dean of Students and the Department of Psychology. Each of these divisions of the University carries part of the financial load through University funds, and part of the over-all supervision. In addition, support has come by research grants from foundations, and by contract with governmental agencies. Fees are collected from nonstudent clients but are turned in to the general funds of the University and do not directly contribute to the support of the Center.

Staff. There are sixteen staff members on salary. Most of these have faculty appointments in psychology and one has an appointment in the Committee on Human Development. They devote part of their time to the counseling service and research in the Center and part of their time to their departmental teaching. Almost all of these staff members have their doctoral degrees and a number of years of clinical and counseling experience. In addition there are approximately twelve courtesy appointees on the staff. These are individuals who are for the most part completing their doctoral training in clinical psychology or related fields. They have had from a few months to several years of clinical and counseling experience.

Clients. The Counseling Center sees approximately 700 new clients per year. Slightly more than half of these are students. Of the nonstudents some are children who come for play therapy, some are parents of the children, and others are adults from Chicago or out of town. Almost all clients are self-referred. They learn about the Counseling Center in a variety of ways and come in because they seek help for themselves. The service is open full-time.

In carrying through the service function there has never

been any focus upon specific types of problems—academic, vocational, marital, religious, and so forth. The focus has always been upon dealing with the individual as a person involved in many relationships. It is believed that these relationships improve as the person becomes more deeply able to understand and accept himself.

Method and Philosophy. The method and philosophy of counseling is in general a client-centered one. Rather than attempting to provide specific solutions to the problem presented by the individual the Center relies upon his capacity to become aware of the factors in himself which underlie these problems. It has been found that though the individual comes in concerned with a problem, he soon begins actually to work on himself—that is, to work toward the achievement of a deeper insight into and understanding of himself and a reorganization of self to include these new insights.

Fee. The nonstudents who pay a fee arrive at the amount on the basis of their own decision, which is reached in conference with the counselor and with the information provided by the suggested fee schedule sheet.

Length of Contact. The usual length of each interview is forty-five or fifty minutes. However, some of the counselors have experimented with interviews of double this length when clients have so desired. When the Center was first opened, cases averaged four to five interviews in length. As the Center has been longer in operation and counselors have become more experienced, the average length of cases has increased steadily, so that at present cases run from fifteen to twenty interviews per case.

ACTIVITIES OTHER THAN INDIVIDUAL COUNSELING

Education. Many of the staff are faculty members in psychology and carry various courses, but they are particularly responsible for the sequence of training courses in counseling and have other seminars concerned with personality dynamics and research in psychotherapy. Training courses in counseling gradually increase in intensity until the students are carrying counseling cases under supervision, recording their interviews, and discussing these interviews with their supervisors.

Research. It is probable that the staff members devote at least 30 per cent of their time to research. At the present time a very comprehensive group of correlated studies is being carried on, financed by a foundation grant.

Records. In the service function no records are kept of the interviews except those which the counselor may wish to keep for his use. These would be his own property and would not be filed in any central file. For the research work a good many interviews are recorded, and these are kept under code with all names and identifying material changed when the interview is transcribed. The general card file of clients does not contain their code name, and every effort is made to keep their code names and the real names disassociated.

COUNSELING AND GUIDANCE SERVICE OF THE MERRILL-PALMER SCHOOL
71 Ferry Avenue, East, Detroit 2, Michigan
(January 8, 1951)

History, Auspices, Support. The Counseling and Guidance Service of Merrill-Palmer School was organized in September, 1948, when the Advisory Service of the Family Life Department and the Guidance Service of the Psychology Department combined to form a single operating unit. In September, 1949, a psychiatric social worker, Mrs. Clara Lyndon, was appointed as full-time director. A consulting psychiatrist meets weekly with staff and students for case discussion and analysis. A steering committee of staff representatives serves as a consultative body for the discussion and approval of policy. The Counseling and Guidance Service offers diagnostic and treatment services to children and to adults. It has a threefold function, as do the other Merrill-Palmer Services: needed service to the community; training in counseling and guidance for Merrill-Palmer graduate students and for social work students from the two schools of social work in Detroit; and providing data for research in interpersonal relationships.

Staff. In addition to the director, whose experience has included family casework, child guidance, and family life education, members of the Family Life and Psychology Departments of Merrill-Palmer serve part-time as staff members.

Clients. During 1949, 179 clients were seen and presented the following problems: 16 parent-child relations, 30 marital-premarital, 35 testing, 98 various child adjustments. In addition, a premarital counseling program for a group of engaged couples was conducted by the Family Life Department. Data on percentage of women, and the religious, economic, and education breakdowns, are not available. This service is restricted numerically by staff limitations; additional service is rendered through consultation to organizations interested in developing counseling programs.

Method and Philosophy. The counseling base is necessarily broad and flexible enough to include varying approaches and techniques. Because one of the primary functions of Merrill-Palmer is training, there is opportunity for study of family relationships and for experimentation in clinical procedures. The method is essentially that which underlies any form of counseling; namely, offering to the individual a relationship within which he can best, in terms of his own needs, work toward some solution of his troubling situation.

Fee. Fees are on a flexible basis, and range from 50¢ to $5 per hour or are waived entirely. Specific fee in any given case is determined by the ability of the individual or the family to pay.

Length of Contact. The usual unit of time per interview is one hour but variation is possible. No data available on number of interviews per client.

ACTIVITIES OTHER THAN INDIVIDUAL COUNSELING

Education. All members of the staff who engage in individual counseling teach one or more courses in the school—in interviewing and counseling, phases of clinical psychology, marriage and family life education, and marriage counseling—that are of direct or indirect relationship to the training of students in individual counseling. Courses are offered for engaged couples, expectant parents, and for marital and parent-child guidance of parents of small children.

Research. Research is currently being undertaken jointly by Dr. David F. Kahn of the psychology department and Dr. Robert A. Harper of the family life department.

In-Service Training. Graduate students interested in marriage counseling are required to take the basic courses offered in the school. They also have experience in social agencies and the public schools in and around Detroit. When deemed ready, students begin counseling under close supervision.

FAMILY LIFE DIVISION OF THE DEPARTMENT OF GENERAL STUDIES—UNIVERSITY OF MINNESOTA
Minneapolis 14, Minnesota
(November 30, 1950)

History, Auspices, Support. Marriage education and counseling at the University have been closely associated since their inception. Student interest and need led a committee, appointed by the president in 1943, to recommend a credit course in Preparation for Marriage to be taught by a qualified person, who would also do part-time counseling on premarital and marriage problems in the Student Counseling Bureau. The first course was offered in 1945, and the instructor joined the student counseling staff. The Family Life Division was established in 1947, with Mrs. Dorothy T. Dyer as chairman.

Staff. All five staff members of the Preparation for Marriage course do counseling as it develops from the teaching situation and referrals from students. They are chosen for the dual role of counselor-teacher from their major fields of psychology, social work, and sociology. All have had several years of teaching, group work, and individual counseling experience in academic settings or social agencies. They are all married and are parents. Psychiatric consultation is available through the Student Health Center. Supervision for the counselors is cared for by periodic case review with the director. There are also frequent consultations among the marriage counselors.

Clients. Counseling is available to any student, their spouses or fiancés. If the client is a member of the marriage course, appointments are usually made with the instructor of his section. Students or faculty members referred by other college personnel usually contact a counselor through the Student Counseling Bureau, whose director is a Ph.D. in psychology. The 290 clients seen in 1950 represent chiefly upper and lower middle class families, with men and women in about equal proportions and age range from seventeen to under forty years.

Method and Philosophy. The techniques of counseling are eclectic and vary with individual counselors and the particular client's situation. Interviewing is frequently supplemented by various tests and inventories. While couples may be seen together or separately, it is common procedure for each partner to have his own counselor. Counselors try to help the client to achieve greater insight into his problem so that he himself will be free to make his own decision. Consultation with referral resources on the campus and in the local community make the counselor's service more effective.

Length of Contact. Sixty minutes are allotted for each interview and the number of contacts per client range from two to one hundred and fifty.

Fee. While students are not charged a fee, a nominal fee ranging from $5 to $25 is charged for the occasional noncollege client.

ACTIVITIES OTHER THAN INDIVIDUAL COUNSELING

Education. Leadership is offered to discussion groups and speakers are furnished to clubs, P.T.A., church groups, and other community organizations. This aspect of service takes 10 per cent of staff time.

Research. The research program centers on evaluation of methods, techniques of teaching and counseling, and prediction of success in marriage. Joint staff projects, as well as individual research problems, are constantly being carried on, for example, development of an attitudes scale—a ten year study evaluating the validity of the focus of the marriage course.

In-Service Training. The summer graduate course includes opportunities for field work.

THE MARRIAGE COUNSELING SERVICE
Florida State University
Tallahassee, Florida
(December 11, 1950)

History, Auspices, Support. The present Marriage Counseling Service is a direct outgrowth of the University's marriage education program. Consultation service has been provided regularly in connection with the functional marriage courses, which had their inception in 1930. The University has recognized the value of such consultation and has designated as university marriage counselors certain well-trained and experienced professors who teach in the area of marriage and family living of the School of Social Welfare.

Staff. The counseling staff includes four professors who are trained and experienced in marriage counseling practice. All of the counselors have advanced degrees in sociology, theology, or law, and all have had advanced study in psychology in addition to several years of marriage counseling experience. Other clinical facilities of the University are utilized in the Marriage Counseling Service, such as the University Health Service, the Human Relations Institute, and the services of the psychiatric social worker of the School of Social Welfare. A full-time university psychiatrist has been employed to serve as consultant to the Marriage Counseling Service, Human Relations Institute, and University Health Service.

Clients. Approximately 200 clients receive counseling each year, about 75 per cent premarital.

Method and Philosophy. The philosophy of counseling in the Marriage Counseling Service is eclectic. Each counselor is sufficiently oriented to the various disciplines such as psychology, social work, and psychoanalysis to be cognizant of the value and place of each of them, and to make referrals when needed.

Fee. Inasmuch as the Marriage Counseling Service is a part of the University program and the counselors are salaried faculty members, no fees are charged. Four consultation rooms are utilized and the service is open full-time.

Length of Contact. Client interviews are usually one hour in length and client contact varies from one to fifty interviews.

ACTIVITIES OTHER THAN INDIVIDUAL COUNSELING

Education. Members of the counseling staff are engaged in teaching on the campus and conducting family life institutes in communities throughout the state.

Research. None.

In-Service Training. Through the facilities of the Marriage Counseling Service, practicum for advanced students in the doctoral program in marriage and family living is being provided under the supervision of staff counselors and with the consultation of the University psychiatrist and the psychiatric social worker.

MARRIAGE COUNSELING SERVICE
Furman University, Greenville, South Carolina
(November 10, 1950)

History, Auspices, Support. This Service was established in 1949 and is offered through the office of the director of personal guidance. Support comes from the regular college budget and, at present, plans for a long-range program are awaiting more adequate funds from other sources.

Staff. The director, Aaron L. Rutledge, who holds a doctorate in clinical psychology, has a background in the ministry. In addition to experience as an army chaplain, he was chaplain in a state mental hospital where he did therapy, as well as counseling with people from the community. A local psychiatrist, other physicians, and suitable faculty members are used for referrals.

Clients. The service is available to students, university staff, and their families. While it is not advertised to the public, many persons come for help. During the past year 704 clients were seen, of whom 60 per cent were women. Ninety-eight per cent were Protestant, less than 1 per cent Catholic, and less than 1 per cent Jewish. Approximately 60 per cent came for premarital guidance.

Method and Philosophy. Counseling is thought of in terms of the person as a whole in his environmental setting, including his own philosophy of life. The aim is diagnostic and therapeutic and not merely for immediate adjustment. Psychological tests are used where indicated, especially with children. Special use is being made of group therapy in counseling young premarital clients. It is felt that most problems are caused by emotional immaturity, that if some of the conflicts are handled, the emotional life reopened to growth, and some information and guidance offered, most people are capable of reaching a better permanent adjustment.

Fee. Those not from the University campus are not charged a set fee but may, if they wish, pay a nominal amount to the "Clinical Aid Fund" used to provide further specialized help (usually psychiatric) for students who cannot afford it. Students and faculty are not charged a fee.

Length of Contact. The average interview is between forty-five and fifty minutes. The number of interviews per client ranges from one (where only referral is indicated) to whatever number is indicated in the particular case.

ACTIVITIES OTHER THAN INDIVIDUAL COUNSELING

Education. A course in social psychology and one in emotional development each semester; consultant to Family Service Organization in city; conduct one course per year for nurses of local hospital; institutes for local Y's; institute for human development annually for local school leaders; family emphasis weeks in local churches; resource person for local teachers and P.T.A.'s. (This work is done evenings by the director.)

Research. The director is continuing a five year project entitled "Guilt, a Psychoreligious Analysis," begun in a mental hospital, and now being checked with cases of a more average nature. The first three chapters of a report on this project will appear shortly in journal form. Personality surveys are made on all incoming students, and a project to analyze the reasons for dropping out of school is under way.

In-Service Training. At present in-service training is limited to a few courses in the fundamental principles of guidance, with emphasis upon emotional problems. Plans are under consideration for enlarging the service with the hope of utilizing local clinical facilities for supervised training of a few select students.

MARRIAGE COUNSELING SERVICE
School of Education, Pennsylvania State College, Burrows Building, State College, Pennsylvania
(November 10, 1950)

History, Auspices, Support. This service is a functioning part of the Psychological Clinic and was established in 1940, but had existed on an informal basis from 1937.

Staff. In addition to the director, Clifford R. Adams, Ph.D. in psychology, there are three counselors, two with Ph.D.'s in psychology in addition to many years of counseling experience, and one who has nearly completed requirements for a Ph.D. degree. The counselors also accept private cases. The chairman of the psychology department participates to the extent that his time will permit. A psychiatrist is available to assist with those cases requiring psychiatric attention. There is a close working relationship with local physicians who are responsible for many referrals.

Method and Philosophy. The client's basic problem is determined in the initial interview at the Psychological Clinic. If it revolves around sexual or other marital adjustment difficul-

314

ties, it is referred to the Marriage Counseling Service. Other types of personal problems are handled by the regular staff of the Clinic. A close functioning relationship is maintained between the Clinic and the Counseling Service. Diagnostic tests, including premarital prediction and marital adjustment, are regularly utilized.

Clients. While the service is not restricted entirely to those associated with the College, it is largely restricted to student couples and faculty because of lack of facilities for expansion. Approximately 40 per cent of the case load is comprised of individuals or couples seeking premarital advice. Approximately 300 clients (including couples taking compatibility tests) were seen between September, 1949, and September, 1950.

Fee. Fees to students are nominal and the same is true for faculty members if the number of interviews required is three or less. Thereafter a charge of $5 per interview is made.

Length of Contact. The average interview approximates one hour. The average number of interviews is three, although contacts with some clients have been maintained for as long as five years.

ACTIVITIES OTHER THAN INDIVIDUAL COUNSELING

Education. All senior counselors do some teaching, largely courses in preparation for marriage, counseling techniques, and therapeutic methodology. Through Education Extension, a correspondence course in preparation for marriage is available. Special summer workshops in family life education are conducted on the campus. Other institutions wishing to initiate such seminars are provided with leaders. Lectures are also available for academic or community organizations desiring such services.

Research. A continuing program of researches is maintained, some devoted to specialized projects satisfying requirements for masters' or doctors' theses, others, by senior staff members, devoted to longitudinal studies extending over a decade.

In-Service Training. Not until one year of graduate clinical internship in educational and vocational counseling has been completed is any student, however mature, permitted to do marriage counseling. During this second year, such counseling is carefully supervised by a senior clinician. At the beginning of the third year of the graduate program selected students, who have demonstrated competence, are permitted to counsel with a minimum of supervision.

PRE-MARITAL COUNSELING SERVICE
Stephens College, Columbia, Missouri
(December 14, 1950)

History, Auspices, Support. The Pre-marital Counseling Service at Stephens College was started in 1934. It was a natural concomitant of the development of a course in marriage education started the same year. There was one instructor-counselor and his counseling was, in a sense, extracurricular, since it was not recognized administratively. The counselor had no private office, met his clients in classrooms, other offices, and tearooms in after-class hours, and the number of counselees was small.

The Pre-marital Counseling Service under the directorship of Henry Bowman, Ph.D., is now recognized administratively as one of the regular counseling services available to students. The counseling done, however, is still in addition to a regular teaching load. Each counselor is a member of the marriage education staff. There is no financial support for the counseling service other than that represented by the salaries of the teacher-counselors. Clients make appointments with the counselor of their choice at any time he may have open.

Staff. The academic background, training, and experience of the three counselors follow: The director has a Ph.D. degree in sociology and twenty years of teaching experience, seventeen of them in marriage education. One counselor has a B.D. degree with considerable background in sociology, fifteen years in the ministry during which he developed programs of marriage education and counseling in various churches, and seven years of teaching and counseling at Stephens College. One counselor, new to the service, is about to receive his Ph.D. in education and guidance after fourteen years of teaching experience, with special attention to the development of the college advising program.

Clients. The counseling service is open to anyone, although most clients are students of the college, a few are "boy friends" of Stephens students, alumnae, students of the University of Missouri, and townspeople. Only a small proportion are married. The counseling service operates only during the academic year. From 200 to 300 clients are seen annually and most make appointments on their own initiative.

Method and Philosophy. The primary emphasis of the service is on premarital counseling. Counseling and teaching are considered two facets of the same process, namely, preparation for marriage. Each makes a contribution to the other in an integrated program. Through counseling, students may be assisted toward the solution of problems too highly individualized to be adequately treated in class discussions. On the other hand, problems frequently met in counseling may safely be assumed to be more common among students than the number of clients presenting them to the counseling service might suggest. These problems, therefore, may be approached, to some degree, through class discussion. Such discussion is often the initial impetus that leads a given student to make an appointment with the counseling service. In this counseling no set, standard method assumed to be universally applicable is used. Preferably, counseling is thought of as adaptive rather than either nondirective or directive in an exclusive sense. None of the staff is trained in medicine and none feels himself prepared to do therapeutic counseling in the strict sense of the term. In any case, however, the client is helped to solve his own problem; it is not solved for him.

Fee. All members of the Pre-Marital Counseling Service staff are regular members of the college faculty; therefore, the service charges no fees.

Length of Contact. Most interviews are for one hour. The

ʋɾ appointments made by a given client varies; the ɹɾity have one appointment. Occasionally, a client has as many as sixteen appointments within two months. Since most clients are Stephens' students, however, total contact is not described only by number of specific appointments. There are many follow-up contacts both in classes and on campus through one and sometimes through two school years.

ACTIVITIES OTHER THAN INDIVIDUAL COUNSELING

Education. The counseling staff teaches a course in marriage education, which is elective. It carries six hours' credit and extends through the year. Each year 50 to 60 per cent of the second year class, to whom the course is open, is enrolled in it. This means 400 to 550 students.

Research. Recently the College sent out an evaluation questionnaire to every alumna who had had the marriage course. Currently a study of alumnae marriages is being made; 20,000 questionnaires were sent out and there have been 10,200 returns.

In-Service Training. The new instructor-counselor is this year going through the entire marriage course, having the same classes as the director.

MARRIAGE COUNSELING SERVICES
Southern Methodist University
Dallas, Texas
(January 26, 1951)

History, Auspices, Support. The Student Counseling Service connected with Southern Methodist University had administrative approval and assistance at the beginning of the school year 1924–25 when the present counselor, H. L. Pritchett, Ph.D., became a member of the faculty of the university. It was officially recognized and provided for by the board of trustees at the beginning of 1928–29. The counselor was then designated "mental hygiene counselor," and his functions defined in terms of personal counseling for all resident students of the university. Until 1944 the counselor was also head of the department of sociology, which position carried with it the usual administrative duties. Counseling, however, was a large integral part of his total program.

In 1944 the services were reorganized, expanded, and officially recognized as a part of the university administrative organization. The title was changed, by request, to "university student counselor." The service became full-time (thirty-six hours weekly), although limited teaching opportunity in the field of marriage, the family, and marriage counseling was permitted. From the beginning, the primary function has been premarital and postmarital counseling. While other student problems occasionally were handled, in general they were referred. With a campus population of 7,000, there are few unused conference periods.

The office is located conveniently for students in a central campus building with adequate furnishings and a reasonable operating budget.

Staff. The staff consists of the counselor who, in addition to holding a Ph.D. degree, has had specialized training in medical and similar fields closely related to marriage counseling; a receptionist-secretary, who is a college graduate continuing in-service training and who may also assist in history taking; and a part-time assistant, usually a senior or graduate major. The latter is used in connection with administering and scoring personality inventories and other diagnostic devices.

Clients. There are almost twice as many premarital as postmarital counseling cases for students. Veteran marriage problems predominate in the latter group. All student conferences are voluntary, although administrative officials, faculty, advisors, class or group contacts, are sources of referral. The counselor includes conferences with student marriage partners under student privileges, no fees being asked.

Method and Philosophy. Preventive guidance is far more important than corrective therapy. The college campus is the optimum time and place for mate selection. Marriage guidance and instruction, therefore, is a student service of paramount importance. Correction of misinformation and destruc-

319

tive attitudes from early life and positive guidance of both campus men and women by classroom, discussion groups, and individual conferences are the major opportunities. The individual conference is the most satisfactory and most frequent means. Contact is continued in terms of student need, cooperation, or in terms of the counselor's responsibility to others. A follow-up program is carried out in terms of brief personal conferences, telephoned reports, or by correspondence.

Fee. The counselor is permitted private practice unrelated to the university in the field of marriage counseling. Approximately ten to twelve additional hours per week are given to such appointments. Fees of from $10 to $15 per conference are charged for these services. Most private cases involve post-marital counseling, but there is a steady increase in the number of premarital counseling opportunities.

Length of Contact. Student interviews are usually one half to one hour long and the average contact is four to five interviews.

ACTIVITIES OTHER THAN INDIVIDUAL COUNSELING

Education. Extra-campus professional lecturing is an extension of university function. The counselor is a lecturer for the Hogg Foundation for Mental Hygiene in Texas in community "Marriage Institutes," and under other auspices.

Research. Constant research is a necessity for efficient work, but an unlimited case load permits little opportunity for research for publication.

In-Service Training. In-serving training in the form of clinical opportunities and professional contacts is constantly sought by the counselor but is not at present offered in this set-up.

MARRIAGE COUNSELING SERVICE
Utah State Agricultural College
Logan, Utah
(February 17, 1951)

History, Auspices, Support. The Marriage Counseling Service was activated, in 1945, in the departments of sociology and social work and co-ordinated with the office of the deans of men and women, the department of psychology, and the Student Health Service. The service is a college function supported by a departmental budget. The physical set-up includes the offices of staff personnel, the psychological laboratory, and the health center. Time open for clients is by appointment and not restricted.

Staff. The staff personnel includes a director, Dr. C. Jay Skidmore, with a Ph.D. degree in marriage education and counseling, and additional clinical training and experience; two social workers; a clinical psychologist; and referral service from the Student Health Service.

Clients. The client population includes any student enrolled at the college and others involved in their cases.

Method and Philosophy. The range of client problems has included those incidental to dating and courtship, and premarital and postmarital situations. The service undertakes the functions of diagnosis (and referral in the case of more serious personality disturbances) and supportive therapy. Most cases involve a combination of personal consultations and classwork. The philosophy of counseling is based on the assumption that the central purpose of counsel is to assist the person (or pair) to grow in the understanding of himself or themselves and of other persons, also in understanding of the situational circumstances surrounding development and probable future circumstances. Counseling techniques are flexible, employing those from clinical psychology, generic social work, and social psychiatry. The point of view of the counselors might be characterized as moderately psychoanalytic. A *minimum* of exhortation and advice is given.

321

Source of Referral. Sources of referral include the office of the deans of personnel, class instructors, physicians, national agencies, and religious leaders. The largest single group of clients come in voluntarily as a result of having taken one of the family courses.

Fee. There is no fee for the service.

Length of Contact. The length of client contact varies from one hour to hours throughout the academic year. A modal length of contact has been four consultations over a period of from four to eight weeks.

ACTIVITIES OTHER THAN INDIVIDUAL COUNSELING

Education. Staff are called on for adult education, and the holding of family life institutes throughout the state.

Research. There is some research.

In-Service Training. Plans are under way for in-service training on the graduate level.

BUREAU OF STUDENT COUNSEL
University of Utah, Salt Lake City, Utah
(November 22, 1950)

History, Auspices, Support. Marriage counseling is a function of the Bureau of Student Counsel, which is an integral part of the Graduate School of Social Work. The Bureau was established by the Board of Regents in 1927 under the guidance of Dean Arthur L. Beeley, to provide a basic service of assisting students with problems of personality adjustment and mental hygiene. In 1947, the services of premarital and family counseling for engaged and married students were included. Financing comes entirely from University funds.

Staff. Rex A. Skidmore, Ph.D. in sociology, is the director of the Bureau. The regular staff members include two psychiatric social workers both with M.S.W. degrees, a generic caseworker (M.S.), a home economist (M.A.), and a psychometrist (Ph.D.). Each staff member teaches at the University in his respective field and spends between one-third and two-thirds of his time working at the Bureau. A psychiatrist is available for consultation on more involved problems. All of the staff have had three or more years of experience in working with marital and other personal problems.

Clients. About 300 students use the service yearly. Of these, approximately two-thirds seek premarital counseling. The age range of the first hundred clients was from seventeen to thirty-two years, with twenty and four-tenths being the average.

Method and Philosophy. The approach to counseling is eclectic, with the individual counselor being left free to work in the manner he chooses within the framework of supervision and staff conferences. Through interviews and tests, clients are given opportunity to develop rational self-direction regarding their feelings, problems, decisions, and plans. The Bureau is especially interested in assisting young people prepare for marriage in a mature manner. This is an interdisciplinary approach which welds the resources of psychiatry, psychology, social work, sociology, and home economics.

An applicant is first interviewed by the director or a counselor, who either works with him directly or refers him to another counselor. Psychological tests are usually administered if the client is willing. Supplementary resources such as projective techniques are available if needed. There is a weekly staff meeting to discuss more difficult cases. In addition to regular staff, a psychiatrist, the Dean of the School of Social Work, and the social work students at the Bureau attend.

Fee. No fees are charged and services are limited to students and their close relatives or friends.

Length of Contact. Forty-five to fifty minutes are allowed for each interview. The average number of interviews per case is from five to seven.

ACTIVITIES OTHER THAN INDIVIDUAL COUNSELING

Education. Individual staff members present lectures and lead discussions on marriage and family living before various clubs, school classes, religious groups, and other community organizations. One staff member is participating in a weekly television show centered around problems of courtship and marriage. The Bureau also assists in supervising a family life institute at the University of Utah each summer.

Research. Research is a major function of the Bureau. Each staff member is working on one or more projects related to the marriage counseling processes. In addition, plans are being formulated to make some follow-up studies of the counselees.

In-Service Training. The service is used as a fieldwork placement for one or two social work students each quarter. These students are assigned cases to handle under supervision; they also participate in staff presentations and discussions.

MARRIAGE COUNSELING CENTER
Ohio State University, Columbus 10, Ohio
(November 2, 1950)

History, Auspices, Support. The Center was established in October, 1948, although for several years prior to that time marriage counseling was being done with two or three counselors operating somewhat independently of one another on a part-time basis. The need was felt for (a) premarital and postmarital counseling for students at the University and their immediate families, (b) training facilities for students preparing to do counseling in conjunction with teaching, mainly at the college level, and (c) research into the various aspects of marriage counseling. The first director was John F. Cuber, Ph.D., and the present director is Merton Oyler, Ph.D. The service functions under the Department of Sociology and receives its budget mainly from this department. Research funds are allotted from the University Development Fund.

Staff. Counselors are all members of the staff of the sociology department, mostly with a Ph.D. degree or working towards it. Five people are now giving part-time service, none of whom is trained professionally as a counselor.

Methods and Philosophy. The philosophy of counseling has been eclectic from the start. There is and always has been great variation in the concepts of counseling held by the various staff members. Procedures, therefore, are also varied.

Clients. In the first year of operation 60 per cent of the clients came for premarital counseling, and the remainder were experiencing marital difficulties.

Fee. No fee is charged.

Length of Contact. The average interview lasts one hour and the number of interviews per client has ranged from one to fifty.

ACTIVITIES OTHER THAN PERSONAL COUNSELING

Education. No data available.

Research. Several projects are under way but as yet there are no results to report.

In-Service Training. No data available.

Subject Index

Subject Index

Center for Sexual Advice, 5
Central Conference of American Rabbis, 11, 55-56, 252
  attitude toward marriage counseling, 55-57
Change, effects on family, 15
Chi-square statistical test, 87, 213
Child development, studies in, 9
Child spacing, 187; *see also* Planned Parenthood
Child study, 45
Child Study Association of America, 45, 257-58
Cincinnati Social Hygiene Society, 60, 255, 297
Clergymen, as marriage counselors, 5, 26-29, 53-59
Client, follow-up of, practical suggestions, 39-41, 117, 149, 196
  medical referral of, 175, 195
  procedure for application of, 180-81
  psychiatric referral of, 156, 195-96
  time limits for contacts of, 192-93
Clients, of a Marriage Council
  age and sex changes after 1940, 215, 218-19
  age differences, 93-96
  age, effects of, 98
  age of, 76-77, 104, 105
  areas of similarity, 101
  characteristics of, 73-102
  changing marital status after 1940, 222, 223
  changing referrals after 1940, 215, 221-22
  changing sexual difficulties after 1940, 224
  compared with population base, 103-11
  comparison of men and women, 87 ff.
  differences in sources of referral, 100-101
  education of, 79-80, 107-9
  education of, after 1940, 219
  educational differences of, 96
  length of time married, 97
  marital status of, 80, 82, 109-10
  mixed marriages among, 78
  number of years married, 80
  reasons for coming, 83-86
  religion of, 78, 105-7

residence of, 75-76
  seeking help after marriage, 85-86
  seeking help before marriage, 84-85
  sex differences in, 90-92
  sex of, 76, 103
  use of counseling, 112-76
Climacteric, female, 98
College courses on marriage, 6, 32-33
Community organizations, and marriage counseling, 35, 45-72
Conservative rabbinate, 57
Consultation centers, 5
Consultation Service of the Maternal Health Association, Cleveland, 53, 255, 282
Council, Marriage, *see* Marriage Council of Philadelphia, *also* Marriage and Family Council, Chapel Hill
Counseling, *see* Marriage Counseling
Counseling and Guidance Service, Merrill-Palmer School, Detroit, 62, 254, 307
Counseling Center, University of Chicago, Chicago, 61, 253, 304
Counseling Service, Boston, 60, 253, 299
Counseling Service, District of Columbia, 60, 253, 303
Counseling services, listed alphabetically, 252-56
  reports on, 257-325
  see also family counseling services
Counselor, academic training, 23, 32, 65
  attitude of, 186
  attributes of, 180, 193-94
  considerations for, 188-89
  contributions of, 180
  personal qualifications of, 66
  professional qualifications of, 66
  reliability of statements by, 191
  role of, 202
  unethical, unorthodox, 23

Dependency, public, extent of, 14-15
Depression, economic, 14, 20
Divorce, 3, 4, 17, 19, 161

Educators, as marriage counselors, 5, 22, 29 ff.

Family, and its members, 19

328

Maternal Health Association, Cleveland, 53

Maternal Health Center of Philadelphia, 221, 222

Menninger Foundation, 53, 70, 253, 285

Mental disease, 3

Mental health, goal of, 1, 50-51, 229

Merrill-Palmer School, 34, 62, 254, 307

Metropolitan Life Insurance Company, 96

Mid-Century White House Conference, 16

Mothers' Health Center, Brooklyn, 52, 255, 279

National Association for Mental Health, Inc., 50-51, 251

National Catholic Welfare Conference, 11, 251-52

National Committee for Mental Hygiene, 50

National Conference on Family Life, 23-24

National Council of the Churches of Christ in America, 252; *see also* Federal Council

National Council on Family Relations, 31, 45-46, 65, 251

National Marriage Guidance Council, 37-38, 244

National Mental Health Act, 10

National organizations, related to marriage counseling, 251-56

Ohio State University, 62, 324

Pearl Harbor, 211

Pennsylvania State College, 62, 256, 314

Physicians, as counselors, 5, 24-26, 205-6

practical suggestions for, 29-31

Planned Parenthood Federation of America, Inc., 51-52, 251

interest in family problems, 51

standards of, 52

Pre-Cana and Cana Conference, 55, 289

Pre-Marital Counseling Service, Columbia, Missouri, 62, 254, 316

Pre-Marriage and Marriage Counseling Service, Richmond, 49, 256, 272

Premarital counseling; *see* Marriage Counseling, premarital

Preventive approach, 2

Protestant Churches, 57

Rabbinical Assembly of America, 57, 252

Rates, birth and the war, 16

divorce, 17

marriage, 17

marriage and the war, 16

Religio-Psychiatric Clinic of the Marble Collegiate Church, New York, 59, 255, 295

Research, effects of, in analytic psychology, 10

in counseling, 199-201

in delinquency, 9

in family counseling, 70, 75

in fertility, 10

in marital difficulties, 48

in marriage, family life, and child development, 8, 9

in population, 10

in prediction, 9

in sex behavior, 9-10

in social casework, 10

Roman Catholic Church, approach to counseling, 53-55

Saint Michael's Hospital Family Clinic, Milwaukee, 55, 256, 286

Schedules; *see* Background Schedule, Marriage Counseling, Use of

Science, of human relationships, 3

of Marriage Counseling, 229

Semantics, 177

Separation, 161, 172

Sex Knowledge Inventory, 191

Sexual advice, Center for, 5

Sexual Hygiene, League for, 5

Sexual adjustment, case of, 138, 157

effects of war, 152-66

effects of age on female, 98; on male, 99

Sexual information; *see* Information, sexual

Sexual maladjustment, case of, 118

Social Hygiene, 59, 62

331

Subject Index

Southern Methodist University, 61, 256, 318
Stephens College, 62, 254, 316
Stanford University, 6
Swarthmore College, 32

Teachers, as counselors, 29-31, 39
  practical suggestions to, 39-41
  training for, 34
Technology, invasion of home, 4

United States Public Health Service, 10, 151, 200
United Synagogue of America, 57
University education, 60
University of Chicago, 6, 61, 253, 304
University of Minnesota, 62, 254, 309
University of Utah, 62, 256, 322
Utah State Agricultural College, 62, 256, 321

War economy, 14

War, impact on marriage counseling, 210-27
  effects on the family, 210-11
  effects on young people, 227
  outbreak of, in 1941, 21
  prognosis for next decade, 227
World Federation for Mental Health, 24
World Health Organization, 229
World War II, demands on families, 16, 20, 63
  counseling following, 167-76
  and use of Marriage Council in Philadelphia, 216-17
  summary of impact on, 226-27

Young Men's Christian Association, 35
Young Men's and Young Women's Hebrew Association, 35
Young Women's Christian Association, 35

332

Index of Names

335

Index of Names

336